ONLY
HUMAN

ONLY HUMAN

An Operating Manual for Seekers and Sensitives

ISRAEL BOUSEMAN

For more information, email only.human.wisdom.training@gmail.com

ISBN: 979-8-88759-663-1 - paperback
ISBN: 979-8-88759-665-5 - hardcover
ISBN: 979-8-88759-664-8 - ebook

Only Human Wisdom Training

What if your potential was much greater than you ever realized? What if it's a blessing beyond belief to be born human? What if all we need are a few pointers to begin to actualize that potential and begin living richer, fuller lives than we'd ever imagined?

This is what Only Human Wisdom Training is all about. If you'd like to know more, or if you'd like to gain clarity around your personal journey, feel free to reach out. To join the Only Human community, or if you'd like to speak with me directly, you can contact me at: onlyhumanwisdomtraining.com

ISRAEL BOUSEMAN

DEDICATION

This book is dedicated to my father, my first teacher and guide. He raised his sons with a love of God and Truth and a wonder for the living world. He nurtured our minds and hearts with a rich diet of myth, philosophy, and honest inquiry.

John Kirk Bouseman, the White Wolf, inspired growth, depth, and critical thought in generations of misfits. He taught us to mean what we say and say what we mean. He encouraged us to open our minds, to look at everything that we can and find what works for us. This book is part of my journey to do just that and to share the fruits of this exploration with all those who might benefit from them.

My father laid the foundations in me for the medicine path, the path I now walk. And, along the path, I have encountered so many beautiful teachers and companions. I do not have space here to name you all, but I give you all thanks for the gifts you have given me and the growth you inspired.

Blessings and good journeys!

CONTENTS

INTRODUCTION

"If, in the distant future, someone hears these words, then perhaps it is not too late. There is a world above. A magnificent world to which you can return if you have but the courage. Find the blade, and you shall find your freedom!"

– Quoted from *Starchaser: Legend of Orin*

We stand at a crossroads, one which we feel in the depths of our souls, and one which concerns the fate of every living being on this planet. What we do now determines our future, individually and collectively.

But the world has grown so big in some ways, and so small in others. It's small in that we reach every part of it, digitally and physically, with an ease unimagined by our forebears. It can feel as if all has been discovered and there's nothing new under the sun. And the world has become large in that the forces set in motion are so huge, backed by so much momentum, that it sometimes feels impossible to change course or choose a new direction. What can one person do in the face of nations and corporations, when faced with circumstances set in motion generations past? How could a drop make a difference in the face of the ocean?

But it is not impossible. With every choice, we create our future. With everything we say, everything we do, we leave a mark upon the world. We each have the power to create, to leave a mark that merits the gift of life we have been given. And yet so many of us feel locked-in to lives half led. We can all too easily be left with pale shadows of the richness life has to offer, our creative energy drained and channeled into the creation of things we don't care about.

The good news is that we can all return to a life of deep fulfillment, one in which we create beauty, where we leave a mark upon the world that reflects what we believe in and what we truly have to offer the world. We don't need to quit our jobs or drop away worldly things to begin this journey, though there's no guarantee where the path will lead. All we really need to do is show up to our bodies, our lives, and our living moment.

What you do matters. And this doesn't mean that it's time to get into politics or take up some activist or humanitarian cause. These things all have their place, but there is a much deeper offering we can give the world. Our conscious, healthy presence. We can show up in our lives and in the lives of those we care about. We can start choosing, actively, what we would like to create in our personal experience, in this moment. What kinds of feelings and stories we'd like to feed, what practical decisions align with our values. We can show up, and it makes all the difference.

One person waking up to their own power, to the choices they make each day and what those choices create, is like a candle which can light other candles. When we dedicate ourselves to knowing ourselves and healing what we find there, we step into a much better position to show up in our lives, to authentically be there for ourselves and those we care about. In healing our lives, we promote healing in our loved ones. And the spiral widens, gaining momentum along the way.

Our Shamanic Heritage

The word shaman often conjures images of tribal witch doctors and primitive cultures. But this perspective is ethnocentric. It is a holdover from generations of cultural arrogance in the West. When encountering tribal people, Western colonizers viewed them as ignorant, even deluded. Western peoples discounted the traditions of tribal peoples as nothing more than superstition. As a result, it has taken centuries for the vast wisdom of tribal culture to be embraced by Western society.

Every culture has its own unique trajectory of growth. And each path of growth offers unique ways of understanding the world and relating to it. No cultural perspective is better or more true than another. They all offer helpful perspectives for certain conditions. That said, it's high time to revisit the spiritual and living traditions of these other cultures to see what they have to offer us. To see how they can enrich our own culture and encourage healthy growth.

One thing stands out in my own investigations into shamanism in history: it goes back as far as people do. There is not a single tribe we have encountered which *does not* have some form of shaman. Every living tribe, and all those that we have records of, had a place for the medicine man, the tribal priest, healer, and sage, the medium between the visible and invisible worlds.

All of this sounds deeply mystical, and it is. At the same time, consider the role of the therapist. The therapist helps their patients to manage their relationship with the invisible world. Consider any high ideal, any principle worth dying for. Justice isn't the sort of thing you can break down into atoms and molecules. Justice lives in the invisible world. The world of thoughts and emotions. The invisible world is more practical than we sometimes realize, and it touches every aspect of human life.

Humans are incredibly gifted at recognizing patterns. We have phenomenally delicate senses, far more nuanced than the feedback we consciously access. And we have amazing processing power of a unique scope and type. We often use the smallest fraction of these abilities in our daily lives. And it is a tragedy if we come to believe that this small fraction is our whole potential.

We are born into this world knowing nothing of what we're capable of. We stumble joyfully into our most basic discoveries as children. As we grow, we learn to work with the world, and with ourselves, in the way that we have been shown. And slowly, the discoveries stop, and we get the world nailed down into something regular and predictable. The wonder slows to a drip, and we start playing the script.

But this is just a resting place along the path. For those who wish to see further, there is wonder beyond imagining in the invisible world, powers and ways of relating to the world that we may never have suspected. An entire medium of experience, with its attendant battleground, that we participate in each day, each moment. This is the world of the shaman. And, at a fundamental level, it is the core of all human experience.

The shaman is not just a figure in tribal culture. The shamanic archetype is part of the very fabric of human experience. There will always be those driven to see deeper, to understand the ways of the world beyond the surface. To make sense of the world in their own personal terms, rather than simply the terms borrowed from their culture. There will always be those among us who see the world differently, and who ask different questions and come to different answers.

There will always be shamans, so long as there are humans. This is not a cultural lineage, though there are many shamanic cultural lineages. Essential shamanism, at its core, is the human spirit waking up to the living story. Learning to mediate that story rather than to be mediated by it.

We need the shamanic archetype in human society because change is constant. We are always growing, always in flux. No approach is perfect; no one perspective answers all questions we encounter. We need those who think outside the box for those times when the box isn't working. We need trailblazers and wayfarers so when the ship is sinking, we have some alternatives to explore.

In the pages ahead, you will hear many references to Eastern, Western, and tribal spiritual traditions, perspectives, and practices. References to the fruits of shamans from all cultures, even when those shamans were called priests, or monks, or scientists. Because our relationship to the inner world, to the invisible world, transcends culture. It transcends all division. We are all enlivened by the same spirit, sharing thoughts and feelings more directly than we have imagined.

Shamanism isn't a lineage. It's what happens when humans wake up and create a personal, conscious, and artistic relationship with their inner worlds.

Who is this book for?

This is not a book for the average person. In fact, this book is not written for a person at all. It's written to the seed of consciousness within each of us. It is a clarion call to those of you ready to grow, to attune more fully to the consciousness expressing itself through you.

If you feel completely fulfilled in your life, if you're engaged with the business of living in a way that inspires joy, clarity, and grace, then you won't need these lessons. And, if your idea of success is a corner office, or a big bank account, or even to just continue doing what you do each day until you can finally retire, then the path these lessons describe will not appeal to you.

The average person will resist change and growth, especially if it requires a shift in perspective. That's fine. Everyone is on their own path. We're all here for a unique, personalized journey. Some of us will find a comfortable place in life and hunker down, see it through to the end. But some of us are driven to push further.

There are some of us who just have to ask: Why? How does it work? Why is it like that? Where did it come from? There are others who feel the hugeness and wonder of the world in ways that go beyond our descriptions and definitions, who *know* that there is something more to our lives than the things we see upon the surface. And others who experience the world in subtle but powerful ways that they must account for somehow, just to make sense of their own experience. And others still who have striven for the symbols of success as described and achieved these things, only to find that they didn't bring the promised happiness.

Some of us are called to go deeper. It's not better or worse than any other calling. And it's not a path that anyone would choose unless they find themselves unmet by anything tangible their lives have to offer.

Simply put: waking up is hard. We spend so much time running from our pain and our challenging feelings, so much energy. When we start to truly get to know ourselves, we have to come face to face with all of that, to really feel it. And it takes effort. Humility. A willingness to call bullshit on ourselves, again and again, and to look openly at all the things we are most afraid of seeing in ourselves.

That's loads of work. Lifelong work. So, most people prefer distraction. We stick with what's working until it doesn't work anymore. The marriage that finally reaches its breaking point, or the job that feels more hollow every day. Eventually, things wear thin. The path of awakening calls to us when we finally tire of these distractions and start seeing through to the pain beneath.

Then we hit a crisis. What we were doing isn't working for us anymore. And we need to change things in order to move forward. But how? What happened to begin with? How did we get into this situation, and how can we get in the driver's seat of our lives moving forward?

If any of this sounds familiar, then this book will offer tools, techniques, and an understanding of your mind and body to help you make this transition.

This book was written to fill a gap in our modern education, a missing piece that becomes more vital every day. We learn so many definitions, so many ways to perform in society. But we rarely learn about the business of living, feeling, growing. We rarely learn about how our stories form our world, about how to use the connection between mind and body, about our values, about how to live a life of fulfillment and purpose on our own terms.

Each of us, as human beings, is gifted with both an organic processor unlike anything we have been able to construct technologically and a body linked to this processor in very specific ways. When we understand the relationship between body and mind, both function more efficiently. We begin to integrate the various aspects of our being into a single, powerful force. This brings with it massive benefits in every single area of experience. The development of a conscious mind-body connection is a superpower, and it's just the beginning of the journey.

Humans are beyond amazing, verging on the miraculous. We are capable of so much more than we suspect. Each one of us has the potential for savant-level skills, genius-level pattern recognition and comprehension, even conscious direction of the autonomic functions of the body. We share our stories and dreams with one another, and they become the dreams of the world, the container of our existence. Just *being human* is so big that words can't do it justice.

Learning to be human in a way that works for us is the hardest thing anyone can do. And it's also the only thing truly worth doing, in the end. It sets the stage for the highest degree of growth, creation, and connection available to us. The lessons in the pages ahead offer tools, knowledge, and perspectives to make sense of the journey to consciousness. To understand the battleground and engage with this opportunity, this life, with open eyes.

As you move forward, please keep this in mind. Don't believe me. Don't believe anything you've heard, or even what you tell yourself. I encourage you to look with your own eyes, with fresh eyes each time, to make sense of the world in your own way and bring your own dream to life.

We are not here to borrow meaning from others. We are here to learn to create meaning in ways that work for us. We are, each of us, artists of our own lives, given a lifetime of practice in which to refine our approach. Try, instead of believing, to understand, feel, and experience.

THE ROAD AHEAD

When you first begin learning a martial art, you are taught how to stand. How to walk with this new stance. And you may wonder, why waste time with that? I already know how to stand and how to walk.

In a martial arts class, we learn stance so that we have a strong foundation, and we learn to walk with this stance so that we can move this strong foundation around as needed. As they say, "Bad hands, needs work. Bad feet, bad kung fu." Every move begins from the ground up.

In the seven modules of this training, we begin with breath. But why? We all know how to breathe already, right? I mean, if we weren't breathing, we'd die.

And this is true. But it is only the beginning. Just as we can learn to have a stronger foundation by standing in a particular way, we can guide our mind and our inner experience by breathing in a particular way.

With each module, we tune in to a layer of our experience. We learn to navigate this realm and fine-tune our relation to it. This is not a matter of knowledge, although knowledge can help us to make sense of it. It is a matter of practice. A living practice of consciousness that extends into every aspect of life, deepening and gaining momentum as it goes.

This journey begins in the outer world and uses outer world language familiar to all human beings: the breath, the emotions, the attention, story. No one is excluded from this journey on the basis of culture or beliefs. At the same time, these lessons lead to the cultivation of an absolutely unique path. We are all given different gifts with which to stand in service, and the flowering of each of our life paths will reflect these gifts.

In this training, you will learn to enter the meditative or journey state at will and without props. You will learn to hold your center amidst intense emotions, to healthily self-parent and to make emotional sensitivity a blessing rather than a curse. You will learn to harness the creative force of your attention and direct it to your will. And you will learn to meet yourself with love and acceptance. And that's still just the beginning.

This is knowledge that should be made available to every human being from birth. And that begins now, with you and others reading these words and putting these stories into practice. It begins by ensuring that those who awaken are met with love and guided to healthy, life-affirming relations with themselves, with others, and with the world. Armed with this knowledge, we can begin making a healthier, more loving world, one person, one interaction, at a time.

The Shaman's Journey

The shaman's journey takes us through the invisible world, a world of thoughts and feelings, of strong passions and holy ideas. A realm of pain and inspiration.

The shaman's path takes us away from everything we know. In order to take this journey, we need courage all out of proportion with reason. Courage enough to find a Truth that others don't understand, and may not even believe in. The Truth Against the World.

This Truth is not against the world in such a way as to set us at odds with it, though it may seem otherwise at times. This Truth, which is found in personal experience only, sets us at odds with the way others understand the world. We will be forced, again and again, to make decisions based on growth rather than security. We will be driven by our own inner needs to grow past our limitations, to step into a bigger, more vital realm of experience. And finally, we will be led by our own pain, by our conscious engagement with our lives, to a desire for meaningful service to the world.

While we remain with the herd, we have company, confirmation. Validation. Security. While we follow the script laid out for us in life, we can justify our behavior to others. We can speak to others in terms they understand. And if that works for you, by all means, do your thing. But the one thing the herd does not offer is individuation. In individuating, we come to an understanding of life on our own terms; we learn what we value and we learn to serve those values, even when the herd is moving in a different direction. This path requires exceptional character and strength of will. It also cultivates this strength in those who make the leap.

Society teaches us what we need to know to fit in to society. And there's nothing wrong with that. It's necessary for the human race to continue and for our culture to be maintained. The next step in our development is up to us as individuals.

Our culture is a patchwork blend of unconscious agreements, shared stories so distant from the physical world as to border on delusion. A person who can see the social story as no more than one of many valid perspectives is often challenged in relating to those who see it as the world. But it is just such an individual who can spearhead change when it is required.

The shamanic archetype is one name for the inner force which calls us to awaken. To look again at the conditions of our lives, to see where we have made choices and what those choices have led to. When the shamanic archetype begins to blossom in an individual, they become a trailblazer, exploring the world in personal ways, engaging deeply with their lives. When we begin looking with our own eyes at the world around us, we become a wayfarer, a guide to others, tuned in to both the needs of our society and new ways that those needs might be met. Consciousness is powerful in beautiful and unexpected ways.

On this journey, we learn to interpret our lives in much the way we might interpret a dream, looking at the outer details as reflections of our inner being. And we learn to hack this relationship between the inner and outer worlds, adjusting inner conditions to make outer conditions more likely, and vice versa.

We first come face to face with all the ways we self-sabotage, old patterns that we cling to unconsciously. This is the journey through the Lower World, the realm of the personal subconscious. After a lot of work in reclaiming our personal power, we move on to the Upper World, to the place of holy ideas like Truth and justice. We learn what we value, what we serve.

After all of this journey through the intangible, the shaman's path leads right back where we started from, right back to the visible and the tangible. The Middle World. We take what we have learned about ourselves, about the world and our relation to it, and put it into practice. We create in alignment with our values. We tell stories and take action, dreaming the way forward and then actualizing that dream.

This is not the specialized knowledge of some few, not specific to any culture. It is human, accessible to each person who feels called to it. That said, consciousness is not a toy or a weekend getaway. It is the center of the human journey.

Shamans are scientists and artists of consciousness. And, whenever a human being begins paying attention to their experience, to the relation between their inner and outer worlds, they begin their own conscious journey of discovery and creation.

The Invisible World

It may sound strange to hear of the invisible world. After all, what is it? I'm familiar with what I can see and hear and touch and smell and taste, but what about the things I can't? Is there really an invisible world at all? Maybe it's all just matter, and everything else is an illusion.

If you're thinking this, you're not alone.

But perhaps the invisible world is not such a foreign idea. After all, storytellers craft tales in the invisible world that entertain and inspire. Scientists peer into the invisible world, divining its mechanisms and using this to determine how matter will behave under different conditions. Lawmakers craft social agreements in the invisible world that determine the organization and interaction of people in society. Everything that we feel and think is invisible, and yet it has a profound effect on our experience. In fact, our experience itself is invisible.

All meaning resides in the invisible world. And, though physical correlates can be associated with it, consciousness itself is invisible. We have our invisible self, the spirit within each of us, bringing life to our body, the *Being* experiencing the feelings and sensations generated by interaction with the world.

The visible world is important. It is the medium for our experience in the body. But the invisible world is equally important, just as the feeling and intention behind a touch can mean as much as the touch itself.

To understand the invisible world a bit better, just think of a book. Books are wonderful things. Within a book, a story can be found. But it would be misleading to say that the book actually *contains* the story. The book actually contains a sequence of symbols. When we engage with those symbols, we interpret them based on agreements we have learned in the form of language. The symbols transform, in our inner experience, into words, and then into an entire series of events and interactions playing out.

In the visible world, it is only a book. But in the invisible world, it is a portal to a story, to a collection of thoughts and experiences, a way of seeing the world, of growing, of framing and responding to the challenges of life.

If you were to grind up the book and break it down into its most basic elements, you wouldn't find a story. The story comes through symbol and representation. It is not found in matter, not housed in the physical world. Instead, the story is *expressed through* the physical.

This is the nature of the invisible world. It is a world of information, meaning, and feeling. Information is reflected in the way matter forms ordered and sophisticated arrangements. Information is evident in the patterns reflected in living things and throughout every aspect of the natural world. This order is reflected at every level, in the DNA, in the brain wave oscillations, in numbers and physical laws, in the archetypal journey of the story. Information guides matter to unfold and take certain shapes, to respond in characteristic ways.

When one begins to understand the invisible world, they begin to see that their thoughts, emotions, and intentions are as important as their words and actions. They begin to see that every bit of the world is a reflection of nature, of the divine, of the patterns and structures inherent in ourselves and the universe. Stories, numbers, and archetypes are living denizens of the invisible world. Plato's forms and Kant's categories of cognition are configurations of living information.

In the invisible world, our stories are alive and they grow alongside us. Strong dreamers share their tales and shape the inner experience of all who hear them. We are all shaped by the stories of our culture, and we craft new stories with our lives to add to that which came before. We play these stories out in our relationships, across generations, and between nations and cultures.

When we can't see the invisible world, we tend to get a bit out of balance. Everyone is quite busy with their own concerns, and with the fears that keep them focused or the rewards that make it worthwhile. It takes someone who sees the whole formed by the group, who sees the ecology of stories generated in society, to bring everyone onto the same page from time to time. Such an individual can release pressure and offer a healthy focus by working with stories shared by all involved. They do so by finding a perspective that promotes unity and serves the needs of both the individuals and the whole.

In comes the shaman, the human who is tuned to the invisible world. Painful or fearful stories, unresolved emotional undertones, secrets and resentments, these things can build up and poison a community, splintering it and fostering conflict. When someone can see these invisible things clearly and help the community to address them, they have performed an invaluable service. Humans are capable of anything when they work together. And we are our own worst enemies when we work against one another.

The shaman is a shaman first because they see these subtle things, both in themselves and others. And next, because they have chosen to stand in service to their community in the highest and best way available to them. Integrity leads us to balance on a knife-edge, to both honor the right of each being to determine their own path and to show up in support of others when it is healthy to do so.

Shaman is not a title. It is a function. It's not a point of pride, but a reminder of the need for constant vigilance and humility, lest we project our issues onto others and play out our own dramas in the worst way possible. To see what others can't is a power. And, like all powers, it should be handled with respect.

This is what the invisible world is all about. And this is what it means to be a shaman, to mediate between the visible and invisible worlds. Those of us who are called to look deeper, to more fully express our potential, are called to step into service to what we believe in, what we value. We are called to bring these invisible things more fully into this visible space, just as an engineer does when designing an aircraft, just as an architect does when designing a house. Just as a teacher does when passing along new ways of seeing the world.

All meaning comes from relation, from the invisible connections we make with people, places, feelings, and ideas. All fulfillment – true fulfillment – comes from doing something that we believe in, from honoring our experience and living our life as the gift that it is. And every bit of this is found in the invisible world.

Transmutation

> *Many a blessing begins as a curse, but all blessings become curses if we disrespect them.*
>
> *-Anonymous*

Sometimes life hurts. More than can be put into words.

Sometimes we go places that are hard to come back from. Sometimes we make mistakes that we regret for years to come. Sometimes we lose people we love dearly. And it all hurts.

There are no words that could take this pain away, nor should there be. There are some pains which would be more of a tragedy to **not** experience. We hurt because we care, because we love. And that's worth more than comfort. It's deeper and more real than numbness or distraction. Pain and love go hand-in-hand, and it's worth it to experience every bit of feeling life has to offer.

We can never escape our pain. But we can transmute it. We can transform our pain into compassion and wisdom. We can change our relationship with these memories, these feelings, from traumatic to empowering. We can free ourselves by letting ourselves process and experience old emotions, and then deciding what we want to do about them. The pain doesn't so much fade as transform into clarity, compassion, and humility.

Here's a massive secret of life: Much of our pain persists for so long because we spend so long trying to avoid it. We get so good at avoiding our pain, we may not even realize we're doing it. We can look straight at our issues and not see them until we're ready to.

Humility shortens the learning curve massively, as does vulnerability and a willingness to look honestly and openly at our own feelings. Whatever it is we're feeling, the longer we resist it, the more intense the crisis when we are finally forced to deal with it. *The only way around is through.*

The past is done and gone. We cannot go back and undo our mistakes or the things that led us to regret. But each mistake holds a lesson within it. And each regret has the potential to show us what we truly care about. Until we are willing to face our pain, we're stuck hurting. But once we open up to feel it, we gain access to it. We can use our past lessons to point the way forward, to show us what we care about, what we stand for, and what we would like to build in our lives.

We cannot escape our pain, but we can transmute it. Resentment can give way to compassion. Ignorance can mature into wisdom. A victim mentality can transform slowly into an empowered relationship with our own lives. We all make our own path, and we can descend as far as we like, as far as life takes us. But as soon as we are ready, no matter how lost we have become, we can begin the slow climb back to truly loving life.

Each challenge we experience could be described as a dragon, a ferocious beast that we must face in order to continue upon our journey. But the task is not to kill the dragon, but rather to tame it.

When we make peace with our challenges, when we face our pain, we tame our dragon. We can then transform it into a strength, becoming a dragonrider, an empowered being in our relationship with our inner world. And one beauty of this journey is that this inner strength is recognized by those around us.

Think about it this way. When you have a problem to solve, would you rather consult a textbook, or someone who's already been through the problem and come out the other side? There's no substitute for personal experience. When you transform your personal challenges into clear, solid life lessons, your words become powerful, resonant. They ring true in the ears of others. There is a subtle but sweeping power that comes from self-knowledge.

Every single challenge we experience – every pain and every shortcoming – can become a lesson. Every challenge we see our way through becomes a point of strength. In meeting a challenge, we gain clarity about what we truly value and how we can act in accordance with those values. Our old pains become sacred wounds, granting determination, clarity, and groundedness and spurring us to stand in service.

When we see life's challenges as obstacles, it's easy to get frustrated or overwhelmed. But when we instead view them as training, as opportunities to access old pains and outgrown stories, the landscape changes. Instead of a minefield of issues, we get a living jungle that inspires us to grow in every way possible. To become aware of our blind spots. To learn how to hold space in a way that works for all that we care about, even in the moment and under pressure.

Every time you rise to a challenge, you become better at meeting that kind of challenge in the future. And every time you rally in the face of adversity, you train yourself to keep going when the going gets tough. Slowly, slowly, through life's challenges, we grow. We come to know ourselves more deeply and express more of our potential. We begin shaping our lives to reflect what we truly want and value.

The Psychology of Initiation

When we change from one way of relating to the world to another, we do so through an initiation. A woman becomes a mother through the initiation of pregnancy and childbirth. A marriage is a different kind of initiation, an entry into life as a couple. In both cases, life before the initiation looks very different from life afterward. The initiation marks a transition point, an "entry into" the new life from the previous.

Some initiations are more subtle. We are initiated into a new situation when entering a new job, or new school. We are initiated into the family of a lover when they bring us home to meet the folks. We are initiated, in some way, into the role of an adult from that of a child, and later, from adult to elder. These life changes are rarely honored in modern society, but they are massive for the individual involved. And, when we do a ceremony for the initiation, it helps the community to participate in the individual's journey, to honor the changes in their life.

The core of an initiation is not the shift in the outer world, but that in the inner. A ceremony may symbolize initiation in some cases, as in the instance of marriage. But many initiations occur with little to no fanfare, and some without a hint of warning. When we begin to wake up, we experience an initiation, an inner change. We begin to look deeper than the surface, and our entire relationship with ourselves and the world begins to change to accommodate this new dimension of experience.

This may sound abstract and appealing, but it rarely feels that way. It's said that changes in life first tap, then knock, then bowl you over. The longer we resist the change, the more intense it will be when things finally come to a head. In the case of a shamanic initiation, a growth into a deeper and more conscious relationship with self and world, this transition often takes the form of a crisis. It may be a challenge to our health, to our emotions, even an existential crisis. But things come up, and we feel we can no longer continue as we have.

This is a beautiful moment, and a powerful opportunity. But it's not easy, not by a long stretch of the imagination. When we go through the deep challenges of life, we have to be patient and remember to breathe. We will be assaulted by all our fears and insecurities, by stories filled with our old emotional toxins, all the things we had tried so hard to avoid. All the things we didn't want to see. And we just have to breathe and allow it to be what it is. Allow ourselves to feel the feelings and learn whatever lessons can be learned in this moment.

Moments like these can feel like forever, like they will never end. It might seem like we'll never feel ok again, like things are always up in the air and it's always running, like it's an endless grind with more pressure building behind it all the time.

But one of the only constants in life is change. These things will pass. And we have a say in how things will feel – in how things will work for us – from here on in. What we are shown in these depths helps us to know what we truly value, what we care about, and how we would like to conduct ourselves. These experiences, when we come out the other side, offer unusual strength, grace, and faith.

Nothing worth doing is easy. But if you find yourself going through a challenging transition, remember, you are the watcher at the center of your being, viewing all of this and learning from it. You are the one who chooses. After this feeling has passed, you will still be.

Moments like this are priceless for knowing what you truly, authentically want. They help us to see what is meaningful to us, what really matters. Challenges can offer clarity and show us how to use our creative energy in ways that work for us.

Initiation is a fancy word for something that happens naturally in the psychological and emotional development of a human being. When we use a conscious ceremony for initiation, we are honoring the change in our lives and setting an intention to participate consciously with this shift in our inner world. And we can do this whenever we meet a major challenge in life. We can recognize this challenge for the initiation that it is and rise to meet it like a warrior.

This is much easier said than done, and one thing which is of huge benefit in this is story. Humans use stories to make sense of the world. A healthy narrative framework can help an individual to make sense of the challenges they face. A solid, life-affirming myth is an ideal frame for individuation.

One simple way to begin building a true myth is by recognizing how all of your life's challenges have forged you into the person that you are today. And, in the process, by recognizing how you forge yourself with each action, word, and breath, with each movement forward.

A significant degree of freedom is to be found in choosing stories that bring our conscious and subconscious minds together and get them acting in unison. This is what myth can do, in a deeply human and personal way.

I encourage you to delve deeply into the stories of your ancestors, whatever myths hold resonance for you. These stories explain the world and how a human being stands in relation to it. Read them like you would look at a dream to find the meaning. They are wise oracles offering deep insight into human life. Into *your* life.

Remember that the stories that you read, those you hear from others, those you watch, all stories behave just as myths would in our inner mind. They prime us to make sense of the world in certain ways.

Our stories show us the world beyond our immediate senses. They show us how human beings behave in response to specific challenges, and how those responses play out. Engage consciously with the stories you take in, seeking out symbolic insight and healthy heroes upon which to (mostly unconsciously) model your behavior.

The Battle for Power

Whether we know it or not, each of us is engaged, each day, in a battle for power. This is not power in the traditional or conventional sense. In fact, we may never even be aware of our power or of this battle. We might drift our way along from one moment to the next without much thought about it. But no matter our degree of awareness, we choose, create, and shape the world a tiny bit with each moment, each decision, each bit of attention or will we spend.

This power is not measured in terms of money, or strength, or social consensus. It comes from the ability to choose. To decide, I will do *this*, I will not do *this*.

These choices are often made unconsciously, sometimes without us realizing that a choice exists. Consider a time, for example, when someone hurt your feelings. That hurt was a choice. But it didn't feel like it. It was a product of how you were invested in the situation, how you perceived and interpreted their words or actions. There are many choices in this process, but it can feel as if there was no choice at all, as if our hurt feelings were the only reasonable way for us to respond.

In this case, we have given our power away. To the person in question, to our mental image of ourselves, to our stories and dramas. Although we had a potential choice about how to engage, how to respond, we perceived and responded reflexively, acting out old patterns.

Until we reclaim it, our will, our authentic choice, is not our own. It is, for the most part, bound up in ideas and stories. Excuses and histories and self-limiting beliefs. To reclaim this will and once more have an authentic choice is the work of a lifetime.

Just think for a moment. How much of what you do is what you truly want to do? And how much do you want to do that you feel you cannot? How much of your life is a survival pattern created by reflex and necessity, and how much of it is an intentional journey?

Any habit which you feel you cannot choose is a habit to which you have given your power. If you are called to unconscious response, if you are triggered, it's because the trigger touched upon something to which you have given your power. Some idea, story, habit, perception, person, that you have charge around. Any belief you have about the world is your belief because you have invested your will in believing it.

We give our power away with our attention, with our interpretation of experiences, and with our active choices (or lack thereof). We give our power away when we stop speaking up for ourselves or start hiding. When we maintain secrets or lies. When we do not take care of ourselves. When we believe others' words more than the reports of our own senses.

We give our power away when we want something and cannot be content without it. We give our power away when we fear something and avoid facing it. When we cling to habits, or ideas, or memories, or anticipated futures, while unconscious of the life we lead in the moment.

It's easy to give power away. It's hard, very hard, to reclaim that power. Just think of a time when you were trying to quit a habit. Or when you took on that diet and exercise plan. Or when you stepped away from that relationship that wasn't good for you. Or when you stopped following the script and began deciding what you want to feel, experience, share, and build in your life.

In any instance, reclaiming our power from old habits, limiting stories, and unresolved emotions is hard work. To do so in the service of consciousness requires lifelong commitment and vigilance.

Every fixed story, every bit of unconscious charge, colonizes a little bit of our power, of our will. The battle for power is a process of watching our own behavior. Watching our choices and where we place our attention. Before we act, considering. Is this what I really want to do, what I really mean to say? And, after the fact, reviewing. Did those actions or words line up with my values? Has my time been spent in ways I find fulfilling? In ways that build the things I want to build with my life?

There's always room for improvement, so the battle for power is never over. No resting on our laurels. It's about the journey, not the destination. Although this battle will never end, and although it will one day claim our life, each day that we wage it consciously becomes a day fully lived. To the best of our imperfect abilities, we step forward and meet the challenges life throws our way.

Power over others is an illusion. Meaningless at best, and a trap at worst. Power in the world evokes resistance and fades all too quickly. Power within, the power to choose, the power to engage with the world as we will, this grows with time. It grows subtly, in the depths, until we realize that we have more choice than we thought possible. Our words, thoughts, and deeds gain depth and we come to life, moving from merely surviving to thriving.

The end goal is a world where people can communicate and collaborate in a healthy way. Where we make the world more kind, more healthy, and more alive by our interaction with it. Where we foster the growth and healing of the human spirit while making space for the unique needs and contributions of the individual. But, in order to create collectives such as this, conscious collectives, we must first have conscious individuals.

The best thing that the individual can do for society, for themselves, and for those to come, is to wake up to their power and choice. To meet their pain, learn their values, and act accordingly. To see the battle for power in which they are engaged, and to meet that challenge with spirit.

We each meet this battle on our own terms, in our own way, with challenges uniquely customized to our strengths and weaknesses. We are accountable only to ourselves in this journey, though the consequences impact everyone we touch. It's not a race, and this battle will not end until we die. Perhaps not even then. And, even though the work will never end, every scrap of power reclaimed leads to a fuller, more fulfilling life.

But be warned. The deepest parts of our beings are absolutely committed to growth. Once we engage in the battle for power in the service of consciousness, we have committed to growth at all costs, even when it is unpleasant or uncomfortable. Even if we would rather stay small or play it safe.

This isn't a battle we walk away from without grave consequences. Often the very crises that led to our initial awakening come back with even greater force, leading to a domino collapse of all the things we cling to in resistance to growth.

That said, all any of us have to do is show up, *really* show up, to this one moment that we're living. Everything else stems from that.

Power and Integrity

> *With great power comes great responsibility. With small power comes... great responsibility.*

Humans are social beings. We are connected in a living web that includes not only all human beings, but also all other beings on the planet. This interrelation of all of life is one of the keys to wisdom and is the source of all practical morality.

Before we have come into our power, questions of morality are just a list of *should's* and *shouldn't's*. A collection of rules and laws to govern our behavior. Once we begin to exercise our will in the world, we create consequences. We impact those around us with our words and actions. And, in some way, the consequences of this impact work their way back to us, often in amplified form. All of life is interrelated, intimately and inextricably connected.

Thus we have a very practical reason to use our power with integrity. To act with consideration for the impact of our actions upon ourselves, upon others, and upon the world. Any misaligned application of power will lead to imbalance, conflict, and unsustainable situations.

Imposing, manipulating, exercising our will beyond healthy boundaries or using excessive control, none of these things are effective in the long run, and all of them come with serious downsides. But power applied with integrity evokes respect and trust. It becomes a foundation upon which healthy collectives can be formed.

Every single one of us wields power in the lives of others in countless small ways. We can make the lives of others harder or easier. We can contribute to a bad day or help turn it around. We leave echoes in the lives of others even with a casual conversation or a smile in passing.

It may seem like none of these things matter. They don't make a difference, right? Wrong.

It mattered to that one person. It has mattered to you before. That one conversation that just really hit home. Someone helping when they could have stood in your way. We all work together to create the conditions we experience in society. When we think that other people don't matter, or that the little conversations we have don't influence others, we tend to treat others with indifference. And we get treated with the same indifference. And it snowballs, leading to a numb society, rife with casual cruelty and disrespect.

What can one person do? One person can treat others with respect. One person can use their will, their voice, their power, with integrity and with honest care for the mark they leave upon the world. One person can touch others, inspire them. Even the biggest things in life begin with just one person showing up, speaking up. And every single one of us who make it a practice to use our power, our will, in life-affirming ways, every single one of us shines a light into a world that badly needs it.

To act with integrity is to act with your whole being, with a consideration of both heart and mind, alongside the practical needs and constraints of the body. When we act out of alignment with our values, we are making a decision with only a part of our being. We are not acting with integrity. But, when we take these values into consideration, the things we truly care about, the things we truly serve, we can direct all of our efforts and form all of our stories in relation to these things. We bring our entire being into alignment with itself when we then follow these values with action, in the highest and best way available to us. This is how we cultivate integrity.

Integrity requires both compassion and humility. Compassion, because we are social creatures, because we are imperfect and would like to receive compassion when we err, and because we must offer the same to others if we are to sustainably relate with them. Humility, because we will be shown, time and again, ways that our old patterns lack integrity. And we will be given opportunities, time and again, to humble ourselves, to reclaim our power and make new decisions more in line with our whole being.

It is easy to make destructive and selfish decisions. But it is not fulfilling over time. And it creates consequences that we never really escape. Integrity is the alternative. To use our power in ways that honor what gives us life, that honor all the things upon which our life depends. In doing so, we will often be required to overcome selfish and limiting perspectives, desires, and habits. The tradeoff is an inner freedom and clarity of purpose, alongside closer, healthier, and more meaningful connection with our world.

Freedom and The Ego

Each of us meticulously constructs a role, just like a method actor. Unlike a method actor, however, we do it unconsciously. And we convince ourselves so deeply that we come to believe that we *are* the role. We build this paper-thin legend, and then wrap it around an experience that's so big it doesn't fit in a box. We build a story of self, an ego. This is not the Ego, the I Am presence at the center of our beings. The little "I", the ego, is a story about who we are, where we came from, who we're connected to, and what's possible for us.

When the story wears thin, when we experience a crisis that would force us to change our story, the ego feels threatened. We learn to color in the lines, to maintain our role and resist deviation from established boundaries, even when we feel moved to a different form of expression. We create our role unconsciously, parroting those around us, refining this role reflexively based on the validation we receive from others. And we forget we're playing a role.

At this point, we believe that our ego, the story that we have about ourselves, is the same as the "I" we experience. We want to hold on to that I, to what makes it worthwhile and valuable. We want to protect it. So we tend to cling to our story of self, thinking that the two different things are one and the same. If we find out that we're not as well liked as we thought we were, not as capable, if we suffer shortcomings in the eyes of others, then our story of self is in trouble. The ego feels threatened. And, *if we think we are our story, we are compelled to respond to this threat.*

Freedom comes when we can move beyond our story of self and into the experience of Being. And this comes when we recognize that we are connected intimately and inextricably to every aspect of our inner and outer worlds. We come to a point where fulfillment is found only through honoring this connection, through standing in service in the ways available to us. We can then take on our role consciously, in service of what we believe in and in support of the living world which surrounds us.

To put it simply, we find our freedom by dedicating ourselves to something more than our own bodies, our personal enjoyments and concerns. We find fulfillment and purpose in crafting an ego that allows us to stand in meaningful, healthy relation to the world.

The key is not to eliminate the ego. That will only happen for brief moments, anyway, as the ego is a working interface to frame our practical relationship to the world. The key is to recognize that our ego is a role, a tool that we use to show what we're about, to express our values, to voice our principles.

The ego allows us to care passionately about a person or cause. So choose consciously. Wisely. Choose with your whole being. Get to know your needs and values, and observe as you craft your ego with each story, each face you present, each message. We build this legend for ourselves as much as for others. And then we inhabit the legend, filling it and living it.

What kind of legend do you want to build? How can the very way you live your life, the very way you hold space, be an inspiration? How can it be an expression of what you stand for? How can you show up, in your perception of yourself, in the social space, and in the tangible things you build in life, as the person you would like to be?

Build your ego, your legend, consciously, knowing it as the tool that it is. And, when your growth outpaces your legend, allow it to die. Let your old stories about yourself go. Make space for new stories to come in to frame your relation to the world in new ways. The ego dies, and the ego is reborn, brighter and more aligned with who you are right now, with your needs and desires in this moment.

This is one of the deepest and most powerful expressions of freedom. To be able to inhabit egos and cast them off, as necessary, consciously, without attaching to a specific story of self. When we learn this kind of freedom, we learn to not take ourselves too seriously. We know that we don't know everything, so we must keep an open mind. We know that we are always growing and changing, and what described us yesterday will not describe us tomorrow. And we have learned to use this knowledge to remain open, fluid, changing with the dance of life.

To craft one's expression of self consciously is high artistry, and to do so aligned with our values, living out those values with meaningful service, this is a masterpiece.

Personal Journey, Collective Healing

There is a word used by the Quechua tribe of South America: Ayni. Ayni could be defined as "right relation." It involves reciprocity and the interconnectedness of all life. When we hold ayni sacred, we see our connection to the community, to nature, to the universe, and we strive to act consciously and with respect on all of these levels. We become aware of the exchange of energy that is occurring between ourselves and every aspect of our surroundings, and we strive to make this exchange balanced and healthy.

Words are powerful. They frame the way we see the world, the way we understand and connect with our values. When we learn a word like ayni, we are given a different lens through which to view our relationship with the world. Instead of viewing ourselves as separate from the universe, we can begin to see that we are inextricably connected to everything around us. We start to notice how every act impacts the people around us, the web of life and culture that sustains us.

Humans have become extremely powerful. Clever. Advanced. Whatever you want to call it, we have the capacity to shape the world. And we're doing it. One decision at a time. People come together to form nations, corporations, movements, they vote with both ballots and money. Every single thing we do creates something, leaves some mark. Even if we're just doing our job, just following orders. We are using our creative energy in service to that job or those orders, shaping the world in tiny but inevitable ways.

We have become so numerous and so technologically advanced that we have the capacity to destroy ourselves and much of the life on this planet. We relate to one another and the world unconsciously, without truly understanding the power we wield. Most of all, we feel separate, isolated. It can feel as if it doesn't matter what we do. A culture with unprecedented power and an attitude that what they do has no meaningful consequences is very dangerous and thoughtlessly destructive. And, though we once thought that technological power would solve all the world's ills, we're now finding that increasing our technological power simply amplifies the consequences.

If the human race is to avert self-made disaster, we need a miracle. And no one is coming to save us. If this miracle is to come, *we* are responsible for it, each and every one of us. We need as many humans as possible to wake up to their power and begin creating, with every choice, a world which is life-affirming, one which unites us and promotes ayni. This is the solution, the miracle. Individual awakening, followed by collective action. Beginning with the smallest things – the way we show up in *this* moment, for ourselves and for those we care about – and working our way up from there.

All of the most beautiful, most aligned things we can offer the world begin with inner work. They begin with looking inside and finding the pieces of gold hidden in the challenges. We can try to help others or change the world before we have done this work, but often our projection hinders the good we might do. Once we begin truly healing, this is shared with the world in countless invisible ways, through the well-timed word or even the slightest gesture. We share our meaning with others, both consciously and unconsciously. Healthy meaning promotes healthy growth.

Many of the deepest transformations in the life of the individual or the culture begin with stories. We have played out the usefulness of many of our past stories, those which emphasized progress and profit. We need a new story, and shamans are storytellers, weavers of the invisible threads of ideas and emotion. We need a story that:

- Makes consciousness central, rather than incidental,
- Is inclusive of all humans,
- Promotes ayni (right relation),
- Is empowering and liberating,
- Supports individuation, actualization, and personal fulfillment, and
- Helps us to link personal fulfillment with conscious collective action.

Those of us who feel compelled to look deeper, to wrestle with our demons and make peace with ourselves, to stand in service to the world, we are here, in part, to tell a new story to the world. One which addresses the gaps in the current story. When we commit to our own healing and growth, we begin making meaning in different ways and sharing this new meaning with others.

In cultivating consciousness, we inspire awakening. In reclaiming our personal power, we inspire others to dream and make those dreams real. In finding freedom from old habits and patterns, we blaze a trail to authentic choice for ourselves and those around us.

The key to service is respect. *All beings deserve respect.* And, when we view others with respect, we will strive to act with consideration towards them. We make them just as important to us as the things we want for ourselves. When truly standing in service to the world, the end **does not** justify the means. Doing something with respect and integrity and failing has a more beneficial impact on the world than doing something harmful or deceitful for great intentions. Respect all life, and your decisions are far more likely to be healthy ones.

How to Make the Most of this Book

This work springs from a lifetime of study of humanity, consciousness, and spirituality. It is written to offer a path to reconnection with ourselves, with our bodies, our potential, and our living experience. The lessons are presented sequentially, and taken together, they offer a comprehensive review of the human experience from the perspective of consciousness.

Furthermore, it is not a work of theory, but of practice. These perspectives and techniques can place you in a position to engage more deeply and more meaningfully with your inner world, and to enjoy all the benefits that result from it. But you will gain these benefits only to the extent that you are willing to put in the work.

All real change happens through experience. So, this book was written as an accompaniment to a training course which offers a solid foundation and support in deepening your journey of self-knowledge and self-actualization. We all walk the path in our own way. That said, it can be incredibly helpful to have a strong understanding of the human mind and perception. It's also vital to share with other living minds to work through things and learn in person.

Human beings can be amazingly resistant to growth. We can fool ourselves, refuse to see what's right in front of us. Because of this, it can be extremely helpful to go through this journey with guidance from someone who's walked the path. Words, even the most perfectly chosen words, veil truth rather than revealing it. So there is no way to write these lessons in a way that will speak to everyone, or in a way that is impossible to misunderstand or misapply.

However, there are some people, myself included, who prefer to teach themselves, rather than to be taught by others. For those stubborn individuals, please consider taking one module per month.

Read them all, if you like. Or simply work on one at a time. But for the span of a month, I encourage you to review a single module and do the practices each moment, each day, and in the background. Just like learning a musical instrument. Do it until it begins to become natural, reflexive. The work you put in during this foundational phase will pay exponential dividends later on.

So, for the first month, work on rhythm. Notice the breath. Feel the beat. In everything, at every moment. Learn to change your own rhythm with breath, with focus and intention. Learn to enter the journey state at will, and begin exploring what self-guided meditation and inner work can offer. Form within your mind a place of power to act as an interface for inner work. Train yourself to slow your rhythm and center yourself in times of pain, triggers, stress, and when high function is required (intelligence, memory, dexterity, creative application, conscious communication).

For the second month, explore your emotional charge. Listen to the wisdom of your feelings. Learn how to hold space for yourself to feel and release old emotional charge. Learn to host the temple of your inner being and self-parent in healthy, life-affirming ways. Learn to check in with yourself and use your subtle feelings like a compass to guide you. Train yourself to step back and consider, rather than to be pulled into unconscious reaction. Learn to tap in to helpful emotions intentionally.

And so on, until every bit of the practice has become inscribed upon your lens of the world.

This is only a suggestion, but one intended to help you get the absolute most out of these lessons and out of this phase of your journey.

MODULE 1 - RHYTHM AND CONSCIOUSNESS

Intro to Rhythm and Consciousness

Imagine, for a moment, that you had never seen a radio before. A friend brings in an old radio, one with a tuning dial. Once it's plugged in, turned on, and turned up, music comes on. For a person seeing it for the first time, that's a moment of wonderment, magic beyond comprehension.

Now imagine that you've spent years listening to that radio, sometimes liking the music playing, other times not so much. But hey, at least it's making noise. And then the same friend that dropped off the radio comes to visit. They notice that you have music playing and ask why you chose that style of music.

"What? What are you talking about? That's the music playing. How could it be anything other than what it is?"

In response to your bafflement, the friend steps over to the radio, turns the knob, and changes the station. All of a sudden, different music is playing. And again, you have experienced a miracle. The music, the whole feel of the space, has changed in ways you never realized it could. More than that, you see how you could change the dial yourself, how you can change the music any time you want.

In the Twenty-First Century, we no longer use analog radios with dials and tuning knobs, but perhaps the image will still serve as an example. What if your brain was, in certain ways, similar to the radio just described? The brain is a sensitive organ, capable of picking up a host of subtle signals and interpreting these signals – in some as yet undefinable way – into a sphere of sensory experience, a medley of thoughts, memories, and feelings. What if we had the capacity to tune the function of our minds, to change the knob and hear different music? What if we've been listening to classical for our whole lives, never realizing that we had the capacity to listen to jazz?

These days we know more about how to craft and engineer materials than at any other time in history. However, we are just as clueless as ever about the nature of consciousness, how to navigate and work productively with the conscious experience. Each of us, as human beings, is in possession of an organic computer more powerful than anything we have created digitally.

And that's just the beginning. Our minds speak to and inform the function and growth of our bodies. We engage with an entire world of words and meanings that are invisible to a microscope, but powerful enough to direct the course of cultures and nations. The human being is in possession of an instrument unlike any other, and like the radio described above, it came without an instruction manual.

To bring this home a bit further, think back to a moment when you were on fire, performing perfectly, in flow. And now, try to think of a time when you were engaged in the same task but felt off. Having to struggle a bit, overlooking things, losing track of things. This is a personal, experiential example of how your inner tuning can affect you.

Often, when we're a bit off, we know to push harder, to double down and force through to the finish. But what if it was possible to shift from scattered and ineffectual to focused and clear, *at will*? If this is possible, why is it not part of our basic education?

Like the individual in the example above, we were never taught about tuning our device. "What's that, anyway? Life is just what happens to us, right? And we just deal as well as we can?"

But there's a bit more to it than that. Life is as much about how we react to what happens, how we engage with our moment, as it is what happens to us. We have the capacity to change the station, after a fashion, and engage differently with the task at hand, with the moment of experience.

The key to tuning our minds is rhythm. Shamanic practices the world over have used the drum as a foundational journey tool, and for good reason. The body itself is a drum. We have the drumbeat of our heart, the bellows of our lungs, and the electrochemical activity of our brain, all coming together to form a three-part rhythm. These drumbeats are linked together and tend to echo one another.

Our whole experience is tuned to these rhythms. When we are excited or nervous, the heart rate and force of contraction increases, as does our rate and depth of breathing. Invisible to the naked eye, the rhythms of our brain waves follow this train, coloring our inner experience, bringing up feelings and connections that fit with our current moment. So, when our heart rate and breathing slow, so too does the rhythm of the electrical activity in our brain.

The Science of Brain Waves

But why does this matter? Well, time for a little science lesson. The brain speaks to the body via electric signals sent through neurons. When viewed as a whole by an EEG, these electrochemical signals form wave-like patterns known as brain waves. There are five categories of brain waves, classified by their speed: Delta, Theta, Alpha, Beta, and Gamma, listed from slowest to fastest. Brain waves are measured in cycles per second, also known as Hertz (Hz).

These waves change constantly as we move through the day and they correspond with our actions, thought patterns, feelings, and state of mind. As indicated in the table below, each brain wave rhythm is associated with certain functions or qualities of consciousness.

For the most part, the average person spends their lives with the Beta frequency dominant. This is the brain rhythm associated with problem solving, planning, and responding to immediate threats. The mind is alert and the concentration is sharp. The body gets signals that it needs to be ready for action, so the sympathetic nervous system charges you up, and you're ready to figure out how to survive.

This is a perfect response in the wild, when faced with a natural or physical threat. And it's also good for logical planning and engineering, working with processes and structures. However, if the body is constantly primed for threat, it begins to wear down and eventually enters a state of chronic fatigue from overstress. The mind tires from constant exertion as well, just as we've all felt after a period of draining or monotonous mental work.

To top it off, more intense concentration doesn't necessarily mean more awareness. Just think of any time you were so engrossed in a book, movie, or game that you missed what was happening in the room around you. Beta brain waves are associated with intense concentration on a relatively small slice of the external environment. Internally, this requires more effort to maintain and is more prone to missing details peripheral to the focal point.

On a neurological level, when your brain is working faster, many parts of your brain are functioning at once, each performing its individual task. High frequency and low amplitude reflects many activities performed closely together. Lots of activity, but less cooperation between different parts of the brain.

As the brain rhythm slows, different parts of the brain become entrained with one another. They begin to cycle together and operate as a more integrated unit. Frequency drops, but amplitude increases as the waves of electrical activity reflect more of the brain working together, more neural networks firing at once.

When the brain waves slow to the Alpha rhythm, between 8 and 13 Hz, the inner experience is often described as a relaxed, light meditative state. When the brain is operating in this way, we have access to a wider range of awareness.

For example, consider the difference when you are focused intensely on something, and when you are watching the sunset, just letting the experience wash over you. Odds are, you'll be more aware of everything around you when engaged lightly watching the sunset. Plus, you might notice that *aha!* moments come more often when you slow down and create a bit of space.

Slower brain rhythms correspond to creativity, higher-level intuition, improved cognitive function, better memory and recall, lower stress levels, and better overall health, just to name a few benefits. Nothing beats the higher brain rate for intense focus and problem solving, for keeping on our toes when faced with practical challenges. However, we can use slower rhythms for learning, communicating, high-level performing, doing deep creative or intuitive work, and improving the health and function of the body and immune system.

So, the question at hand, at least to my way of thinking, is how to make use of these characteristics of mental function to improve my quality of life. If these benefits exist from tuning the brain and being to different rhythms, how can I begin to access and make use of these benefits?

Let's take a look at how we can learn to change and direct our brain rhythm. Without drugs or machines, using only the tools that every human being is born with.

Frequency range	Name	Usually associated with:
> 40 Hz	Gamma waves	Higher mental activity, including perception, problem solving, and consciousness
13–39 Hz	Beta waves	Active, busy thinking, active processing, active concentration, arousal, and cognition
7–13 Hz	Alpha waves	Calm, relaxed yet alert state
4–7 Hz	Theta waves	Deep Meditation/ Relaxation, REM sleep
< 4 Hz	Delta waves	Deep dreamless sleep, loss of body awareness

Tail that Wags the Dog

How can we internally direct our brainwave frequency? The short answer: we move the piece we can. Everything's linked together. And breath is one of the key regulators of whole-body rhythm. So, by slowing or changing the phases of the breath, we can exercise a specific influence on brain wave frequency.

Here's an example that helps me to make sense of this phenomenon. Just think of a dog. For those who've spent time around dogs, you've all seen that a dog will tend to wag its tail when it's happy or excited. It might seem a silly question at first, but have you ever wondered if the dog is wagging its tail because it's happy, or if it's happy because it's wagging its tail?

Have you ever noticed that dogs will also wag their tails when they are nervous? Just as cats often purr both when they're happy and when they're trying to self-soothe. The physical behavior and emotional state become associated in our inner experience. When you consciously use an associated physical behavior, you can trigger the emotional state. In simple terms, smiling can lead to feelings of happiness, just like feelings of happiness can lead to smiling.

Since all of our internal frequencies are linked, you can lead them all by leading one, just like a herd of cows can be guided by directing the lead cow. Move one, the others follow.

Breath is the easiest internal rhythm to access directly. We breathe both consciously, like when we take a breath on purpose, and unconsciously, like when we keep breathing while we sleep. Breath itself is such a fundamental physical process that it forms a natural meeting point for conscious and subconscious awareness. Breath is always with us, in every moment, as long as we live. It is the optimal tool for conscious self-regulation and self-mastery.

However, maintaining concentration upon the breath can be challenging at first. There are a few time honored techniques that help to keep focused and maintain a specific rhythm. You see, our bodies and brains tend to sync up with rhythms we see, hear, and feel in the external environment. Shamanic drum techniques make use of this to create a foundation for journey work, for guided meditation and visualization. Using a physical drum is powerful, both in directing one's own journey and in learning how to guide others.

Our brain rhythms become entrained with music that we hear. This is a beautiful thing to note, as we are at every moment influenced in subtle ways by our external environment, often without even realizing it. Listening to slow, soothing music is helpful for slowing brain wave frequencies, especially instrumental pieces that can help you to maintain concentration while relaxing.

That said, no external methods can substitute for an internalized method of self-regulation. When you can shift your own mindstate internally without having to be in a particular environment or listening to a particular type of music, you'll benefit much more from the ability.

Internal Biofeedback

All of our internal rhythms are tied together. When we shift one, such as the breath, all other rhythms follow. In fact, it goes even further than this. Over time, you can become familiar with the feeling of different rhythms, different states of mind, and use the feeling itself to guide the rhythms. Breath is key here, but the feeling itself, the specific inner state and subtle somatics of the body, becomes the feedback for self-regulation.

In effect, this is the foundation of a practice of internal biofeedback. Traditional biofeedback teaches one to exercise control over their autonomic processes, such as heart rate or skin conductivity. For example, the student might have their heart rate monitored and displayed in symbolic form, such as a panel of lights that light up as the heart rate increases. Over time and with practice, the student learns to use intention to light up more lights, or to make lights go out. Eventually, the student is able to direct heart rate intentionally, even without the feedback of the panel of lights.

By learning to use our breath and feel our rhythm, we begin to tune in to feedback from the body itself. We can learn to exercise greater awareness of and influence over autonomic processes, even without machine readouts or chemically-altered states of consciousness.

This takes time, but not as long as one might think. It also takes practice and continual refinement. However, this practice offers massive potential for self-directed growth, accelerated healing, pain management, improvement of immune system function, and a host of other benefits.

The Journey State

The entire focus of this first module is to provide tools and information that give you access to the journey state, at will and without external props. And in the pages ahead, you will hear many mentions of the journey state, the meditative state, even the prayer state. At times, these terms may even be used interchangeably, though there are subtle differences between the states of mind that they describe.

For the sake of clarity and disambiguation, the meditative state is a term which can be accurately used to describe a focus on the inner world, rather than the outer. A light meditative state brings relaxation and helps to balance the body, while remaining fully aware of the body and the conditions that surround it.

As we go deeper, into a medium meditative state, we remain aware of the body and its external conditions, but have the capacity to focus deeply on an intended question, visualization, or shift. This could be described as the prayer state.

Finally, when the meditative state is taken deeper, it could be described as a journey state. In this state, visualization can become more vivid and the subconscious tends to color more of our impressions of our inner space.

On the psychological level, the meditative state is a shift from an outward focus of attention to an inward focus. On the physical level, the meditative state accompanies a slowed brain wave pattern. Since our brain wave frequency is linked to both our breath and heart rate, the meditative state is experienced when breathing and heart rate slow and become steadier.

One central benefit of the meditative state, whether light or deep, is that it helps us to create space within. In this space, the conscious mind is more receptive to the subconscious. Different parts of our being are able to communicate more effectively with one another. This opens up access to information and physical operations normally out of reach of the conscious mind.

Although the journey state may sound abstract, complicated, and mystical, it is natural to all humans. We enter the meditative state when we daydream and in the moments between sleep and awakening. When we experience *aha!* moments and when we enter the flow state for high performance, like when playing intense sports or challenging pieces of music.

We experience the journey state when going through a guided meditation, or whenever we relax and devote our attention to visualizing deeply and thoroughly. We also enter the journey state naturally when gravely sick or injured, and our time spent in this way is a part of the natural healing process.

It is part of our birthright as human beings to experience the meditative state and to make use of different states of mind to optimize our health, cognitive function, emotional balance, and physical performance. This completely natural state of mind provides a framework for meaningful interaction between our conscious and subconscious minds.

Our subconscious mind directs the function of our body and carries a record of everything we've ever seen, heard, felt, and experienced. Because of this, it can be incredibly helpful for the conscious mind to have access to this information and to have a say in the subtle operations of the body.

There are two details of our mind-body connection that highlight the potential of the meditative state. First, remembered or visualized imagery triggers neural patterns in much the same way as physical sight. So we can activate the brain with visualization just as we could by actually being in a place or actually moving in a specific way. Memory and visualization, on a neurochemical level, are just as real to us as physical sight and experience.

Next, consider the placebo effect. This is a well-documented and securely established interaction between mind and body, in which mental effects, like expectations or beliefs, are translated into physical effects and conditions.

The placebo effect demonstrates that the mind tells the body how to grow. Furthermore, it shows that it is our subconscious expectations that are felt and expressed through the body, rather than our conscious intentions and rational expectations. This makes a personal relationship with our own psychology central to our growth. If we wish to make conscious, intentional use of the mind to promote physical health and function, then we must bring the conscious and subconscious functions together.

Our conscious minds usually feel like they run the show, but an honest assessment will show that most of our conditions in life are the result of unconscious choices rather than conscious intentions. It is a deep journey to bring these subconscious impulses into the light of conscious awareness. Although this is not an easy or quick task, each scrap of insight we gain into ourselves offers greater freedom and the realization of greater potential.

When I was young, my martial arts teacher told me a story which helped me to understand how to make use of the meditative state. He told of a P.O.W. held captive in the Alps. This soldier enjoyed golf, so to occupy the time of his captivity, he played a game of golf in his head each day, visualizing every bit of it as clearly as he could, the landscape, positioning of the body, the feel of the swing.

Now, he was never a very good golfer, but since he enjoyed it, this was a great way for him to spend his time. And, after his release was secured, he returned home and played the best game of his life. His visualized practice translated into a real increase of skill.

We were taught to practice our martial arts forms in our mind when unable to practice physically. And, amazing as it might seem, this mental practice translated into physical ability. But this is just the beginning. Memory experts use visualization to construct a mental palace, an envisioned storehouse of memory triggers arranged intentionally and associated with specific meaning. The use of visualization can be hacked in this way to improve memory and recall. This is a fragment of the skill used by shamans the world over in the construction of an inner place of power for the journey state.

The mechanism which makes the journey state effective for bringing conscious and subconscious content into contact with one another is the same as that used in free association or in the Rorschach test. When we enter a meditative state, we make space for the subconscious mind to color our inward voice and inward perception. We create a framework upon which we will naturally tend to project things that have been felt but not fully understood. Things that have charge in our inner realm bleed into our subconscious choices in visualization. The feel and color of the space we envision, the tone and content of the voices within, all of this is created by conscious and subconscious intention working in tandem.

A key element of the interaction between the conscious and subconscious functions of our being is the use of symbol. The subconscious mind speaks in a language of symbols, images that indirectly represent or signify aspects of our experience. The conscious mind can learn the language of symbol and use it to express intentions to the deep mind. To put it another way, symbol is the natural language by which the little "I" of our conscious mind speaks to the big "I" of our whole Being.

Our symbols are, in part, learned from those around us, cultural and personal interpretations established by learning and inner agreement. For example, we learn that *this* word has *this* meaning. It soon becomes automatic as we hear the sound of the word and instantly associate it with meaning. We absorb a language of symbols from our culture, many of which are arbitrarily chosen to meet the specific needs of that culture.

In part, though, these symbols are universal. All humans have a natural language of universal symbols or archetypes (things like hand, mouth, mother, father). These archetypes are reflected in our personal perception and addressed in some way in our cultural narrative and mythology. From this perspective, all mythological or narrative frameworks could be described as a collection of symbols in interaction with one another. When we learn a specific mythology, we take on a map of symbols which help us to navigate the inner realms.

These maps are potential and participatory, which means that we each create our own unique relationship with this symbol framework. We could perceive our inner world in any way we can imagine. This imagining becomes a framework which allows us to engage meaningfully with it *in the way we have imagined.*

One implication of this is that these maps are effective even if they have no connection to the nature of the world in itself. By perceiving the inner world through the lens of a specific map, we will be able to meaningfully engage with our inner realm in the manner that the map offers.

Our mythology offers roadmaps and trails through the infinite. It gives us the ability to symbolically express physical, mental, emotional, and energetic abstractions. And, since observation leads to effect, by visualizing these abstractions we can interact with them directly.

As mentioned above, the depth of meditation, the frequency to which we slow, has an impact on our inner experience. If we slow down slightly, just take a breath and exhale long and slow, and relax, then we enter a light meditative state. This state helps us to center our awareness in the body.

As soon as the body receives our attention, it will tend to shift slightly, moving further into balance. We may adjust our position to get more even and aligned. We may notice points of tension and begin to ease these spaces in our body. These adjustments happen naturally as soon as we perceive them, so a light meditative state helps us to naturally balance and reset the body.

If we take this state deeper, such as with closed eyes, a body scan, and a countdown, we go into what we might as well call a medium meditative state. In this space, we still have complete awareness of the body and its immediate surroundings. However, our attention is drawn inward and images tend to slow down and become more vivid in the mind's eye.

This makes the medium meditative state ideal for active visualization. We can visualize healing or growth in the body, for example. Or we may visualize physical training in this state, and find that the benefits of this practice translate surprisingly well into physical skill. This medium meditative state is also ideal for working through high-level cognitive processes, such as synthesis and analysis. This is the *prayer state,* and *intentions expressed at this level have a powerful impact upon our lives.*

If we then take this state deeper, slowing further, engaging with the visualization on the screen of the mind, we move into a space that combines the elements of waking and dreaming. This can be called the *journey state*.

It can be very challenging to get to this depth intentionally without falling asleep and to maintain the depth and track of the journey. These things become easier with the right kind of practice, and they are more natural for some people than others. But every single person can learn to enter the journey state intentionally and guide their own journey. Every person who does learn this will experience profound and unique benefits from the practice, first and foremost from the use of intention to shift mindstate and the use of relaxed focus to maintain a desired mindstate.

The journey state is extremely powerful for looking inside and discovering parts of ourselves, voices, feelings, that we never knew existed. Some of these parts will be hurt, stuck as children, hiding in the shadows until we meet ourselves with love and reclaim this portion of our psyche. Some will be strong and wise in ways that our conscious story of self is not, and these voices will point the way to our highest growth.

In the journey state, we can take a challenging feeling that has come up and give it space to play out within, let it show us the lesson it brings. We can set an intention to meet a teacher or guide within, and converse meaningfully with this figure in our inner space. We can literally journey with ourselves in any way that we can imagine, and, with proper training, can get grounded guidance and insight from these experiences.

RHYTHM AND
CONSCIOUSNESS PRACTICES

As this is the first set of practical exercises in this course, I'll offer a bit of a preface. Learning the body and the body-mind connection is similar to learning an instrument. At first, even the simplest techniques require focus and effort. After some time, they become more natural. Eventually, they become effortless.

Over time, we learn different techniques and add them to the repertoire, and eventually we're making amazing music. The first days of practice will always seem worlds apart from the skill cultivated over time. Each of these practices is a step in the development of a skill which can transform your life. Nothing worth doing comes without effort and dedication, and it will take some time for the full benefits to become apparent. But it will take no time at all to begin to see the first fruits.

Practice 1: Notice your breath

You are breathing every moment you are alive. If you were to stop breathing, you'd die within minutes. And yet for the average person, nearly all of this breathing is unconscious. We might go days without really noticing our breath.

Consider this: a human being cannot sob when taking smooth, even breaths. Another: we cannot have a panic attack when taking smooth, even breaths. Try it out. When sobbing, the breath becomes ragged and uneven. As soon as the breathing smooths, the sobbing stills, and we create a bit of space around the emotion in our inner experience.

When having an anxiety attack, the breath becomes rapid and shallow, sometimes verging into rapid and deep. If you are able to slow and soften the breath, the inner experience lessens in intensity and the anxiety attack passes.

In both cases, the rate and depth of breath is a key contributor to the inner experience, the tail wagging the dog.

In order to gain benefit from changing your rhythm, you have to be able to notice your rhythm in the moment, when life is actually happening. This first exercise is to practice paying attention to your breathing. Every time something important happens, every time you're preparing for an intense conversation, every time you get hurt or triggered, *notice your breathing.*

This will be extremely difficult at first. It is a practice of creating awareness around our breath, and the average person's awareness is wild and untrained. Only by coming back to it again, and again, and again in the midst of life's challenges, will we make it a habit, a reflex we can draw upon when we need it most.

Notice your breathing and notice how you're feeling. Make the connection. Breath is the first lesson we learn in life, and one which takes a lifetime to practice properly. The more consciousness you bring in to your breathing, the more aware you become of the impact of your breath on your inner experience.

Notice if your breathing is deep or shallow. Notice if you are breathing into your chest or your belly, or both. Notice if you have tension in your body that impacts your breathing. Are you breathing through your nose or your mouth? What is your posture like?

When we begin paying attention to these things, we naturally tend to make subtle shifts, straightening the posture, relaxing tension, breathing into the belly instead of the chest. This exercise, though, is more about making it a habit to tune in to your breath. And, once you do, *relax*. Every time something important, painful, challenging, triggering, etc. happens. Breathe and relax. This exercise is surprisingly powerful, as it teaches you to be conscious when you most need to be.

Practice 2: Four-Part Breathing

For this practice, you will need to have a few moments where you can sit or lay down comfortably without interruption. This will be a prerequisite for a number of the meditational practices. Creating a small space in your schedule for quiet and self-care is an extremely healthy practice in itself. It doesn't matter where or how, just that you have a few moments each day to be with your own thoughts and feelings.

Four-part breathing is a simple technique used in both yogic and shamanic traditions. With your body at rest, in a neutral position, inhale for a count of four. Hold for a count of four. Exhale for a count of four. Hold your lungs empty for a count of four. Repeat.

That's it. That's the entire technique. You can, if you like, lengthen the count evenly, such as extending all phases to five or six counts. If it is difficult to manage a count of four, look into proper breathing, diaphragmatic breathing, yogic breathing, etc.

We often carry tension in our bellies that restricts our breathing. Relax your stomach as much as you can and let it expand as you breathe in. You may wish to massage the solar plexus lightly to help release tension. You may notice you need to adjust your posture or position in order to breathe easily and steadily. Listen to your body.

This practice is as effective as it is simple. Breathing is powerful, and after a few rounds of four-part breathing you will notice your awareness shift. Just lightly, but enough to make you more aware of what's happening in your whole being, what thoughts or emotions or sensations are coming up.

You will often hear me use the term "tuning in". Some traditions describe this as "listening within". Our bodies are always responding to the environment, synched up with signals that we are not consciously aware of. Often our thoughts are so loud that they get in the way of what we're actually feeling or experiencing. We are, all of us, brilliant in ways that we have not yet imagined. In order to tune in to that brilliance and make use of it, we have to listen within and let it come forth.

Four-part Breathing helps to create space in our inner experience, to quiet our thoughts so that we can tune in to our feelings, the subtle signals of our bodies, unmet needs, ideas waiting to be brought forth, etc. In practice, it can be like getting a foot in the door. One tiny bit of stillness in the chaos of the mental chatter. And, once you know what that stillness *feels* like, you can learn to return there. The more regularly you practice, the easier it will be to create space within.

Practice 3: Alpha State Meditation

This practice is a strong foundation for all meditation, visualization, and journey work. It takes time to master. However, just as with any skill, it becomes easier and more natural. Eventually, this practice will let you enter a meditative state at will, within just a few breaths.

Meditation can be used to recover from physical or emotional pain. It can deepen your capacity for learning and memory, and offer a platform for reviewing thoughts and experiences. It can be used to release stress, help the body return to balance, and access the flow state for times of high performance. The meditative state is also ideal for moving subtle energy and promoting deep emotional healing, as well as for evoking transformation (healing, specific directed change, grounding and attuning, etc.) in your experience.

Find a space where you can focus uninterrupted for a few minutes. (You may need a half-hour or more for this exercise at first.) Sit or lie down in a relaxed, neutral position.

Breathe slowly, deeply, and evenly, into the diaphragm, belly relaxed. Count down with each breath, beginning at 100 and going down to 0.

As you count, do a body scan. Spend one breath releasing tension from the toes, either tensing and releasing, or just allowing tension to flow out with the breath. Spend the next breath releasing tension from the ankles, then calves, all the way up the body, one small bit at a time.

After the entire body has been scanned and all tension released, continue breathing down. Don't rush the count or become impatient.

That produces the opposite of the desired effect. Just breathe, and with each breath relax a little bit more.

It's likely you will fall asleep or find your mind wandering whenever you try this practice, at least in the beginning. It requires quite a bit of focus and mental discipline, especially at first. But it becomes easier. If you find that your mind has drifted, just bring it back to the practice. If you run out of the time you've set for yourself, just try again tomorrow.

Once you are able to take the count to zero without falling asleep, you may notice a sense of lightness or openness in your inner experience. Each person describes their experience differently, so simply pay attention to how you feel. Take note of the subtle sensations of the body, the quality of the inner experience. Whatever you notice in this space, this is the feeling that accompanies a slower brain frequency for you. This state of mind and body – this inner orientation – is the foundation of your meditation practice.

After lingering in this state for as long as you like – or have time for – bring yourself back up with the breath. Deepen the breathing and begin to count upward with each breath, going from one to five. With each breath, feel and envision a bit more light, life, and energy entering your body. This part often feels as if coming from the depths of the water all the way to the surface and then emerging. Open your eyes, get some movement into the body, and then move on to whatever you'd like to do next.

Practice this exercise daily. After a short time, you may notice that you feel completely relaxed and aware well before the count finishes. That's the whole goal of the exercise. Shorten the count, then, however much seems appropriate to you.

In my own training, I used a count of one hundred until I could reliably enter the state without losing concentration or falling asleep. Then I reduced the count to seventy-five. Then fifty. These days, for deeper meditation or journey work, I prefer to use twenty-one as my starting count. However, when engaged in healing or intuitive work, I often simply close my eyes and slow down. Within a few breaths, I'm there.

This is an intense training, in that it requires dedication and patience. However, you will begin to notice a heightened awareness of your body and your inner state within a week of beginning the practice. More than that, this is a streamlined practice that helps you to access the journey state reliably and without props. In the journey state, we begin to engage with aspects of our unconscious processes that would otherwise be inaccessible.

You may wish to use this state to reflect on a current challenge, to envision the body functioning healthily, to envision a place in your mind that serves as your sanctum sanctorum, anything, really. When the slower brain rhythms predominate, there is better communication between the conscious and subconscious functions. So, you can visualize your intentions in this state (a conscious process) and they will be heard and responded to by the whole being (including the unconscious processes).

It doesn't stop at consciously directing autonomic processes. Our subconscious stores all of the information we have been exposed to over the course of our lives. It processes multifactorial equations at lightning speed, all without taxing conscious awareness.

Just think for a moment about what you could do with better communication between your waking consciousness and the reserves of your unconscious knowledge. Learning becomes easier. Performance moves from taxing and awkward to effortless and graceful. And deeper awareness of the subtle signals of the body puts you in touch with an invaluable stream of feedback from your environment.

The purpose of this exercise, however, is just to practice entering the journey state. Baby steps. Just as with practicing an instrument, you will progress more quickly and consistently by mastering one small technique at a time.

It is likely that few who read this will have the time or motivation to practice this technique properly. Those that do will experience a deepening of awareness and conscious ability to shift their mindstate to suit their needs.

True freedom comes when we know (and feel) the choices we have. It comes with the capacity to respond rather than react. And it begins within, with the capacity to tune our own minds as we will, regardless of external circumstances.

A few final words regarding this practice:

Consciousness is personal and subjective. So, working with one's inner state is as much an art as it is a science. We each develop our own relationship to our inner experience. With a practice of awareness, we can each find personal ways to align that inner state with the needs of the moment.

I personally like to enter a light meditative state prior to giving a lecture or listening to one, before meetings, before a challenging experience, and when I've been sick or injured. After an intense situation to reflect and process what has occurred. For clarity in the midst of challenge. Just to name a few.

For those who take the time to program their minds and bodies with this reflex, you will discover many more benefits and uses than those I've described.

Meditation is a tool to align the human engine to its natural potency. It is a means to deepen our conscious awareness of every facet of our experience. And it's not surprising that breath is so central to meditation, as breath and rhythm are fundamental to each moment of our experience. Just by taking time to breathe and get still, we can begin to see benefits in every area of life.

MODULE 2 - EMOTIONAL WISDOM

Introduction to Emotional Wisdom

> *"We live in a world that distrusts feelings. Over and over, we are reminded that feelings are not as important as reason. That feelings are childish, irresponsible, and dangerous. We are taught to ignore them, control, or deny them. We barely understand what they are, where they come from, or how they seem to understand us better than we understand ourselves. But I know that feelings matter."*
>
> – Quoted from *Sense8*

We live in a global culture that favors objectivity. We are taught to give more value to facts and hard evidence than feeling and emotion. And, for many purposes, this is a fruitful bias. It's important to be able to discuss practical matters in terms that apply equally to each of us, regardless of our subjective reactions to the situation.

That said, all of the juiciness of life comes from our emotions. Everything that makes life meaningful, everything that makes it worth living, all of that matters to us because of how we feel about it. If we were successful at purging our emotions for the sake of logic, we'd be left with a dry, barren inner world, always winter, and never Christmas. We may distrust our emotions, but none of us wants to live without feelings altogether.

To take it a step further, logic and reason are not as clear-cut and sacrosanct as we might like to believe. We often encounter situations in the world that don't make sense to us, those that occur for reasons we don't understand. We also view the entire world from a single subjective perspective. When we see our logic and reason as solid and reliable, we are assuming that our mental model of the world – our one vantage point – *is the world itself.* Without even thinking about it, we assume that this world is the same for others as it is for ourselves.

To understand this a bit better, consider this. Our exercise of logic masquerades as impersonal, impartial. Objective. But we never truly think objectively. We are not motivated objectively. We experience a subjective world, rather than an objective one. Our stories about the objective world are logical abstractions, helpful, but removed from personal experience. When we believe logic above feelings, we give our true feelings cover to pull the strings unnoticed.

Emotion can also offer clear, actionable insights into the situation at hand. Just think of any time you've known something intuitively, by feel. For each of us, there are times when these feelings come up and prove to be correct, even without evidence. Our feelings can actually tune us in to aspects of the situation that were invisible to our logic or reason. This in itself demonstrates the value of the emotional feedback we receive from within.

The challenge is that, while our hunches, intuitive hits, and emotional reactions sometimes lead us to solid knowledge, sometimes they cloud our perception and distort our understanding. We've all had situations in which we were upset, angry, sad, or afraid, and couldn't think clearly. We've all seen the same (fundamentally human) responses and behaviors in others. So how can we learn to navigate the emotional space, to listen to the wisdom of the heart without being overwhelmed by its intensity?

The first step is to look more closely at the emotional experience. Our emotions speak their own language and follow their own logic. By learning this language, we can tune in to a range of subtle feedback regarding our environment, our needs, and our inner state. With greater awareness comes more freedom and deeper clarity around our needs and values.

Emotion is closely linked to the foundation of our personal experience. By becoming conscious of our rhythm in the moment, we begin to become conscious of the moment itself. Which is beautiful, so long as we can maintain it. And then something comes along and triggers us, and we're full on into the reaction before we've had a chance to consider a response.

Our emotions add force and motion to our inner experience, and they can either waylay or supercharge our intentional action. Our emotional charge has a powerful influence on our course through life and on the things we experience. Emotion, in general, is subtler and far more powerful than our conscious choice.

No handling of intention or will in the inner experience is complete without a discussion of the feelings that underlie, motivate, and direct the will. When the conscious will and emotions are at cross purposes, emotions often win the conflict. When we set our sights on a particular outcome, our emotions provide force to make it happen. It's our emotional relation to a person or situation that makes it meaningful to us. Our emotions are often wiser and more in tune with our true needs than our conscious understanding.

As with all things, understanding supports wise action. Let's take a look at a few models of the emotional experience to see how we can navigate these waters most effectively, how we can listen to and dance with our feelings, making them a blessing and a strength.

Cognitive Models of Emotion

As we move into the next section, I'd like to present a concept that helps us to make use of perspectives without getting lost in them:

The map is not the territory

Human beings make sense of things with stories. We build conceptual models of the subject we are exploring, and then use these models to predict how the subject will respond in the future. None of our models is perfect. The world is huge and complex, and no matter how well-considered our conceptual framework, it will always fall short of the nuance and detail of our experience.

With this in mind, consider the value of a conceptual model. It helps us to make sense of the world, of the aspect of the world which we are working with. It helps us, in some way, to navigate the experience of life. None of these conceptual models will be True, in the way that philosophers prefer, that absolute, unchanging truth that is equally applicable to all times and all people. However, each model that we use to make sense of the world helps us to do something, to engage with the world in a specific way.

We often learn about the world in conceptual terms. We inherit ideas and perspectives from others that help us to make sense of the world beyond the envelope of our immediate experience. However, our concepts can become so compelling to us that we refuse to see things in our experience which contradict our understanding. We often become so attached to our preferred perspective that we blind ourselves to what we are actually seeing and feeling.

To make use of conceptual models without getting trapped in projection, it's important to remember that each conceptual model is a story about how we relate to the world. No story is True. All stories are tools. If you find that a given way of looking at things is not working for you, the most efficient way to respond is to adjust your understanding. To shift your perspective.

This happens naturally as we grow and learn, but we can be extremely resistant to this kind of change if we confuse perspective with Truth. For the purpose of this conversation, try to look at each of the following models as *a* way to understand your emotional experience, rather than *the* way.

The Buddhist Perspective of Emotion

I'd like to begin with the Buddhist view of emotion, a perspective which offers simplicity and clarity to an otherwise labyrinthine subject. Buddha is often misquoted as saying, "Desire is the root of all suffering." While this is close to the mark, it misses something important.

Buddha's teachings are strongly psychological in nature. He taught that all suffering arises from ignorance of our true nature. This ignorance manifests in two main forms: desire and aversion. From the Buddhist perspective, all that we experience is a projection of our own being. Who we really are, is consciousness, which is complete, impartial, and all-embracing.

All resistance that we have to what we perceive (aversion), and all addiction to certain perceptions over others (desire), result from ignorance. From an identification with the apparent, with the body and the forms of the manifest world. It is this ignorance of our true nature that causes us to pull towards some things and push away from others. We base our sense of self in outer stimuli rather than inner experience. But our true self is the I AM core at the center of our experience, untouched by the constant fluctuation of the outer world.

To explore this further, imagine that at your core, you are a point of consciousness. This point of consciousness inhabits a body at the moment. This body has access to a collection of sense impressions. In (an imagined state of) complete balance, none of these perceptions can drive us to action. We have a choice as to how to respond to these stimuli.

However, in practice, we find ourselves attracted to certain sense impressions and avoidant of others. Just consider a time when you saw something you wanted, whether a physical object, or a situation, or an idea, and lost perspective in the pursuit of this thing. Addiction is an extreme example of this tendency.

Now consider a person, situation, or thing that you absolutely cannot stand. Even better, perhaps there was a food or activity that completely turned you off when you were younger. Then, at some point, you tried it and found that it wasn't as horrible as last time or as you had imagined it would be.

If you can find a situation like that in your personal history, then you've felt the coloration that aversion can add to otherwise neutral sensory stimuli. And you've experienced how your feelings around these stimuli can change, how you can experience that stimulus differently as you release aversion around it.

The Buddhist bias is that consciousness is True and Real, while the body and the senses are fleeting and ephemeral. From that perspective, the physical is less Real than consciousness itself. Whether this is true in an objective sense, it offers exceptional clarity on the level of our individual psychological reality. The stronger our desire or aversion towards a particular set of stimuli, the less functional freedom we have in interactions with that aspect of our lives.

If you've ever overcome an addiction, you can understand very well the impact of desire on freedom. The same can be said of any aversion or avoidance in our lives. On a fundamental psychological level, freedom involves being able to take in sense impressions without being moved into reactiveness. Freedom means having a choice as to how to respond.

Sense-Story-Charge

It is useful, after a fashion, to boil the entire spectrum of emotion down to attractive and repulsive forces. Emotions are complex, multifaceted, and constantly in flux. By abstracting them into elements of charge, we can take a step back from the specifics of our experience. This lets us look at how emotions move us into action, how they influence our perceptions. However, it can be taken one step further.

On a fundamental level, the human experience can be broken down as follows: We have a core of consciousness, an I AM sense that we carry with us throughout our lives, regardless of what is happening in our outer world.

We also have a sphere of sensory experience, the multiple streams of information that come to us through the eyes, ears, tactile senses, taste, and smell. This includes the subtle somatic feedback from within the body.

Somewhere between this core of consciousness and our external sense perception is a layer of thoughts and emotions. These thoughts and emotions form a framework through which we interpret sensory information.

All emotions can be described as charge, just as in magnetism, both attraction and repulsion are expressions of magnetic charge. Charge, in terms of emotions, speaks to their ability to move us into reaction.

When we have charge around a particular person, situation, or thing in our lives, this charge conditions our dynamic; it sets the tone for our relation to that aspect of our world. Furthermore, all charge is personal. Nothing is inherently happy or sad. It becomes so because of what it means to us, because of where we stand in relation to it.

Our thoughts, though they include separate categories like personal history, learned information, and imagination, could be described simply as story. Story, in this usage, means both concept and context.

When you define a word, you offer a story about what that word means to you. When you think of a memory, this memory is a conceptual story about where you have been, what you have done, and how this history sets the stage for your current experiences. Learning, in the Western sense, depends heavily upon absorbing specific stories about the world, and then using these stories to predict future interactions.

This cognitive model could be broken down as: *sense-story-charge*. In our relation to the outer world, we have a collection of sense impressions. Populating the inner world, we have story and charge. Story is our conceptual context in relation to specific aspects of sense experience. Charge is the emotional quality attached to this conceptual interpretation. One benefit of this model is that it helps us to distinguish between story and actual sense experience. Story is personal interpretation, and subject to personal redefinition.

Another benefit of this perspective is clear handling of emotion as charge. By viewing the nuanced emotional spectrum as a degree of charge, we perform a calculus of consciousness. We may not be able to understand what specifically we're feeling. We could (unintentionally) make an infinite number of equally compelling and equally false stories about the feeling to explain it to ourselves. This gets confusing.

However, if we pay attention, it should be pretty easy to recognize that charge has come up. Plus, we are often able to note the trigger for that charge. We can observe the charge, and the trigger, and then make space to tune in to what's coming up for us. Over time, we begin to notice the patterns and come to understand ourselves better. We become more aware of what our emotions are telling us in the moment. Thinking in terms of charge can sidestep the maze of story and offer clarity around our emotional reactions.

A side note which has been helpful for my own understanding is the view of emotional charge as similar to gravity in the inner world. Gravity is an attractive force which, according to some views, causes space itself to curve around the point of greatest mass. Similarly, when we have a powerful charge around an aspect of sense experience, we are primed to see it.

This is the mechanism of the Rorschack or inkblot test. When shown a potentially random image, human beings are more likely to see things that line up with their emotional charge. Emotional charge attracts our attention, conditions our perception, and warps our entire perceptual framework around the areas of greatest emotional intensity.

Consider your personal history once more. Have you ever gotten angry with someone, convinced that they had acted wrongly towards you, only to calm down later and view the situation in a different light?

In a moment of anger, it can be extremely difficult to see that there is another perspective. After the anger has faded, things can look very different. In some instances, we may even have a hard time understanding our previous mindset or behavior. Our whole view of the world can shift in ways that make the world appear radically different.

With this in mind, you might consider how processing old emotional charge might influence our perspective and comprehension. Each time we clear a point of charge, we also clear out a point of distortion in our understanding. In the wake of an emotional release comes deeper clarity and a wider awareness of ourselves. We often get more growth from dealing with our feelings than we do by absorbing more information.

Four (or Six) Basic Emotions

Just as the two previous models, this perspective is an oversimplification. However, it can still be extremely helpful for interpreting the language of the emotions. From this perspective, the four basic emotions are: mad, sad, glad, and afraid. In other words: anger, fear, joy, and sadness. Each of these emotions influences us in a particular way, readying us for a specific type of interaction with the environment.

According to this model, anger tells us that our boundaries have been crossed. Healthy anger helps us to stand up in defense of ourselves and our loved ones. Fear tells us that we need to take action. Healthy fear motivates us to take action to ensure safety for ourselves and our loved ones. Sadness is an indication of unmet needs. Healthy sadness helps us to become aware of these needs so that we can meet them most effectively. And, finally, joy tells us that what we are doing is working for us.

From a biological perspective, we can include two more basic emotions: surprise and disgust. Surprise is an indication of the unexpected and the need to pay attention. Disgust is an indication that what we are doing is *not* right for us.

All of these things are relative, subject to our interpretation of the triggering stimuli. The same news might bring joy for some and anger for others, depending on what it means for them. Regardless of the specific context, the emotion is an in-the-moment reaction to our situation, as we perceive it.

This and other representative models are helpful in gaining insight about our experience, to put words to feelings. However, there is the danger of confusing these models with reality. Emotions are far more nuanced than charge, than love and fear, or any set of basic, fundamental emotions we can lay out. Each person and each moment of experience is unique.

On the level of application, though, all of these models can help us to make sense of our situation and navigate it. Ideally, we can strive for both self-awareness and cognitive flexibility. We can try to be aware of the perspective that we are using and consider how well it works for us in the given situation. At times, a shift of perspective can offer more insight and better results.

Triggers and Emotional Processing

One thing which makes emotions so confusing is that they often seem out of place, irrational. Just think about a time in your past when your feelings were hurt unintentionally. Perhaps a friend or loved one mentioned something that you were sensitive about. And, all of a sudden, an emotional storm rages through completely out of proportion with what's happening in the moment. This is the kind of experience that leads us to distrust our feelings.

One key to remember about emotions is that they are, from one perspective, messages from the whole being to the conscious self. Just think about your alarm clock. For many of us, our alarms tell us when to wake up. If we hit the snooze button, the alarm will go off again in a few minutes.

The alarm is intended as a signal for the conscious mind, an indication that it's time to begin the day. If we choose to put the message off for later, it will come back up, not at the time that we originally set, but a few minutes after we hit snooze. And, with some alarm clocks, this will continue to happen until we wake up and dismiss the alarm properly.

We have the capacity to hit the snooze button on our emotions as well. Sometimes we do it with distraction, or story, or numbing out, or any of a number of other coping mechanisms. If we are capable of pushing our emotions out of our conscious awareness, they become suppressed. They recede into the subconscious where we don't have to look at them.

But suppressed emotions are not gone. **What we resist, persists.** They remain within our psyche, distorting our perception of all aspects of life linked to this charge. Sometimes this distortion is subtle, and we are often blind to it until we begin to process these old emotions.

Because of the wealth of repressed emotions that we tend to carry around, it can be difficult to distinguish between genuine emotional messages about the current situation and old emotional charge. We get triggered, in part, because the situation reminds us viscerally of a situation linked with an old charge. And that trigger is a blessing if we are able to recognize what's happening. **If we can feel it, we can heal it.** Without such triggers, unresolved charge remains invisible to us, coloring our experience and influencing all of our choices from behind the scenes.

Consider a situation in which you've been triggered emotionally. There are two ways that we can go. One: we push the emotion back so we can deal with the needs of the moment. Two: we allow ourselves to fully feel the emotion itself, breathe through it and allow the intensity to fade. The emotion is a message. When you allow yourself to feel it through and *listen within* for any thoughts that come up in connection to it, it is as if you receive the message. Until the message is received it will continue to circulate.

So, for example, if we are able to push the feelings away with story or distraction, they will only pop up again and again, often in disguised form. If we try to control the feelings with a narrative, that narrative requires effort to maintain. It requires sending the mind down that chain of associations again and again, retriggering the emotional flash each time.

In some of the most challenging situations, we can take an emotional flash – which in itself lasts only a few seconds – and turn it into a habit, a way of life. Our narrative (intended in this case to protect us from a feeling that we don't know how to handle) can set our emotional experience on a continuous pulse. It can seem as if we don't know how to feel any other way, as if we're stuck in a state of fear or sadness or irritation.

The only way out is through. No story, no matter how awesome or where it came from, can do the work of processing our emotions. There is no substitute, no shortcut. You will be plagued by your old emotional charge until you stop running and allow yourself to make peace with the feeling. Until you can slow down, create more space around this emotional message, and take actions informed by it. The good news is that feeling your feelings and processing your emotions takes less time and energy than running.

The benefits of emotional healing are too numerous to list. They include greater clarity around the situation, greater freedom, and a dramatically improved sense of wellbeing. The challenge is that, on an unconscious level, we'll often do everything we can to avoid coming face to face with our fear, sadness, anger, shame, etc. Being real with ourselves is a lifelong journey, and perhaps one of the most difficult ones we face in this life.

Emotions and the Art of Consciousness

> *"We are healed from suffering only by experiencing it to the full."*
>
> — Marcel Proust

Growth is a journey in expansion. Just think back to how you perceived the world five years ago, ten years ago, as a child. Many of us, during a phase of our growth, decide we've got the world figured out. We know what's up. And then we continue to grow, and we realize that there is more to the world than we'd realized. As we grow, our perspective changes, our scope widens, and we take more of the world into account.

If we are able to look back with honesty and self-awareness, we will recognize in hindsight how our emotional charge has distorted our perception. We may even be able to take the next step, to recognize how all of our – as yet unseen – emotional charge is still distorting our current perspective. In the process of resolving old emotional charge, we can begin to recognize that this old charge came not only from what we experienced, but also from how we interpreted that experience.

All meaning and charge in our experience comes from a specific alignment of the inner experience with the outer experience. We are not just passive victims of circumstance; the creation of meaning and charge is participatory. In other words, it's not that the outer situation *made us angry*. Instead, we unknowingly align with a perception of the situation that evokes anger within us.

The upside of this is that we can review the experiences of our lives and come to a deeper understanding of them, turning triggers into awareness and challenges into strengths. We can consciously participate in the creation of charge and meaning that work for us, rather than against us.

One benefit of emotional awareness as described thus far is that it paves the way for accountability. Accountability to ourselves for our actions, choices, words, and how we are living our lives. Before accountability, we take the role of the victim, dealing as well as we can with the situations life throws our way. As we take on accountability, we accept responsibility for where we are in our lives, and we begin to see how we can take action and make choices to move our lives in the desired direction.

Processing old emotional charge dramatically changes our perspective. It offers more awareness of how we came to be in the current situation and helps us to see how we can navigate similar situations in the future. For the purposes of growth and self-development, emotional healing is more effective at promoting true growth than any amount of information we learn.

The question then, is how can we best approach emotional healing? The short answer: with patience, compassion, gentleness, and acceptance. And, in equal measure, with an honest willingness to deepen our knowledge of ourselves and to hear the messages our emotions are sending. So, with that in mind, let's look at the body, our most intimate and fundamental medium for emotional expression.

Physical Correlates of Emotion

Although the body and mind are often discussed as separate subjects, they are intimately linked and they affect one another reciprocally. Each of us, as human beings, for every moment of our lives, exists as body and mind, emotion and energy. Everything that happens to us is experienced on all levels of our being simultaneously. We perceive and respond mentally, physically, emotionally, and energetically all at once.

In order to clarify this idea, I often return to the image of a pin through four sheets. The first sheet is physical, the second emotional, the third mental, and the fourth energetic. The pin binding them together is the being. Whenever an emotional pressure occurs, it's as if the sheet is tugged. Because of the pin, the pressure from one sheet is referred to the others, and a characteristic pattern of tension develops across all four sheets.

An emotional pressure shows up in our story and perception as gravity and in our bodies as tension, rhythm, and set. This influence is reciprocal, with both story and conditions of the body influencing our experience of emotion, just as they are influenced by them.

In essence, our bodies act as an interface between our outer perception and our inner consciousness. They reflect both states intimately. Our bodies, in their own way, shine a window into our hearts and minds. With baseline muscle tension, facial expression, body language, and breath, our bodies align moment-to-moment with our emotional charge and the focus of our attention. Plus, since we have voluntary control over aspects of the body, this provides an avenue for influencing the inner state, just as we saw with the use of breath to influence brain rhythm.

Every emotion you experience has an impact on your body. Some common expressions are tension in specific areas of the body, body language, and facial expression. When an emotional reaction becomes chronically suppressed, it tends to manifest as emotional armor. Our whole posture, set of the face, and body language project our emotional state to others and reinforce it in our inner experience.

One benefit of understanding this is that an awareness of the body can be used to tune in to our emotional state. The most challenging emotions tend to hide from our view, so it helps to have a medium like the body to tune in to things hidden from conceptual awareness. A balanced, relaxed body reflects an easy flow of emotions. *All tension in the body has emotional associations.*

By tuning in to the state of the body and learning to breathe relaxation into these spaces, we can bring the emotions closer to the surface, giving us an opportunity to process them. Clearing tension in the body helps to release emotional tension from the psyche. The body is often a more direct route to old emotional charge than the mazes of story we erect around our feelings.

But it doesn't stop there. Every emotional state is accompanied by its own unique feeling in the body. By paying attention to the body language and muscle tension associated with certain emotions, we can prime ourselves to tap in to these emotions. We can, with practice, access resource states like joy, calmness, patience, creativity, enthusiasm, inspiration, and confidence, at will. By adopting the body language of confidence, we can prime ourselves to feel confident, just as smiling primes us to feel happy.

We can even take this one step further and anchor these states by associating them with sensory stimuli. An imagined image and sound, along with a physical sensation (like a mudra or a tap or a pat in a certain area of the body) can be linked in meditation to a specific resource state. It anchors the emotional state to a sensory trigger so that it can be accessed at will.

Anchoring emotional states is helpful, in the beginning. It allows us to exercise a specific intention and tap in to a specific charge. Over time, we can cultivate a heightened moment-to-moment awareness of our feelings and their impact on our bodies. The subtle signals from the body help us to both tune in to subtle emotional undertones and navigate to desired emotional states.

It's important to remember that our emotions are our friends. They are wise messengers cluing us in to things our conscious minds tend to overlook. Emotions are not amenable to control, per se. However, we can cooperate with our emotional nature. We can learn to dance with our feelings, and, in time, come to see them as guides and allies.

With that in mind, eliciting specific emotional states is far easier when we have a clear playing field, when we have addressed the loudest emotional concerns prior to introducing a new intention. We come to the point of diminishing returns quickly when we try to ignore, judge, or repress our feelings. The first step is to listen to and honor what arises from within.

Charge, Karma, and Manifestation

I'd like to take this opportunity to share a perspective of emotional charge which links it to both karma and the Law of Attraction. Again, this is a story, a way of making sense of things. If it helps to shine a light on your own navigation, then use it as you see fit.

Imagine that your perception exists as a field, a bubble of energy which surrounds you. Everything that you perceive is experienced through the medium of this energy. When this field is clear and even, the stimuli that enter your field are neutral. They can be perceived without moving you to reaction. However, when strong emotional charge is linked to an idea, person, situation, or thing, it is as if the energy in your field is magnetically drawn to this aspect of your experience.

Out of a random collection of stimuli, each of us is most likely to have our attention drawn to points of strong emotional charge. The focus of our attention colors both our perception of external events and our interaction with these events. Specific emotional charge leads to a specific dynamic, a specific way of relating to that person or situation.

Since the emotional charge is often unconscious, it can seem as if our life just magically gravitates to these kinds of situations. Or, if we are lacking in awareness around this area of experience, we may simply come to assume our experiences reflect the Truth, the way things are.

In the Eastern perspective, this phenomenon is called karma. In the West, it is most often described as the Law of Attraction. The emotional charges we carry in our field put us in resonance with certain types of experience. We are then more likely to selectively perceive these aspects of experience and become drawn into relating with them in specific ways.

From this perspective, the law of attraction is not some superpower for us to master. It is simply a description of energetic resonance and its place in the navigation of our personal experience. Using this phenomenon consciously requires us to clear old emotional charge so that new opportunities, new ways of relating, can replace the old.

From the perspective of the Law of Attraction, emotion could be considered the engine of manifestation, the force that brings this new situation more fully into our experience. That being said, our unconscious emotions are constant and pervasive, often powerful enough to counter intentional manifestation, should they be at odds with conscious intent.

Similarly, it can be tempting for those with a Western background to interpret karma in terms of metaphysical judgment and punishment. However, with a psychological perspective of karma as unconscious emotional charge, we have something we can actually work with. Few among us will honestly claim that they can remember other lives than this. However, each one of us can use the framework of our experience in this life to become aware of the charge we carry and clear it from our field.

For Empaths

There are some among us who would describe themselves as empaths. These individuals tend to be highly sensitive to their own emotions and to the emotional undercurrents of their interactions with others. Whether this is an inherent tendency or a response to life events, empathy can be both a blessing and a curse, and it can be powerful enough to shape relationships and life choices. This is an aspect of human experience often overlooked in our upbringing, so I'd like to offer a few tips that can help make sense of it.

First of all, humans are social creatures. We are biologically hardwired to tune in to others of our species. When people interact with one another, they tend to sync up on several levels.

Consider a few examples: When women live together in the same house, their menstrual cycles will tend to line up. When conversation is flowing between two people, their heart rate, rate and depth of breath, and body language will tend to match one another. When two people spend time around one another, they develop a shorthand communication where a single word can convey a depth of meaning. Depending on the degree of our interaction, we synchronize in momentary, daily, or monthly cycles.

Much of this synchronization takes place without conscious intention, often without any conscious awareness of what's happening. Our bodies and our inner states are tuned in to a host of unconscious details. We become entrained with others by reflexive attunement to these unconscious signals. So, whether you share a conversation or a home, your state and the state of the person with whom you share communicate with one another and find a happy medium.

When an individual is more aware of this emotional pressure and inner response, they tend to be sensitive to the subtle emotional fluctuations of others. This supports compassion and consideration, often to a fault. Because of this, those with a strong sense of empathy can easily manifest as codependent or as people pleasers.

Empaths also tend to be sensitive to strong emotions and more comfortable with one-on-one interactions than with large crowds of people. Suffice it to say, this is a gift that comes with a price. Aligning with empathy as a gift rather than a challenge requires an unusual degree of emotional and energetic self-awareness.

Most empaths I have encountered have discovered two things naturally, sometimes unconsciously. The first is the ability to tune in to the inner state of someone they engage with. It's almost as if an energetic antenna extends from the third eye and links with the energy field of the other. When energy fields are linked in this fashion, they tend to find a happy medium, like the final temperature when two cups of water are mixed together.

Linked fields act, to a certain extent, as a single field. So, at this point, the empath can move their own emotional state and help the other to move theirs. This often happens naturally when we cheer up a friend or help someone in a state of crisis. This is the second common discovery (adaptation) of empaths, and in technical terms, it could be described as "pacing and leading."

To understand the term, consider a time when you were taking a walk with a friend and adjusted your pace to their own. If, after matching their pace, you speed up or slow down, your friend is likely to do the same, sometimes without even realizing it. This is a beautiful ability in the emotional space and it makes empaths natural counselors, sometimes jumping from crisis to crisis in their social circles.

However, there are a few challenges with this approach. The first is that it's a one-on-one style. Even if we prefer to interact with one person at a time, it's important to have the capacity to handle social situations.

Another challenge is the tendency to spend much of our time entangled with others' fields, perhaps to the extent of neglecting our own needs or basing our identity around our role as a "fixer." Or, in extreme cases, to avoid groups, close connections, and the press of peoples' emotions altogether.

One major breakthrough for me was the discovery that empathy is like a two-way radio. We all receive subtle signals all the time. We perceive and respond to these signals on many levels at once, both consciously and unconsciously. We are constantly projecting emotional messages, just as we pick up the emotional messaging of others. This means that we can tune in to a specific emotional frequency and broadcast it consciously.

With empaths, the antenna is constantly out there, looking for some field to engage with. If there are too many options, the antenna is just flapping in the breeze. The empath then lacks a clear cue upon which to orient their emotional vibration. This challenge conceals one of the greatest gifts of empathy.

Here's a rule of thumb to help tune in to this gift: *When both parties have equal emotional awareness and personal power, the most intense emotional charge determines the whole dynamic, the whole tone and direction of the interaction. In other words, the loudest voice wins.*

But when one person has greater emotional awareness and the capacity to lead their inner state, they lead the dynamic, even against greater emotional charge. When we choose consciously whether or not to engage, and how to engage, we determine the emotional dynamic, even against a louder voice.

In simple terms, if you can keep cool when the other is getting heated, if you can respond with openness rather than defensiveness, then you may be able to shift the emotional dynamic in a different direction. Even if this is not the case, you will be able to maintain clarity in the face of intensity. Being conscious of our emotional state and of what we choose to engage with (resonate with) is a massive step towards personal freedom.

This may seem like no more than common sense. The trick is making it work. The key to this situation is the antenna, the focal point of our awareness. Take the attention, and ground it into the body, into the breath. You can even imagine directing this antenna into the earth, growing roots like a tree. Once you have done so, tune in to the space you hold around you while maintaining awareness of your roots.

We each have a field of energy around us that we tune with our attention and our emotion. We are constantly speaking silently through this field. Tune in to the emotion you would like to communicate in this space. Breath that feeling into your body, into your being. See as the space around you fills with this emotional energy. See it become a sphere that communicates with anything that enters your space. Feel your attention filling this space with the desired feeling, reinforcing the feeling with each breath.

You may wish to try this before engaging with a group setting, or in preparation for an emotionally challenging conversation. One of the main benefits that I've observed is a centeredness and ease in relating to larger groups of people. It's almost as if I qualify the space around me, as if I set the tone for the interactions that enter that space.

Rooting and consciously choosing your emotional vibration is also helpful when meeting strong or unpleasant emotions. This is part of life as a human being, and challenging emotional experiences often hide the deepest and most transformative lessons. That said, it's important to approach them in a healthy way, and when we are ready to do so. Prior to that point, we can feel a bit blasted by excess intensity.

Often, empaths attempt to put up shields to ward off intense emotions or energies. The problem with this approach is that it requires effort, works incompletely at best, and, when it does work, it cuts off our awareness of one of our greatest gifts. If instead, you choose to root your energy, you tune your rhythm to your body and set your own emotional tone. At the same time, this allows you to remain open to the insights and penetrating human understanding offered by subtle emotional signals.

To take the image of the tree one step further, you could imagine emotions perceived in others as winds, pressures directed at the being from the external environment. A strong wind can uproot a tree with shallow roots. But with deep roots, the tree will be more likely to withstand the storm. The tree feels every gust of wind flowing through its leaves, and yet it remains strong and centered amidst the chaos.

One final note with regard to empaths: Human beings are absolute geniuses at projection. So much of what we see in the world is what we expect to see. Although it's important to trust our own perception and do the best we can with the information available, none of us is perfect. No matter how keen our perception, whatever signals we pick up from others are interpreted in our own context, in our own way of making sense of the world. This also applies to intuitive work and any field in which information is being used without concrete evidence.

In practical terms, using information derived from empathic sensitivity or intuition requires discernment. Discernment begins when we recognize the limits of our knowledge and the tendency of words to veil meaning rather than reveal it. We can know what we felt or the subtleties we picked up, but we cannot know for certain the content of the other's inner world. We cannot know what it meant to them.

In addition, it helps to have a clear understanding of healthy boundaries and the right of each person to learn their own way in their own lives. We're all here on our own journey and we all learn at our own rate. Regardless of what we perceive from others, they deserve the space and privacy to handle their life in their own way.

Time spent alone in nature will help empaths to find their center within themselves, rather than in those they care for. And all of the relationships in our lives benefit from centered, clear presence.

EMOTIONAL
WISDOM - PRACTICES

No matter how many books you read or courses you take, making peace with one's emotions is a personal journey. In fact, the entire inner journey is one of experience rather than story. The emotional journey in particular involves becoming aware of our emotions, learning to listen to the wisdom they offer, and learning how to create space within so that we can consciously process them.

A note in moving forward: we can spend decades running from our feelings – distracting ourselves, rationalizing, bypassing, numbing out – and never actually get anywhere. Suppressed emotions are powerful largely because we are not conscious of their impact on our perception and decision-making. And running from our own feelings will eventually exhaust us without ever offering better results.

The easiest way around is through. And the payoff is that in clearing unconscious emotional charge, we open up our perception in unexpected and empowering ways.

Practice 1: Acknowledge - Identify – Release

Sometimes we get triggered and we need to keep moving. Maybe some friction came up in the workplace or you've got a set of nerves when heading into an interview. In either case, we don't have time for a lengthy process and we have to continue working, or get to the interview on time, or whatever it may be. At these times, it helps to be able to address what's coming up in a healthy way and let it go so that we can get the job done.

Acknowledge - Identify - Release is a simple yet effective technique to both cultivate awareness around our emotional state, and teach us to set aside feelings that are counterproductive to the task at hand. This technique consists of three steps and is, for the most part, self explanatory.

1. Acknowledge

One of the big challenges with handling emotion in the moment is that we often launch into reaction before we realize it. Perhaps we've gotten good at icing over little irritations, or ignoring the little bits of sadness that come up. Then something happens that strikes us in just the right way and the emotions flood over us. We might find that we're reacting before we even know it. Words of anger, perhaps, or outbursts we later regret.

A big factor in this process is that shoving feelings down can become automatic. We may not even realize we're doing it. In order to unlearn these emotional habits and retrain healthier ones, we must learn to notice when we're triggered. And, because we'd all like to see ourselves in a good light, sometimes owning up to our triggers, even to ourselves, can be challenging. It takes a willingness to honestly look at our own behavior and our own inner state, a commitment to looking within for the sake of growth.

So, Step 1: Notice when you're triggered. Just notice. We don't need to know exactly what the feeling is, where it came from, how it got there, any of that, to simply notice that we have some charge coming up. If we are able to notice our triggered state, we are much less likely to react unconsciously in ways that we will later regret. At the very least, it will give us a clearer view of what we're working with.

2. Identify

This one is tricky. Primarily because the emotions are not processed mentally. And yet the intellect tends to make sense of things in order to establish a sense of control over them. The intellect defines things so that we know where we stand. This is helpful, functional, practical, and there is a place for it. But that place is not to create a story about our feelings so that we feel better about them. Still, in the moment, it helps to be able to link the feeling with a trigger, to have some understanding of why we're feeling it and what to do with that energy.

So, for this step, simply try to connect the emotion with the thought or situation that evoked it. For example, when I heard *this* comment, I felt *this* emotion come up. You might even be able to classify the emotion as anger, or sadness, or shame, or grief. **If you can name it, you can tame it.** The key to remember is that this is just a handle for the moment. If you can get a clear view of your emotional state, and hopefully your trigger, for even a brief moment, it will soothe the intellect and allow you to move forward more easily.

So, Step 2: Identify. I am feeling angry. Or, I am feeling afraid. Or, I noticed a feeling come up when this situation occurred. Since we often judge our own emotions, it can be helpful to accompany our identification with a supportive affirmation: "Even though I feel (whatever you've identified), I deeply love and respect myself. The words are just a way of training a feeling response. Many of us have a harsh and unkind inner critic, so these affirmations can help to counter this influence with a healthier approach.

3. Release

Emotions don't actually go away for good when we push them away. If we push hard enough with denial, distraction, and story, then they hide out in the subconscious and subtly influence our perception, communication, and decision making. Feelings repressed far enough can act as if they take on a life of their own, as if they have their own personality and agenda. Feelings repressed this deep often have massive, life shaping impacts on us.

Suppressed emotions influence us in exactly the same way, though to a lesser degree. They tend to manifest as distortions in communication, dysfunctional patterns in relating, and chronic challenges in specific areas of life.

All of this occurs when the conscious mind tries to ignore the messages coming through the emotional channel. When the conscious mind takes the responsibility to listen to these messages, to feel them in full and act accordingly, then the message has done its work and can be released from the psyche.

For the most part, this requires quiet time, creating space within, breathing, listening, and feeling. However, in the moment, we can consciously set aside the feeling (relax and release) to put ourselves in the state most conducive to the task at hand.

To consciously set an emotion aside temporarily is an act of intention. The degree to which this intention is successful depends in part upon how much we have been able to look at the emotion head-on and engage with it before consciously setting it aside. Simple language, if you ignore the triggers, don't acknowledge the message, and never take time for review, this won't work for you.

If you begin to take the time to notice when you're triggered, you'll be able to handle these triggers much more consciously. And when we make a practice of making space in the moment to understand our emotions as well as we are able to, we slowly begin to see the patterns in our triggers. When we also take time after the fact to review and process our feelings, then we find that emotional management techniques like this become much more effective.

Self-knowledge blended with practice leads to skill. Each time you practice responding in this way, it will become more natural for you. Over time, it becomes as much a way of being as it is a practice.

The final step in this process is to review our feelings later. To sit down and get quiet, slow our rhythm and make space within. When we do this, things pop up. They may be stray thoughts, random details. Sometimes important details that we missed in the moment come to our attention in retrospect.

Once we open the door, unresolved emotions and feelings will tend to come up as well. When they do, you can act as if that feeling were a child in need, and that it is your responsibility to meet that child with care and love, but not with indulgence.

When we meet our emotions like this, it can feel as if we create more space around them, as if we step back from the intensity and gain a bit of clarity. The emotions don't go away, per se. They still point out things that matter to us. Our hearts guide us through life with a compass of personal values. But from this space, we are able to respond rather than react, to consciously choose how we would like to use the energy of that feeling.

Practice 2: Listening Within & Checking in

Listening within is an essential technique. We are often taught to look outside for answers. We look at what we believe, what we've learned, what we've pieced together, and what others tell us. These are all important streams of information.

For matters of an emotional nature, though, that's like trying to understand an orange by looking at a photo of one. While it takes time to become familiar with our inner world, there is no better window into it than our own network of story and charge.

Listening within is simple. However, the inner world is often full of swirling thoughts and chaotic emotional charge. For many of us, this can be an uncomfortable space. We often use distraction, routine, and story to lead our attention down safe and familiar tracks. And when the thoughts flow through, we can tend to chase them along like a small, excitable dog.

In this space, the thoughts are more in control of our experience than anything else. We walk the tracks laid out for us by our stories and spend a good bit of our time on autopilot.

In order to listen within, we must first slow. To do this, begin by placing your body in a neutral position. Then soften and slow your breath, slow your rhythm, and close your eyes. When we close our eyes, we shift our focus to the things we perceive within, like our thoughts, feelings, and inner somatic sensations. Just take a moment, breathing, slowing down, and letting yourself get still. And then listen to whatever comes up.

Often, I find myself slowing down and listening within to review recent events and recent emotional charge, or to review an area of my life that has been challenging in the past. I often have a new insight that can be explored more fully by listening within, so I use this space to allow it to come clear in my mind. I may listen within for guidance about decisions or planning, or when seeking clarity about my current circumstances.

We can listen within passively, just by slowing down and making space to hear whatever comes up. We can also use this ability actively to explore a specific question or line of inquiry. Simply set the intention to tune in to a particular feeling, event, or subject when beginning the practice. And then breathe, allow yourself to become still, and listen to what comes up. This is not about control, so much as priming yourself with the intention prior to the practice.

The value of this practice is that it can shortcut long mental processes and years of heartache. Often our minds work furiously to protect us from things that challenge their preferred viewpoint. We can spend long years taking circuitous mental routes to get to things that were staring us straight in the feelings all along. We can't control our emotions, and ignoring them doesn't work well or forever. But we can dance with them, let them show us where growth is possible, and create space around them to approach this growth in the best way.

A check-in is a quick moment where you drop out of story and into your body. Just breathe and pay attention to the subtle signals of your body. If you need something, like food or water, a check-in gives you space to notice it. If you're uncertain when faced with a decision, a check-in can give you fresh eyes and help to shine a light on things the mind has overlooked. And, if you're being sold on a great idea, a check-in can help you determine if this idea is actually right for you.

When we make it a habit to check in throughout the day, we create space to listen within to subtler and more visceral streams of information. We then naturally incorporate this information into our moment-to-moment responses. We act on the information available to us. Supplementing outer evidence with inner intuition offers clarity and helps to orient us meaningfully in the maze of life.

The further you slow your rhythm, the deeper you can listen. It requires a relaxed concentration to slow your rhythm and intentionally tune in to a specific story or charge. This capacity for relaxed concentration becomes stronger and more natural over time and with practice. Eventually, it can offer a platform for meaningful dialogue with inner aspects of ourselves, inner voices that carry wisdom, champion our values, and offer clear lessons.

Practice 3: When was the last time?

This is a more structured process for recognizing triggers and making sense of our emotions. Even if you prefer unstructured processes, you may wish to try this approach to see the benefits it offers. It involves personal reflection, light journaling, and a direct, visceral handling of the emotional energy.

The process of asking one's self a question and listening within for the answers that come up is extremely valuable. It helps us to focus our inquiry and tune in to specific answers from within. This exercise, practiced regularly, will strengthen your intuition and expand your understanding of your journey.

1. Notice that you're triggered.

This is a conscious process for handling emotional triggers. So, it won't do you any good if you're unconscious of being triggered.

It takes time to cultivate awareness around our triggers and our emotional state. Sometimes, we only realize we've been triggered when our behavior leads to conflict. One blessing in this regard is that our experience of the outer world will mirror our inner state. The outer world offers feedback that can clue us in to suppressed emotion.

In simple terms, if things keep going wrong all day, it's likely you're triggered. If the third person asks you if you're alright, it's likely you're triggered. Try to keep note of how things are working for you, and check in when they seem to be off.

The inner state and outer world are often connected together in interesting ways. Try to make space for the possibility that the current challenge is made challenging, in part, by how you feel and respond internally and on a subtle level.

2. When was the last time I felt this way?

When you notice that you're triggered, sit down with a pen and paper. Ask yourself the question,

"When was the last time I felt this way?"

And simply listen to what comes up. No need to figure anything out or understand why. Just listen to the hits that come up and jot them down.

At first, you may have a rush of different moments come in, recent interactions, times at work, with a partner, or in a personal moment. Jot each one down as it comes, even if it doesn't seem connected to the question. No censorship.

After a bit, the hits will slow down. This often reminds me of water slowing to a drip. No need to dig at this point. If it feels like you're reaching to figure out the next one, it's time to move on to the next question.

3. When was the first time I felt this feeling?

This question takes us back further, perhaps to our childhood, school interactions, parents, early loves, etc. We often have surprisingly poignant and vivid early memories linked with challenging emotions.

Again, just ask the question and listen to the hits as they come, jotting everything down without analysis or censorship. And again, just keep it going until the hits slow to a drip. Once it feels like you have to reach for it, move on to the next step: feeling it.

4. Processing the Feeling

Where do you feel the emotion in your body? Just open up to the feeling sense, both of the body and of the emotions, as much as possible. No stories. Just allowing the emotion to be there, letting it peak, ebb, and – in its own time – recede.

This often feels as if some space is created around the feeling, as if it's lessened in intensity. As the intensity eases, we often gain clarity around the feeling. In a less triggered state, we can then explore what, if anything, we should do about the triggering situation.

Sometimes we're triggered primarily by old emotional charge. If this is the case, by processing the emotions, we've received the message. We've opened up to the lesson, and now have a bit of space to figure out how to conduct ourselves most effectively in future interactions.

After clearing old charge, we can often see patterns of conflict or dysfunctional dynamics that we established and maintained unintentionally, sometimes for years. We see that we've been doing it to ourselves, and we begin to see how. This is the core of real personal growth and sustainable self-transformation.

Sometimes we're triggered by something happening at the moment, something that *does* require us to take action. Perhaps our boundaries have been crossed and it is important for us to speak up for ourselves. Perhaps we need to have a fire lit under us to get us moving. Fear can help us to tune in to our sense of need and motivate us to take action. Whatever emotional message is coming in, the process above can help us to gain clarity around it so that we can respond effectively.

One beautiful thing about this practice is that it is **not** about connecting the dots. By asking the questions and writing the answers, we offer the intellect a very specific and helpful role in the process of clearing emotions. Which gets it out of the way so the real work of feeling can be done.

In retrospect, however, surprising themes can pop up. It's amazing how clear our triggers can become when we list the situations that triggered us, rather than our stories about why we were triggered. You are likely to generate several stories and themes from the lists, *aha!* moments that give you a new way of understanding yourself.

These, like all stories, are ways of making sense of the world and of our experience. If it helps, amazing. Just remember that the understanding is an imperfect reflection, always subject to projection and unconscious distortion. Feeling can be met on the feeling level in a way that it cannot be captured in our understanding.

Practice 4: Clearing the Thread

The most powerful long-term emotional practice I've thus far encountered is a meditative exercise, a specific practice in awareness and attention. To enter the meditative state, you can use the alpha rhythm meditation provided in Rhythm and Consciousness. The following exercise can be quite powerful, especially if you have established a strong foundation in the journey state.

For this practice, find a place to sit quietly in a neutral position. Open your field of vision, find a point to fix your gaze upon. Try to take everything in without looking around, widening your awareness around the periphery of your focal point until you can take everything in at once. Practice holding this state softly.

While maintaining awareness of your entire visual field, expand your attention to take in all that you can hear, sounds that you were tuning out, noises in the distance. Again, practice maintaining this state, not listening for or looking at, but letting yourself be filled with the sounds and images.

Once you are able to maintain this, open to all of the feelings within your body and on the surface of your skin. The temperature and the wind, the feeling of the seat beneath you, your body making contact with itself, opening wider until you can receive all of the information streaming in from the senses at once.

At this point, you may have thoughts and feelings arise. You might conceive of each of these thoughts as objects in the distance of your inner view, each linked with you by a thread of feeling and story.

The vibration of this thread is the emotional charge you carry into interaction with this person or situation. The way you perceive it and the way you feel about it. Even before you say a word, you bring this vibration – this story and emotional charge – into your interaction with this aspect of your experience. We unconsciously load the dice for a particular type of interaction.

Allow a thought of a recent or current challenge to come up, and tune in to the thread of emotional charge connected with it. This is your side of the interaction. It is the thread of your thoughts and emotions. You have the ability to engage with them as you choose.

If you are able to release that charge, then you can clear the playing field. You can choose, consciously and authentically, what dynamic and tone you would like to bring into the interaction. More choice means more freedom.

Releasing the vibration of a thread is sometimes known as forgiveness. When we are able to feel and release this charge, it's as if we can finally drop a heavy load. Forgiveness often requires that we humble ourselves, and it can be extremely challenging to our preferred perspective. However, when we are truly able to release our side of a conflict or challenging dynamic, the other side tends to shift in kind. It's often more effective to start healing relationships or challenging situations from within, and then follow up with action in the outer world when we have greater clarity.

Whether you choose to do this meditation with eyes open or with the eyes-closed alpha state, visualization can help to formalize your intentions. So, for example, you might envision the imbalanced emotional charge flowing down through your body and into the earth, returning as balanced, freely-flowing energy.

Or, you could imagine a bank of circuits along the thread that characterizes its current vibration. This was my first way of envisioning this activity. I saw myself pulling out the old circuit board and sending it up to Source, and then replacing it with a fresh, neutral board.

Or, simply feel the charge and breathe space around it, letting it ease into balance. Our visualizations are simply a way to express our intention symbolically to our whole being, so let yourself be creative in dancing with your inner self.

Once you have addressed all that wants to come up at the moment, deepen the breath, count up, and bring your awareness up to baseline.

This space is excellent for helping us to see things that were hiding from the conscious mind. In cultivating emotional wisdom, listening to our feelings is just as important as clearing them, and listening comes first. Also, what's done is done. The past is meant to teach us, not to be worn as a yoke around our neck. We cannot change what has already happened, but we can learn from it and use it to guide our way forward.

Final Words

In moving forward, remember that learning these emotional and cognitive resources will take time. This is a process of learning the instrument of your mind and body. When learning an instrument, we dedicate long hours and years of practice to make techniques natural and fluid. Each time you work consciously with your inner state, you strengthen a habit of consciousness. Each time you face your emotions clearly and process the message, you reclaim wasted energy and gain clarity. The process builds momentum quickly.

Each day, do your best to notice when you are triggered, when your emotions shift or rise into your awareness. Each day, practice check-ins. Each day, give yourself space to listen within. Until all these things become second nature. And, when especially challenged or confused, try out the written process above. Take note of how it feels to listen within and write down what comes.

Clearing the Threads is our first real foray into personal journeying. Learning how to guide our own personal journey opens up our interaction with the inner world. Self-guided journeys offer a personal, customizable means to access and work meaningfully with our subconscious processes.

For the purpose of clearing emotions, the alpha meditation with eyes closed is sufficient. However, when you're ready to begin exploring it, the eyes-open meditation can help to refine your concentration and sharpen your awareness, both of your sense impressions and of your inner experience.

The concept of the thread of emotional vibration can be both empowering and expansive. By envisioning aspects of our inner world in more tangible forms, we are able to engage more directly with them. Even if no such thread exists in the physical world, our conception of it allows us to work with the charge and story content connected to a specific aspect of our experience. The subconscious mind tends to use the language of symbol, image, and gestalt. Conscious visualization can form a bridge, a language spoken both by the conscious and subconscious minds.

No matter how much theory we have learned, the real magic comes in application. As you work with these processes, see how they fit in to your life most naturally. Can you tailor the practice to your own needs, your style and preference? Are you able to feel it, or just understand it? This is a personal journey and each one of us has a unique relationship to our inner world. We are all artists of meaning and feeling in our personal experience.

MODULE 3 - PRESENCE

Introduction to Presence

H ave you ever been in a conversation with someone who felt like they were worlds away? Like they were physically there but not really in the room at all? Maybe you've been there yourself, so focused in one direction that you missed the emotional undertones? If you've experienced moments like this, then you've felt the impact of presence (or a lack thereof) upon your relating.

How about in your personal experience? Have you ever arrived at your destination, only to find that you hardly remembered the journey? Or perhaps you've been reading and realized that you don't know what you just read? The eyes and body keep going on autopilot while the mind is elsewhere.

Our capacity to remain present has a huge effect on every area of our lives. When we are present, when we are in the moment, we are mindful. We are alive to and engaged with what is happening right now. When we are not present to the moment, we're running on automatic. Our reflexes and habits are running the show, and we are at the mercy of our network of story and charge.

Personal Presence

As we become more present, we also become more capable of acting with freedom and intention, of really seeing what's around us and choosing a response. Presence helps us to bridge the mind and heart. It helps us to be clear and alert, even in stressful or unfamiliar situations. It's fundamental to learning, communication, relationship, performance, to all of the important aspects of human life.

In every moment of our lives, we are receiving impressions from our senses, from our thoughts, and from our emotions. When we practice presence, we cultivate the ability to be aware of *all* of what's coming up for us. In returning to an awareness of the body – of the *being* – in each moment, we learn to listen to our bodies and our hearts. We learn to show up in the moment with clarity around who we are and where we're at. We learn to show up for ourselves.

Anything we want to accomplish in our lives, any change we want to make, starts right here and right now, in the moment where we are making decisions and taking action. Any experience we'd like to have or build towards, we can only experience it in our now, in the living moment that we inhabit throughout our lives. Anything we build or create is a result of action taken in the now. Presence is the key to making things happen and enjoying them when they do.

Even if we prioritize long-term goals over our immediate experience, acting with presence, in a sense, has an advantage over focusing *only* on long-term goals. Success benefits from our capacity to see where we are and determine the best possible approach, as well as from our capacity to focus our attention and bring the best of our ability to the task at hand. A practice in mindfulness primes us for effective, well-considered action, but that's just the tip of the iceberg.

Presence in Relating

When we are present in a relationship, we show up for both ourselves and our partner. When cultivating presence in relationship, we learn to set aside our stories long enough to be able to truly see our partner. We learn to drop all the narratives we have running, center our awareness in the heart, and create space for the other, if only for moments at a time.

Presence in relationship helps your partner to feel seen. This is a fundamental need for human beings, a quality which can make or break a relationship. Presence opens the door for authentic, meaningful, and fulfilling connections. In order to practice this, try listening. Get curious about the being you relate with. And, to the best of your ability, try to be open and honest, both with yourself and others. This is a life practice worth every bit of what we put into it.

When we're on autopilot, we conduct ourselves according to habitual roles and internal scripts. We play out patterns that we established long ago, often unconsciously. In the process, we can overlook our needs and desires. To top it off, we can become distant in our relationships, more tuned in to our mental model of our partner than the actual person. Being present helps us to check in with ourselves and our partner *right now*. It helps us to be honest, open, real, and in tune with both ourselves and those we care about.

Although we will explore conscious relating more fully in the next module, remember for now that every single interaction you have with others is an opportunity to practice presence in relating. We bring consciousness into our relating every time we listen, instead of waiting to speak. Every time we savor the time we share with others, rather than filling it up with schedule and distraction. Each time we honestly express what's coming up for us, without agenda or a desire to evoke a specific response.

When people are present with us, it shows us that they care. It shows us that we can trust them and open up to them. And, as we cultivate the capacity for presence, we become better at showing up for others in this same way. Presence creates a strong foundation for a healthy and fulfilling relationship. Without presence, our relationships feel hollow and superficial. And with it, even the most mundane of shared experiences can be a magical moment.

Holding Space

Offering presence to others, giving them your time, attention, and focus, is incredibly powerful as a healing tool. In fact, one of the greatest benefits of talk therapy is the non-judgmental, accepting presence of the therapist. When we feel safe and accepted, we can finally give ourselves space to look at what's coming up within, especially those charged, painful things that hold the most growth.

When a trusted friend is present with us, it creates space for deep emotional healing, space where we can feel safe enough to stop hiding and allow ourselves to feel. And this goes both ways. When we cultivate presence and acceptance in our relating, we learn to reach the person behind the story, to call them to presence as well.

This brings us to another aspect of presence: Holding space. Humans are social creatures. Every moment, we broadcast subtle expressions of our thoughts and feelings to those around us. And, every moment, we pick up similar impressions from others.

Every part of our being reflects our inner state. So, when we have something coming up, it has an impact on our body language, facial expression, and breathing. Add to that our tone of voice, the focus of our attention, and subtle chemical clues like pheromones. All of these signals come together to create a distinct impression.

Even when we are not consciously aware of the subtle impressions we receive from others, we still receive them. And we respond on an unconscious level. Just think of any time you just felt someone behind you, or when a person entered the room, and you noticed a change in the feel of the space. Our senses are more delicate and nuanced than we might expect. We unconsciously register and respond to the presence that others hold, to their charge, rhythm, and intent, even before they say a word.

Just as we instinctively respond to the subtle signals of others, others respond instinctively to the subtle signals we put off. When we become aware of these signals, when we can feel the space that we hold, then we can start to work with it.

It is exhausting and counterproductive to try to mimic the signs of presence or of a specific emotional vibration. Instead, we can learn to tune in to a particular feeling and allow it to be expressed throughout our being, in our words and actions, in the way we hold ourselves and the way we breathe. And presence is inimitable.

First and foremost, however, is to deepen our awareness of the space around us. Everything we see, hear, think, and feel influences us. When you cultivate a living practice of presence, you begin to notice your triggers, your stories, your habits or pain points.

When we set an intention to cultivate presence and pursue that intention honestly, we begin to notice all the things that move us to reaction or trap us in story. We begin to see how people's words and actions impact our presence, and how our presence influences their reactions.

Obstacles to Presence

Cultivating presence is extremely difficult in today's society. We have so many things that press on our attention, things to remember, things to check, and – especially – distractions. How can we focus on being present when it takes all the focus we have just to get through the day?

The answer? Little by little. Presence can and will become a habit, if it is cultivated as a living practice. Every moment is an opportunity to be conscious of where you are, to be aware of what you are doing and how you're feeling.

Though it may take more effort than our unconscious habits, the practice of presence soon begins to show results. The mind steadies and becomes clearer, performance becomes more skillful across the board, and you'll notice massive benefits in communication and relating.

What stands in the way of the cultivation of presence? Consider the things in your own life that pull you away from the moment, the things that move you to unconscious reaction. Consider how you relate to your time, moment-by-moment.

One challenge is the tendency to think ahead or remember previous experiences. Planning for the future is important, and so is remembering what we have learned from past experiences.

However, if we're so focused on the goal that we can't see the situation right in front of us, then we're less capable of handling life's challenges when we need to. If our thoughts about the past intrude and make it difficult for us to accept our life and engage with it to the best of our ability, then they've become an impediment instead of a lesson. We cannot be present when lingering in thoughts of the past or future.

Another common challenge is distraction. We live in a fast-paced society, full of important details to take care of. When at work, we have to focus on the task at hand. At home, we often have other people and their needs, dramas, and preferences. And during our personal time, we tend to focus on activities, games, or stories. In between major activities, we tend to check our phones.

At every step of the way, our attention is pulled towards this or that. Often, we could look back at the end of the day and realize that we've spent the whole time chasing the next thing. Never fully *arriving*, never letting ourselves catch up to where we are.

Here are some of the main obstacles to presence:

Scattered focus: When we move too quickly, it can be hard to keep track of everything. It's almost as if the mind gets pulled in many directions by all of the details. Also, when we make a habit of moving on to the best thing, old thoughts pile up and begin to spill over.

Every human being needs quiet time to reflect and review, to let the contents of the mind settle. As soon as we do, we gain perspective and clarity, and our focus can rest more easily upon the situation at hand.

Ungroundedness: Being grounded means being conscious of your body, aware of your breath, the condition of your body, and the reports of the senses.

We get ungrounded when we go on autopilot. The senses are receiving impressions, but the attention is engaged with something worlds away, just like those moments when you arrive at your destination and realize that you can't remember the drive.

It can be surprisingly challenging to maintain awareness of the body and the breath. One excellent approach is to regularly tune in to one's body and to make a practice of frequent check-ins.

Emotional triggers: Our emotions are powerful and wise. We can either ally with that power and wisdom or be at its mercy. Emotional triggers come up for everyone. We all have things that we're sensitive about, and when people touch those areas, we get uncomfortable, hurt, reactive, shut down, etc.

Our emotional nature protects itself from a perceived threat by mobilizing the emotion that helps us to navigate that threat. But our emotions are wired for caveman standards, so they don't always fit our immediate needs.

Our attention gets pulled like a magnet to emotional charge, to things we react emotionally to. If we listen to our feelings and learn their language, this can be an invaluable self-diagnostic tool. If we're not listening to our emotions, they warp our perception by making emotionally charged details stand out to us disproportionately.

Story: When reacting to an emotional trigger, we often use story as a framework for the charge. Just think of a time when you saw someone again after having had a conflict with them. The story of the previous experience with that individual, and the emotional charge we carry around it, can be so powerful for us that it overshadows what is happening in the present. We can't fully focus on what's happening now when the charged memory of what happened before is taking up so much of our attention.

Story is a means of understanding the world, of being in control of it, at least on a psychological level. When we learn concrete knowledge about the world, we lock it down, get it sorted, and have a clear idea of what's out there. We make a mental model. Whenever someone says, "This can't be happening," it points out that their physical experience contradicts their mental model.

Again, the map is not the territory. Story is all about what's happened before and what might happen in the future; it takes our attention away from the present moment.

Presence and Mindfulness

The key to presence is attention. Mindfulness just means paying attention to what we're doing, where we are, how we're feeling. But this is easier said than done. Our attention is always engaging with something, at least while we are awake. Our attention is drawn to something, focused on something.

Sometimes we direct our attention consciously, while other times it unconsciously follows the most charge in our field of perception. Without training, we often remain only slightly conscious of where we place our attention and of the choice involved in selecting and engaging with a focal point.

In a way, attention is similar to breathing. It's always happening, and we can place our attention somewhere on purpose, but the attention will find its own place if not focused intentionally. We have the capacity to choose where our attention is directed, but it requires intentional effort.

A good bit of all practical learning is figuring out where and when to direct your attention for a specific purpose. Whether it's walking, painting, or writing, we learn how to engage our attention with the task at hand in a way that facilitates the activity.

Energy flows where attention goes. Wherever we place our attention, we tune in to what's happening there and perceive it in greater detail. Whatever we place our attention upon becomes larger in our inner experience. Our attention is the focus not only of our perception, but also of our active response to the situation. And, when we habitually direct our attention down certain channels, these channels become the container of our experience, the shape of our psychological world.

When going through your day, you may wish to make it a habit to notice where your attention goes. Notice the things that demand your attention, and where you feel you're expected to place your focus. Notice whether the attention wants to shift from the focal point or engage more deeply. Notice any feelings that come up in connection with the focal point.

Perhaps most important, take note of where your attention is centered from within. Often, if we tune in, we'll notice our attention centered in our head, behind the eyes. However, it can be centered in the chest or in the belly, and each orientation of the attention will influence what you see and how you see it.

The attention responds to our will, our intention. So, you can shift the center of your attention, from the head to the chest or the belly, for example, by intending the shift and tuning in to the feeling of that region of the body. Belly-centered attention is good for tuning in to personal needs and strengthening the body, while heart-centered attention is good for communication and relating.

Time and Attention

A key concept is that attention is finite. It can be focused or dispersed, but anything that you pay attention to outside of the present moment takes attention away from your present moment. This is not an issue in itself, but it can become one if we devote too much attention to the future or the past. Mostly because the Now is the only moment we actively inhabit. It's the only place we can change anything, do anything, feel anything.

On the level of our psychological reality, anything outside of what our senses and emotions report at this present moment comes to us in the form of a story. Stories are bound up in time, action and consequence, cause and effect. The experience of Now is, in a strange way, timeless. Our senses don't report that we *used to be* hungry. Just that we are hungry *right now*.

We engage with many types of stories. Stories sometimes take the form of memory. We select bits of our previous experience and weave them together in the form of a personal narrative, complete with emotional charge. Sometimes, our stories are the things we have learned about the world. What's happening out there, how it works, why it happens the way it does. Sometimes, they take the form of anticipation, playing out possible outcomes based on previous patterns.

All stories have their place. They show us how things are connected and what they mean to us. At the same time, story is only part of the human experience. Sometimes life is better felt out than figured out. Just think of dancing, or fighting, or making love. If you have to stop to think about what you're doing, then you're missing all the action. Everything we experience happens to us in the Now. As helpful as stories are, they are no substitute for being in the driver's seat of our lives.

Three Scopes of Time

Human beings have three practical relationships with time. Linear time, the time that we agree on in society, what all of our clocks and phones and computers show, is good for making things happen in the outer world. Linear time is a practical and social construct, and it's ideal for planting and industry, good for scheduling and structuring collective activity. While this is a necessary perspective of time for the function of society, it's not very supportive of our needs as individuals.

In learning to be present, we engage more deeply with personal time, with our living now. In other words, with what we are actually experiencing. Now-time (as opposed to linear time) is good for communicating, learning, performing, experiencing, creating. In essence, whenever we have to really up our game, the first step is to pay attention to what we're doing *right now*. Planning and preparation are helpful precursors, but they are nothing without follow through. And follow through happens in the Now.

The third scope of time, the widest and most encompassing, is a bit more abstract. However, you could see it as the long run. There are themes that run through our lives. If we could step back, we would see these themes woven throughout our journey like threads in a tapestry. With each action and each decision, we can consider what we build and what we create, the personal, silent legacy we leave to the world. Seeing our life as a message, as a work of art in the making, can help us to put our time, our will, and our gifts into perspective.

There is far more to this third scope of time. Aboriginals describe it as the dreamtime, a way of relating to time as a circle, all parts present and able to be contacted, after a fashion.

Circular time is evident in the cycles of nature, and it offers deep insight into our journey as a whole. In the waking world, linear time is often more practical. However, when we begin to use the journey space to its potential, circular time becomes invaluable. It offers clarity about the overall structure of our lives and stories, about our relation to others and the origin of our life patterns.

These three scopes of time are also significant for the purposes of learning. You will see them reflected in the structure of the exercises I've offered. When deep learning a new activity or approach, we can make powerful and sustainable progress by combining three approaches: in the living now, active work, and deep training.

In other words, when making a life change, we get the best results when we address that change:

1. In the present moment where that change is applied,
2. With conscious exercises and practice to improve your skill,
3. With long-term slow learning that integrates the new understanding into your consciousness and reflexes.

The Field of Attention (The Luminous Field)

The Field of Attention or Luminous Field is an incredibly helpful concept in dealing with presence. Remember that our attention, at any one point in time, is finite. If we spend attention on one thing, we have less attention to spend on other things. When we focus intensely on one thing, we're more likely to miss other things.

If we were to sit without focusing on anything in particular, we could imagine our attention at that point to be localized in a field around us. It could be seen as a bubble of potential energy, potential focal points for the attention.

When something catches our attention, it's almost as if a thread of that energy extends out to focus on that thing. In the process, some of our potential attention is drawn away from other streams of sensory impressions.

Imagine a bead of water on a pane of glass. Now imagine a thread that leads some of the water away from the drop, pooling it around the end of the thread. On a psychological level, we all exist within a bubble just like this.

In this case, water is used as an image of our finite bubble of attention, centered in our body and in our moment. It suggests both the capacity to shift the attention to different points of our awareness, and how our attention becomes distributed when we focus on a specific detail of our experience. The more intensely we focus on one point, the less attention remains to perceive other things.

To take this a step further, remember that all that we perceive is interpreted (automatically, in part) by our cognition, by the definitions and the meanings we have learned. Our stories form a framework which makes perception sensible to us.

When we see a cup, the function of that cup, the way we have learned to relate to it, immediately suggests itself. We just *know* what it is, as all of our previous impressions come together to form a gestalt, a complex of meaning.

This memory of function and use is a story, a collection of concepts, formed into a specific configuration and attached, in our experience, to the object itself. Our understanding of an object, person, or situation, our understanding of what it is, what it means to us, how it is relevant to us, is a story.

This story is personalized by our unique previous experience, the things we have learned and lived. Elements of this story rise up unconsciously when we perceive the object. We automatically work within our existing story framework to interpret what we perceive.

In essence, these stories fill our field of potential attention. They form a network of lenses through which we perceive the external world and the people we encounter. These lenses, these stories, have a purpose. Each of them helps us to factor in previous interactions with an object or situation and conduct ourselves effectively in relation to it.

However, these stories are often developed and imprinted upon our awareness unconsciously. Although they help us to navigate the world, they can also bias our perception and shape our experiences in ways counter to both our conscious desire and our best interest.

So, to recap, it's as if we have a bubble of energy around us, filled with stories that help to structure sense impressions into meaning.

These stories often have emotional charge attached to them, which acts a bit like a magnet for our attention.

Whatever we place our attention on becomes larger and more detailed in our inner experience.

And, on a slightly deeper level, the rhythm of our consciousness tunes us to engage with the outer world in different ways. Slower rhythms often accompany a more inward focus and grounded awareness.

The medium of consciousness, as experienced by human beings, can be broken down into these four factors: **rhythm and sensory stimuli, charge, story, and attention.**

Our physical rhythm and the reports of the senses form a foundation for the moment of our experience, while our emotional charge colors this experience. Story helps to make it sensible, while attention draws our engagement, our will and conscious focus, to specific points in this field.

Just as our attention can be focused on the external world, on the periphery of this field, it can be drawn to places within it. We may daydream or wander in memory. We may think of stories that we've heard or previous experiences, people and situations from the past, or perhaps ideas about the future.

Regardless of whether our attention is drawn to aspects of our inner world or to objects in our outer world, the same finite pool of attention is distributed between all things filling our conscious awareness. We can only focus on so much at once, whether we're looking inward or outward.

Another key detail of this perspective is that our stories are developed from our previous experiences. From the past. From things that are not happening right now. So, whatever attention is devoted to our stories takes from the attention available to clearly perceive our present experience.

It's a tradeoff. If our stories describe the situation effectively for our needs, then we are primed to respond to the situation effectively. If our stories are misaligned with the situation, then both our perceptions and responses will be skewed. And, since stories are not tuned to the present, we may not even notice it happening.

In simple terms, if we cling too hard to an old story, an old definition, we will only see what we expect, and it will be harder for us to grow and learn.

Ego and Crystalized Energy

There is, for each of us, one story which forms the context of our personal conscious experience. This is our *story of self*, our personal history. Connected with this story are the memories of our past experiences, our triumphs and failures, shames and joys. We have a sense of where we have come from, where we're headed, what we can do, and who we are, all represented in our inner experience in the form of story and charge.

To build further upon our image of the field of attention, we could envision our conscious sense of self as a crystallization of story in our field. Stories structure our sense impressions. The story of self is like a structure that we maintain in our field.

Just like other stories, the story of self has a network of emotional charges associated with it, as well as a specific influence on our perception. Everything we perceive is viewed from this vantage point, in relation to our story of self.

Here's the thing: we learn. We grow. The person we are today is not the same person we were five years ago, ten, twenty. Over enough time, we can come to understand ourselves in dramatically different ways. As we develop and face the formative experiences of life, our story of self faces pressure to grow with us.

We could, for the purpose of this conversation, describe our story of self as our ego. From this perspective, our ego is a crystallized structure in our story shell. It is a story of self which we have developed unconsciously in response to our experiences. This story of self protects us and helps us to handle ourselves in the outer world. At the same time, we have far more potential than we have thus far expressed.

No story of self can encompass who we may become in the future, or who we are *in the living Now*. The Truth of who we are is bigger than our story. We always have the potential to grow and express wider and deeper aspects of our being. In fact, it's inevitable. That's what growth looks like. However, a strong and inflexible story of self limits our rate of growth. It locks us into holding patterns and loops, often without awareness and counter to our real needs.

To put this in human terms, just consider the attractive person who has, for their whole lives, defined their worth in terms of their looks. This may be an effective story of self when they are young. But as we age, the looks tend to fade.

If this individual's story doesn't change, they're headed for a crisis. They can deny the loss of youthful appeal at first, distract or deflect. Eventually, they are forced to redefine themselves, to understand their value in terms other than physical attractiveness. Their crystallized story must be dissolved, and another must be found, ideally one more in line with their current needs and gifts.

Our story of self acts, in our cognitive space, like a network of vested interests. We want to perceive ourselves in certain ways. We don't want to perceive ourselves in these other ways. We need to value our experience, so we find things to value in the terms offered to us. We learn that it's good to be strong, or smart, or accepted. We learn that we are capable of certain things and incapable of others, that certain things attract positive attention from those around us, and other things, negative.

We construct our story of self unconsciously from all of these details. And, once it is constructed, we kind of forget about it. We assume that we *are* this story, and threats to the story are perceived as threats to the being itself.

Our ego, our story of self, is a role we play in the world. And, if this role is working for us, that's awesome. But, for those times that it doesn't, it's important to remember that we can and do change our stories of self naturally as we grow. When we recognize that our story of self is no longer aligned with our needs, we can consciously rewrite that portion of our script.

Think of a time when someone was rude to you, perhaps when someone made a comment that hurt your feelings. In that moment, it's as if these words entered your field and struck against your story of self. When we resist words directed at us, when we are drawn into internal engagement with them, it's because these words strike a point of charge in our story. They evoke feelings, sometimes pleasant and sometimes not so much so.

When we are unconscious of our story, we tend to make meaning automatically. We interpret the things we experience in relatively fixed ways, often feeling, "That's just how it is!"

But the truth is a bit more nuanced. When we begin to spend time being present, engaged with people and situations in the moment, we practice dropping out of story. And we are often granted a fresh perspective in the process, one with a slightly wider scope.

Becoming conscious of and negotiating with our stories is a journey of a lifetime. However, every time we bring a story into the light of conscious awareness, we gain a little bit more freedom.

Many of our stories were learned a long time ago, formed irrationally, full of pain and shame. Many would even sound silly or juvenile if stated outright. But we hold them true at a level that is only visible through intentional introspection. In other words, we have to honestly review our stories, to ourselves and openly, to free ourselves from them.

When we bring these things into the light of consciousness, it can be extremely challenging at first. It's hard to see things about ourselves that we'd rather not see. But all growth begins from where we are right now. Through a combination of both presence and a willingness to process charge, we can turn any challenge into a source of strength and wisdom. Life itself becomes the deep teacher.

Be Like Water

Another helpful image is to *be like water*. This is a subtle practice, and an extremely powerful one. On an energetic level, comments from others could be described as threads or spears entering our field.

In the case of conflict or harassment, regardless of whether it is subtle or overt, it's as if these threads enter our space and we resist. We tense up. And, because we've tensed, these spears strike against that tension. And we feel it. Our emotions get triggered. Our thoughts get hooked into a story. And we step into a dynamic of polarity and pain almost before we even realize it.

We have a choice every time we engage with others. We may choose to give them our attention, to respond to their comment, to take their story into account in our own experience. If we are too attached to our story, then this choice is made unconsciously. But if we can let go of those aspects of our story which resist these words, it's almost as if they pass through our field without striking anything. The claws lose all purchase.

When we learn to be like water, we learn to allow. To allow the sounds and sights that enter our awareness, to allow the words and actions and stories of others to exist without needing to change or fight them.

When we learn to be like water. We learn to let go, allowing these pressures to pass through us. We are the watcher at the center of our Being, and we choose where to take the energies that enter our space. We begin to actualize this choice when we allow the feeling instead of resisting it.

It can be extremely challenging to let go when faced with something in which we have a vested interest. And on a personal psychological level, the answer to this is faith. We often do not know the best for ourselves. Sometimes we want things that are not healthy for us, and sometimes we resist the experiences which offer the most growth. Faith helps us to surrender, to humble ourselves and take uncertainty with grace.

Faith can help us to let go of a need to control the situation, whether this control is exerted upon the perceptions of others or upon our own emotions and circumstances. Faith can help us to see that we are ok, right now, in this moment, and it is enough. We are good enough, and no matter what happens, there will be a way forward.

The faith that I speak of is not belief and has nothing to do with story. It is a feeling. A sense of trust that allows us to let go, to stop fighting ourselves and our world. It comes with acceptance of this moment, just as it is.

When we understand the gift of this one moment, when we feel the depth of the blessing of being alive, there is nothing to fear and no need to control. We can be like water and allow the challenges to flow through our field without resistance.

Growth and Freedom

When we base our self-esteem on the opinions of others, or upon *any* outer world values, then it will often feel necessary to defend our stories. We can feel drawn to engage in a dynamic of conflict, almost as if we have no choice. With ideas delivered to us in words, with situations that cause our stories to chafe. We make meaning automatically based on these imported values, and then play out the same lessons in loops until the stories change. Until we learn how to make meaning in a different way.

It is extremely challenging to tune in to our unconscious stories and realign our perception. It's not enough to understand our story in intellectual terms. We make meaning on a deep and unconscious level, and we feel it before we see it consciously. It's the feeling itself that's the key.

Our stories help us to interpret situations on an emotional level. They help us to understand what the situation means to us. Our stories link our sense impressions with our network of emotional charge. Emotional charge is the driver that shapes our lives, the motive force that leads both attention and will. Fixed perceptions and stories lead to fixed emotional and behavioral response patterns. The network of charge forms the trigger points and the dynamic of these reaction patterns.

From this level, we might as well be machines. When we don't have a choice in our reactions, we don't have freedom. It's down to stimulus and response. However, if we can maintain presence when triggered, if we can tune in to how we are making meaning in the moment, then we become more aware of our choice. This is a big part of cultivating consciousness, of deepening awareness of our self, our situation, our part in creating that situation. And, from this space, we can learn to exert our will intentionally, to respond rather than react.

To cultivate consciousness in this manner requires a dedication to growth. In seeing our stories, we often have to humble ourselves, to recognize how deeply and profoundly we have been the source of all of our own problems. We will also be challenged time and again by the continual shattering of certainty that comes with honest questioning. After all, we don't know very much at all, in the solid, unquestionable, absolute terms we'd prefer.

Honest growth requires looking into the abyss, opening ourselves to depths of experience beyond our words, feelings the mind can't control. And then learning to use the will, reclaiming our power so we can act in alignment with our developing awareness.

This is not a weekend course. The flowering of one's potential takes a lifetime and proceeds differently for each being. That said, every scrap of consciousness that we cultivate means that much more awareness, that much more freedom, that much more personal power with which to create our future.

Some Practical Takeaways

When it comes to the conflicts that can arise between people, responding to the dynamic that's offered to you means meeting the other on terms they set. Sometimes that's good. When people come to us in a friendly and open way, it can be healthy to meet them in this space.

But that's not always what happens. Sometimes we are met with hostility or pressure. Things escalate, ego games come up, and people dance like puppets on strings. This is a waste of time and energy, and it wreaks havoc in relating.

From the perspective of inner freedom, we win when we have a choice. If we respond in a fixed fashion, then we aren't living our choice. It's as if our buttons are pushed, and we respond in the way that we've been programmed. External events trigger internal charge, and we dance. That person's words hurt us, or this situation threatens us, and we react in the only way we know.

In short, when we take things personally, we get locked in to relating with these things in these personal, triggered ways. In ways unconscious of our choice in the matter.

When someone's words hurt you, it means that those words and the meaning you found in them resonate on some level with your unresolved emotional charge. The pain might be triggered by the words, but it really comes from our reaction to them. And, if we didn't hold this charge in our field already, then it would not be evoked by the words. Outer words and situations trigger our pain when we take them personally, when we give those words the power to affect our inner world. Which we tend to do when they strike a point of charge.

To clarify this a bit, think back to a time when someone said something that hurt your feelings. Remember what that felt like. Now, if you can, try to remember a time when you had words directed at you, possibly with the intent to harm, and it was easy to laugh them off. In the first case, it's as if the words struck a sensitive spot. In the second case, for any number of reasons, those words were not given the same power to influence your inner world.

When we are attacked psychologically or emotionally, the impact of that attack strikes against our crystallized story of self, specifically against the pain points locked within this story. The more fixed our story of self, the more we are called to defend this story against challenges and changing circumstances.

Our story is our own. Our perceptions are our own. And we make meaning, our own meaning, in deeply personal and creative ways. Every time something hurts our feelings, it points out to us things within ourselves – pain, shame, guilt, judgment, etc. – that we have been carrying in our field, in our inner experience. Hidden beneath our awareness.

External triggers help to reveal internal conditions. This is the mechanism behind the Rorschach (inkblot) test. Internal charge conditions our perception. We interpret even potentially random stimuli in ways that reflect our network of emotional charge and story.

With this in mind, we can use our emotional triggers as diagnostic tools. Rather than focusing our reaction on the outer object that triggered it, we can focus on how we respond personally. From this perspective, it's almost as if triggering words are messages from the universe which reveal hidden emotional charge.

Many of our stories hide from conscious view. But, every external trigger highlights our personal stories, our old, unprocessed feelings and the tension we hold in our field. Once we realize that, we can use each trigger as a spur for growth and a guide to greater freedom.

In simple terms, we go a long way towards actualizing our freedom when we learn not to take things personally. Regardless of the motives of others, regardless of the specifics of the outer situation, an experience of internal charge is an opportunity to process that charge.

If we can feel it, we can heal it. At the very least, practicing awareness around our triggers and their personal nature gives us a greater understanding of the choices we make (reflexively) in the moment.

The other half of this same insight is the futility of making assumptions. Everything that we see, we interpret in terms of our story shell, our filters. This story shell has been meticulously developed and reinforced over the course of our lives. It is so absolutely personal, for each of us, that it could be perceived as a whole psychological universe. If we were to honestly assess within, we could take note of years of reflection, specific memories, unique perspectives, all melded into something as familiar to us as it is mysterious.

If we then take a look around at all the other people we see, it stands to reason that each of them interprets things through their own framework as well. That others see everything from within the view of their personal psychological universe, just as we do. We often interact closely with others, tune in to how they work, experience them over time, and have a good ability to predict aspects of their behavior. However, much of their inner experience will still be hidden from our view. We can't know what something *means* to another, what it *feels like* to them.

When we make assumptions about the motives of others, we begin to interact with a mental model rather than the real thing. This is useful; it's a part of normal learning. However, these mental models aren't perfect. If we're unaware that we make meaning in personal terms, we can easily assume that a situation means the same to you as it does to me. We take things as they were not intended, and we see them pretty much as we expect to. Much misunderstanding and poor communication is caused by this alone, by interacting with *our idea of another person* rather than the person.

Once we begin to see the stories that we use to make sense of the world, we also become more aware of the stories used by others. This gives us more insight into the inner experience of those we interact with. It helps us to speak another's language. When we see the stories that people live within, we can interact with them on a much deeper level. If we get really lucky, we may actually be able to connect with the being behind the stories.

A Living Practice

Presence is about far more than just performance or relationships. Literally everything we experience happens to us in our living now. Presence helps us to see clearly, to learn more quickly, to see and honor the person we're interacting with. And, when we make a practice of noticing our attention, noticing the space we hold and how we engage with the outer world, we open to a new and unexpected dimension of experience. We begin to see how subtle orientations in the inner world are reflected in our outer experiences.

This is a living practice. Put another way, presence isn't something you practice for a moment and then put down. It's a way of life. Every moment of our lives is an opportunity to wake up to what we're doing, to truly feel it and see it. Said in this way, it could be taken poetically. And yet, this is no more than normal human consciousness.

We often spread our attention so thin across old stories, memories, thoughts of the future, etc., that very little awareness remains. Without even realizing it, we can sleepwalk through life, interacting with our scripts and our mental models, playing out the same loops and holding patterns.

As we begin to pull in those threads and pay attention to what we're doing, all sorts of things just "pop out." We begin to operate at a much higher level, with more awareness, higher functional intelligence, and responses more in tune with the actual situation.

In our interactions with others, presence is largely a practice of dropping out of our stories and centering our attention in our heart. When we are interacting from the head, we see our mental model. By centering our attention in our body, in our heart space, our whole way of relating changes. Our tone, body language, capacity to truly see the person in front of us, all of this tends to improve dramatically. We become more able to truly honor the person that we relate with.

When centering our attention in the heart space, we also become much more capable of distinguishing honesty from deception, openness from calculation. The human intellect can easily be deceived by a compelling story. However, our visceral responses to the world around us are often far more calibrated to what's actually happening around us. We can cut through a Gordian knot of bullshit far more easily by listening with our hearts and bodies than with our minds.

In becoming aware of the space that we and others hold around us, we begin to tune in to a form of basic communication that precedes words and conscious intentions. We can, at times, feel the presence of others without them saying a word. And, if we're paying attention, we'll notice how others' reactions tend to reflect the feeling we hold in our space. Often, human beings will respond to one another's presence without even being aware of it. We pick up the signals subconsciously and orient ourselves around them.

This applies to our interaction with animals as well. Though they do not use words, animals respond to the collection of subtle signals expressed by other animals they encounter. We communicate calm or anger, affection or fear, on this subtle level of universal language. Other animals perceive and respond to this language of motion, attention, and feeling. They take their cue in interaction from these signals. If we are aware of our presence, we can communicate basic things quite effectively without any words, with humans and other animals.

In short, the living practice of presence is a cultivation of awareness around where and how we engage with the outer world. Around where we put our attention and how we interpret the things we perceive. The more that we can see this, the more we can recognize – and exercise – our choices in engaging with the world. We begin to refine our awareness so that we can tune in intentionally to a person or situation.

Even more, we become aware of the tendency for our vibration and story shell to set the tone for incoming dynamics. This offers dramatically more freedom in our internal space and helps us to take a more active part in the creation of our experiences. It helps us to move from the passenger seat to the driver's seat of our own lives.

EXERCISES IN PRESENCE

A s you move into the exercises ahead, consider the three scopes of time. The first practice is for the first scope of time: the living Now. By *getting grounded* and *gathering the threads of our attention*, we practice the nuts and bolts of presence, in the moment when it really matters.

The second practice, *qualifying energy*, is based in linear time. It teaches us how to consciously practice these skills. With time, they become more natural, and our efforts in the moment bear more fruit. In learning to qualify our energy, we learn to hold space in many different ways and to use intention, feeling, and visualization to consciously tune this energy to our needs.

Finally, the practice of *conscious motion* teaches presence in the third scope of time. By cultivating awareness around our motion and attention, we train a reflex of consciousness. The training of reflexes is a deep practice that realigns our perception. We learn to relate to our body and our experience in a different way, and these benefits filter out into everything we perceive and every choice we make.

Remember that the real transformation comes in mastering these exercises. Stories can get us to the gate. They can help us to make sense of the world in a way that helps us to navigate it. The next step, the only way to truly benefit from these stories, is to practice navigating.

These exercises help us to become aware of our attention, our space, our relationship with time and story. They help us to practice exercising our will in these spaces. That's where the magic happens, with awareness, intention, and aligned action.

Practice 1: Grounding and Gathering the Threads

This is an extremely simple and quite powerful exercise. Before doing anything important, before communicating or performing, after being triggered, take a moment. Tune in to your space.

Notice where in your body your attention is centered. Allow yourself to notice any nagging thoughts, anticipations of the future. Observe the state of your being as completely as possible. Notice the things that you want that you don't have right now, things that you maintain a stance of resistance to, all the threads of thought and feeling that move through you.

All of these threads take a little bit of your attention. When we get too caught up in them, we can be lost in stories that have little to no connection with our actual experience in the moment. This is natural, but it interferes with our capacity to show up for life, to savor the moment, to see the other, and to meet the challenge in front of us with all of our resources.

To gather your threads, close your eyes, and allow your breath to deepen, to become slow, soft, and full. Envision all of these nagging thoughts and bits of charge as threads extending out from your center, pulling your attention into scattered bits. Breathe, inhaling energy, clarity. Exhaling tension. If necessary, address any pressing concerns, like consciously acknowledging a task that must be attended to later. And then let them go. Breathe yourself into your body, your moment.

As you do, envision the energy of your attention pulled back in, the thread reclaimed. Breathe and envision gathering them one-by-one until all of these threads pool back together and you return to the sphere of your neutral state. Envision the threads anchoring within your body, even extending down through your legs and rooting into the earth.

Once you have gathered all stray thoughts and rooted yourself into your body, open your eyes and engage with the outer world. As you do, intend the energy that you would like to carry into the outer world. Perhaps you'd like access to calm, or confidence, or creativity, or eloquence. Whatever you need at this moment, tune in to that feeling, and then bring it forth into the task at hand.

That's it.

Remember that the value of a practice is not in its complexity. Try it out. Each time that you do, you will find it a little bit easier. Each time you do, you will gain a bit more freedom, a bit more clarity. And, each time you practice tuning in to a specific inner resource, you deepen your conscious connection with that resource state. You learn how to return there when you want to, when you need it.

Practice 2: Qualifying Energy (Holding Space)

Whether we realize it or not, we're always holding space. We carry our feelings into the space around us, whether we're conscious of it, whether we intend to, whether we want to or not. The choice we have is not whether to influence the space around us, but how. We qualify the energy around us, on subtle levels, with the thoughts that circulate through us, the emotions and desires that color our perception and motivate our actions.

Those around us respond, both consciously and unconsciously, to the physical, mental, and emotional bubble of space around us. The quality of energy in this space determines the tone of the incoming dynamic.

In simple terms, if we're upset and riling for a fight, everything looks like an affront. And, whether we consciously intend it or not, we are far more likely to invite conflict when we're in that mental and emotional space. We set ourselves up for the conflict before we even say a word.

Human beings, on a fundamental level, use their vibration and story shell to filter and align with outer experience. Our attitude, body language, tone, the subtle somatic emanations of our emotions and attention, all of these things call forth a particular response in those we interact with. We prime ourselves and others for specific arguments, patterns in relating, challenge or ease in accomplishing certain tasks, all with the qualities we hold in our space. Both consciously and unconsciously.

When we regularly experience difficulty in an area of life, it's well worth our time to consider the feelings and stories we have about the subject. The way the world responds to us can act as feedback, helping us to tune in to unconscious stories and suppressed charge. And, once we can tune in to this charge and process it, we notice that our interaction in the outer world begins to shift, releasing old patterns and loops. When we qualify our energy differently, our experience of the outer world changes in kind.

In order to hold space consciously, we first have to tune in to the kind of space we want to hold. Slow your rhythm slightly, envision gathering your threads and rooting them. Then tune in to the feeling you would like to hold in your field.

To tune in, place your attention on a feeling or story and let it become larger in your inner space. Perhaps remember a moment in which you felt this way, or simply create space within and allow that space to fill with the intended feeling. Let the emotion rise in you, filling every fiber of your being.

As the emotion rises, let the breath follow it. Allow your body to take on the posture of that emotion. Anchor it into your body and deep into the earth. Then envision the emotion, the specific color, vibration, or feeling of this charge, overflowing the body and filling your bubble of space.

Breathe, envision, and feel this charge pouring out from you and saturating your field. Once it feels strong and solid, engage once more with the outer world. As you do, set the intention to maintain that feeling, to reinforce it with each breath.

That's it. This practice can be used to hold any emotional vibration in our field. We each have different needs and a different relationship with our emotions, so each of us will discover emotional vibrations and emphases most suited to our unique needs and skills.

One powerful practice is to tune in to the feeling of warmth. Supportiveness, kindness, openness, compassion, the feeling of warmth brings all of these things into our field, into our space. This is ideal for creating strong and healthy connections with others, as well as for building and growing things in our lives.

Another beautiful practice is to savor or celebrate our experience, to tune in to the subtle sensual blessings of the moment. We are lucky to be alive, to be able to feel, experience, and grow. Everything that happens in our lives is a blessing. Each moment is so rich with nuance and detail, so full of novelty and promise, that we can fill our space with joy for life itself. In the practice of celebration, we consciously align with all that makes life worth living. And, in sharing this feeling in our space, we invite health, happiness, and friendship.

A final note about holding space: Remember that our emotions are wise messengers. We ignore them at our own peril. Holding space intentionally works better when we've made a commitment to feeling our feelings and process them, and when we regularly make space to do so.

If we allow old and unprocessed charge to fill our field, we will be tempted to bypass our emotions with intention, effort, and story. Intellectual and spiritual bypass are ego games that slow our true growth.

Practice 3: Consciousness in Motion

Practicing presence is one thing when we're sitting down, being contemplative. It's another thing altogether when we're in the trenches, facing the challenges of life. We have to figure things out, remember details, handle stress, communicate with others, and observe the nuances of our inner state in response to all these things. Too much, too fast, and it takes much of our capacity to get through the challenging parts, presence aside.

So, with all that going on, how can we have enough mental space to be present to our current experience and handle life at the same time?

Simple answer: practice. As with all things, presence becomes easier and more natural with practice. As we drop out of story again and again, as we return to an awareness of what we're doing right now, again and again, we train ourselves to presence as a reflex.

This is challenging, to say the least. One of the best ways to begin this journey is to use simple activities – like walking, folding clothing, dishwashing, etc. – to practice paying attention to what you're doing.

Let yourself notice when thoughts come up, things you'd forgotten, things you've done, things you plan to do. And set them aside for the moment. Come back to the simple task, to the motion of your body, the sensations of the experience.

If you practice walking in this way, try to really feel your body. The sensation of your foot as it meets the ground, the shift of your weight as you move. Feel your posture and your breath. This is a practice of being present while moving. It's also a practice of allowing this presence to inform your motion. As you pay attention, you may feel imbalances or misalignments. Let your motion smooth out and strengthen in response to your conscious attention.

The conscious walking exercise described above is a Zen practice. Another practice aimed at the same cultivation of presence is yoga. Hatha yoga is a practice of conscious physical motion as a means to the cultivation of awareness. Tai chi is yet another practice with the same focus, albeit a different emphasis. All of these practices give us the opportunity to practice moving in more and more complex ways while remaining present and fully aware of our moment.

Another expression of this same principle is the flow state. As we get really good at a particular skill, the techniques become natural to us and require less conscious thought. We develop the capacity to be present to the action itself. We stop having to think about it and begin engaging more deeply with the motion and the moment.

When this happens, our state of mind shifts and it's almost as if our attention becomes woven into the task. And as a result, our engagement becomes more graceful, more skillful, more in tune.

The flow state is an inner orientation that permits us to bring all of our skill and knowledge to bear on the task at hand. It permits far higher performance than we can manage when we're consciously planning the details of each move.

In order to practice flow state, it's helpful to develop a foundation of the techniques and processes involved with a given task. However, any task that we use as a practice of conscious motion improves our capacity to be conscious while actively engaged with any task. In the end, conscious motion itself – presence in action – is the gateway to extremely high performance across the board.

The flow state can be described, but there is something about it that transcends any possible definition. It is apparent when viewing those with skill in a musical instrument, or martial arts, or any endeavor which benefits from timing and proficiency. At some point, our practice of the art becomes greater than the sum of its parts and something almost magical happens. In those moments we create something beautiful, even if it is something as simple as a perfectly timed action.

For the purpose of this exercise, take an opportunity each day to move with presence. Pay close attention to your body, your breath, the subtleties of your motion. If you practice yoga or tai chi, this is a natural time to practice conscious motion. If not, find a moment when you're taking care of a chore, like washing dishes or folding clothes. Or perhaps when doing some repetitive task at work, or when driving, or moving from one place to another.

It doesn't really matter what the activity is, and it doesn't need to be the same activity each day. What does matter is that you practice presence in motion every day. Practice paying absolute attention to what you are doing, what you are perceiving. Practice noticing when thoughts or charge intrude on this focus and practice setting them aside to return to focus. Practice letting the attention rest lightly on the task, like the touch of a feather. No overcontrolling, planning, or rushing. One ... breath ... at .... a .... time...

It's highly advisable to take up both a musical instrument and a physical practice, as both offer ample challenge to the practice of presence. Human beings grow through challenge. We need to set goals and strive, to build confidence and find higher heights and more meaningful depths. This particular challenge, when faced regularly, guides us toward embodied wisdom and the highest expression of skill.

The goal is to let the action flow through you with the utmost grace and ease. In order to approach the goal, forget the goal entirely and engage completely with *this* moment, *this* action. Real training in this fashion is slow and painstaking. The payoff of this training, however, filters out into every aspect of our experience. Every single task – every single moment of our lives – benefits immensely from our capacity to see and respond to it in the living Now.

In Moving Forward

In our discussion of presence, we've covered a massive download of information. We now have a visual image of the inner experience. In a way, this is no more than a metaphor. However, it is based intimately upon the body itself, tuned to things all humans experience personally. Ideally, these passages will bring clarity about our inner experience and inspire a healthier working relationship with our attention, charge, and story.

At the end of the day, though, the content offered here is just another story, one of many valid ways of making sense of our experience. Stories can get our foot in the door. Under the best circumstances, they can prime us to relate meaningfully and healthily with our experience. But from that point on, the practice is the teacher.

There are things we can only learn from experience. Once we begin to engage actively with our experience, we begin to understand it in personal terms. The stories we pick up from others are extremely helpful. They are the medium of cultural growth.

That said, at some point in our development we move from cultural education to individuation. When we engage in an active practice of coming to know ourselves, we begin to understand our life and values on our own terms. This is the gateway to living a life of intention and inner freedom.

MODULE 4 - ACCEPTANCE AND ACCOUNTABILITY

Introduction to Acceptance & Accountability

Ok. Time for some of the hardest questions any of us can face. Do you love yourself? Do you love your life?

Let's take it a bit further. Love is a huge word, as powerful as it is ambiguous. How about this: do you like yourself? Do you like who you are? Do you like the life you're living right now? Are you happy?

These are questions that no one can answer for you. No one can tell you what you need to be happy, what you need to feel fulfilled. We are, each of us, individuals with our own universe of desires and emotions, stories and context. Relationships and meaning.

For each of us, the path to true, sustainable happiness involves making peace with the life we lead, and then considering what we would like to do with the life we have.

This is a deeply personal journey, a journey of individuation. It requires us to look inside and discover what we want, what we value, what we believe in, what we enjoy, and then learn how to align our lives with these things.

The Journey of Individuation

There are two huge challenges that all human beings face on the journey of individuation: acceptance and accountability. With acceptance, we stop running from our life as it is. So much effort is lost – and so much challenge created – by resisting ourselves and our lives. Acceptance helps us to let go, to surrender to *right now* and make peace with ourselves.

Then comes accountability, a willingness to accept responsibility for ourselves and our lives. With accountability, we can finally stop playing the victim. We can finally look at what we've done to get where we are in our lives and what we can do to move in the direction we want to go.

This is work. Lifelong work, the kind that we'd all rather avoid at first. And it's an Achilles heel for most of us, a point of hidden weakness and pain in our psyche. Who wants to admit that they might not really like their lives? Who wants to admit to themselves that they might not even like themselves all that much?

But, in the quiet moments between distraction, or when things take a particularly challenging turn, any of those nagging doubts we have about ourselves and our lives come forth with full force. Guilts, shame, self-judgment, personal failures and humiliations, all of those little pains that we tend to sidestep, or numb out, or deflect.

In a big way, it's healthy for these concerns to come up. Just think about it. We are social creatures, raised and enculturated by those around us. We are taught how to handle ourselves in the world, what we can expect of the world and what the world expects of us. By our parents and our peers, we are taught what to value, what is reasonable, what is possible, what will earn the goodwill of others, what is forbidden, etc.

We are (for the most part and often imperfectly) taught what we need to know to function in society. But we cannot be taught what we need to become ourselves, to live a life of intention, a healthy life aligned with our personal values.

We all respond to this early instruction differently. Some of us dedicate our efforts to living in the manner that we've been taught.

Others rebel, doing all they can to live in reaction to those early lessons. For most of us, the approach is a blend of both.

Whichever way we respond, at some point in our development, we realize that what we have just isn't doing it for us. Some life event, some crisis, forces us to reevaluate our lives, and we discover that we've been playing someone else's game.

When we're young, without knowing any better, we try to prove ourselves to our authority figures. We try to fulfill their expectations, or, if they make this impossible, then we try to rebel in some way that establishes our own inner authority, our own self-determination.

These patterns follow us into later life. We can spend years chasing something that deep down, we don't even really want. We can chase success, chase money, chase the perfect body, the perfect relationship, all to fulfill a life script that we wrote unconsciously. Never our minds on where we are, what we are doing!

In the process of trying to live our lives based on the standards of others, unaware of our own needs and values, we can spend decades chasing a carrot on a stick. We can move through life almost blindly, motivated by ideas of an imagined future that we may never reach.

Maybe we're working through our lives just so that we can do what we want when we retire. Or we're putting our own needs and desires on the shelf to devote our time to our partner or friends. Maybe we're chasing the next promotion, or we're putting the time in the marriage for the kids, knowing that it's not right for us or them.

We can spend huge chunks of our lives playing the "until then" game. Just serving time until things are different, better somehow, until this road actually leads me to the promised happiness.

None of these things are wrong or bad. It's beautiful to work long and hard to build something meaningful. It's deeply fulfilling to cultivate healthy connections with our intimate partners and friends, or to put our selfish concerns aside to do the best thing for our children.

The key here is motivation. Anything we do because we should, because we are supposed to or we have to, comes from a place of duty rather than authentic desire. With the best of intentions, we can edge ourselves out of our own lives, filling them up with duty and distraction, habits and loops, holding patterns to create stability and stave off the uncertainty that accompanies growth.

Authenticity

It is good to fulfill our duties and the practical requirements of our lives. At the same time, the energy we bring to these duties has a huge impact on how we are able to meet them.

Just think of a time when a friend was spending time with you because they *had to*. And another time when a friend was spending time with you because they *wanted to*. Try to remember how different these experiences felt.

Consider a time when you were engaged in one task because you were *supposed to* take care of it. And another moment engaged with an activity you *truly wanted to* do. Think about the quality of the final product. When we don't really want to do what we're doing, we must overcome our resistance just to produce something "good enough."

When we authentically want to do what we're doing, we show up. It's almost a guarantee that the things we authentically want to do will receive more focus, loving attention, and fuller engagement with the act. We become present with the task and bring all of ourselves forth to meet it. When we truly value the people in our lives and wish to spend time with them, we are better able to make strong, healthy connections.

Authenticity is a master key to aligning our will to our lives. When we can be honest and real with ourselves about what we really want, we open the door to seeing the blessings we have right now. We can release resistance to our world and devote all that energy to building the life we want to live.

Authenticity is based on acceptance. On an acceptance of our lives, of ourselves, of the situation we're inhabiting and the playing field of our life as it is right now.

We may not be perfect. We may not have the perfect body, or a life history without blunders or shortcomings. We may not have the ideal job, or home, or relationship, or family situation. But, for each of us, this is where we are. This is our life. It's happening right here, right now. And anywhere we want to go starts from here.

The Journey of Acceptance

On the journey of acceptance, we learn to drop resistance to ourselves. We learn to stop chasing validation from others. We stop trying to earn inner fulfillment with outer accomplishments. We begin to listen to our needs, our subtle responses, to give our feelings and desires space to be as they are. We give ourselves space to be heard without judgment.

Everyone, in their secret heart, experiences doubts and fears from time to time. We all feel pain and grief and frustrations. When we run from these things, we can avoid them for a little while. We can medicate our pain points, the things we do not accept in ourselves and our world. We can sidestep our fears and doubts with posturing, or aggression, or story, or distraction. But they never quite go away. They can keep us running, keep us trying to prove ourselves, for the rest of our lives. Without making any progress whatsoever.

We can't get away from the things we feel. The only way to make real progress with them is to face them.

Acceptance is a process – a lifelong practice – of learning to listen to the things we feel and experience. Of slowing down and making space for them in our inner experience. Acceptance is a process of making peace with who we are, what we have done, where we have been, and how we are now. Of moving beyond judgment and criticism of ourselves, of others and our world, and into a place where our efforts can promote health, goodwill, and alignment.

Acceptance begins with ourselves and then moves outward to encompass every aspect of our lives. And, in the process, it frees us from old patterns and blind spots, leaving clarity in its wake. To put it another way, by accepting our lives as they are now, we free up wasted mental and emotional energy which we can then use to move our lives in the desired direction.

From Acceptance to Accountability

When we walk around in judgment and resistance to ourselves, to others, to our situation, it's as if we're digging in our heels in our own life. We may be completely unaware of working against our own interests, but our lack of acceptance actually helps to keep us stuck in undesirable situations. It disempowers us and primes us to handle life events and interactions as a victim, playing small and believing it.

When we learn to be accountable to ourselves, we learn that we are the ones in the driver's seat of our own lives. It begins with acceptance. This is your life. This is your situation. Right now, not some time in the past, some imagined future, or some alternate life where things turned out differently. Our choices have led each of us to this very moment. Our choices determine the path forward. Where do you go from here?

When we are young, we learn the world as it is presented to us, and we begin to play the game as it was offered. We had no conscious choice as to the family we were born into or the situations of our early lives. Sometimes good things happened, and sometimes hard things happened. And we just dealt with it the best we could. This is the role of the victim, not accountable for their lives, reacting, sometimes acting out, in resistance to the situation.

We often take this into our early adulthood, building a life in the way we know how. And, for some time, it works. But eventually, we run into problems. We encounter setbacks, relationships that fall apart, crises of meaning.

In these moments, we are given both a gift and a challenge. The challenge causes us to look at where we are and to ask ourselves if this is where we want to be. It's a wakeup call and it welcomes us to take a hard look at our current situation.

The gift is accountability, which is the ability to show up as a force of intention within your own life. Our crises force us to consider how we got to this moment and what we would like to do about it when moving forward. They give us an opportunity to wake up within our own lives, to stop playing the victim and begin charting our own course.

From Surviving to Thriving

No one is coming to save us. There is no villain in our world that keeps us stuck in lives misaligned with our needs. It's all on us, each one of us, for ourselves. As soon as we are able to accept that, as soon as we are able to take accountability for our own lives, we are able to start moving forward.

It begins with openly looking at our lives and honoring the ways in which they work for us. Perhaps they keep us safe, or comfortable, or connected to people we care about. Wherever we are, we chose to be here, on some level. We may not have been aware of the choice, but we made decisions that led us to this point.

And we're still making decisions, each day, and each moment. We chose this path, without infinite resources and infinite freedom, without foreknowledge and perhaps without a true awareness of the alternatives, but we chose it and we continue to choose it.

When living as we *should*, we learn a survival mentality. Do what you have to do, and then try to fit in enough enjoyment around the edges to make life worthwhile. Whether we learned that *should* from peers or parents, it keeps us stuck.

When we realize that, *should* aside, we chose this path, then we have a different perspective available. We are suddenly given space to ask ourselves some hard questions:

"What do I really want? What do I really care about? Is this the life that I want to live? Is it what I would choose if I had a choice?"

And then remember that you do have a choice.

When making this inner transition, we first learn to align our will with our lives as they are. To let go of some of the need to have what we want and tune in to our capacity to want what we have. We begin to learn contentment.

At the same time, we're still living, learning, growing, building. Making decisions. We still strive to move forward in our lives, in whatever way has meaning for us, in whatever way aligns with our values. And slowly, almost imperceptibly, we shift from a survival mindstate to one that helps us to thrive. This shift is reflected in the situations we create for ourselves in life and how we show up to our lives. We thrive when we live a life of intention, presence, and honest self-review.

Self-Acceptance and Social Conditioning

All the world's a stage, and all the men and women merely players.

-William Shakespeare

Here are some more hard questions to add to the mix:

Whose life are you living? Who's responsible for the life you lead? Who is capable of choosing the life you lead?

Once you let that sink in:

Are you happy? What would it take for you to be happy? Is there anyone out there with both the power and the motivation to make that happen?

From birth, each of us has been educated to live in our society, to interact in a way that ensures our needs are fulfilled. We learn how we should be as very young children, through mimicry and modeling. We follow the examples we are shown, and our parents, educators, and peers teach us the why and wherefore of our traditions and cultural values.

That said, nobody really knows what life is all about, what it means for others, what it will be like for ourselves in the future. There is no one perfect way that all should follow.

We do coexist with others in our society, and it is important that we be taught how to do so in a way that works for everyone. So, we learn social roles in the form of expectations, charged with the emotion of approval or disapproval. And then we internalize those expectations, becoming our own judge, keeping ourselves in line through unconscious anticipations of approval or judgment from others.

This sort of education is important for human beings at the social and tribal levels. It helps to keep us all on the same page, creates a container for our collective experience, and sets clear boundaries to minimize conflict.

That said, one of the beautiful things about being a human is that it doesn't stop there. We can, each of us, discover what we truly care about, what makes life fulfilling for us. We can, each one of us, bring something unique and personal to our experience and share that with others.

Conditioning and the Human Beneath

Our lives can be expressions of beauty and fulfillment, integrity and meaning. This brings with it a subtle but fundamental power. One who lives a life of intention and clarity of purpose, one who is willing to know themselves and express their insight from a place of love, this person garners respect from all those who encounter them.

When you encounter someone who is present, who is at peace with themselves, you feel it. And, since this is such a rare quality, it's magnetic. This is the feeling of someone who knows their soul and lives in close connection with it. Someone who knows themselves deeply and who can sway hearts and minds with clear, empowering words. This is what a human being feels like when they are healthy and awake.

How often have you run across an individual like this? Unless you have been extremely lucky and blessed in this life, it's not likely to have been a common thing. Instead, we are more likely to encounter unreasonable people, those unhappy with their lives and disempowered to change them, those addicted to drama, or story, or relationship, or roles of a wide variety.

It's almost as if we are actors and actresses. We learn our part over time. We learn the roles that are expected of us, and then, after enough time, we know ourselves as the role. We go on autopilot and forget that we're making choices each time. We experience the consequences of those choices, and somehow conclude that that's just how life is.

On autopilot, the aware, present human drops into the background, and the habitual emotions, thought patterns, and behaviors run the show. We play out little dramas to ourselves and those around us. We go through the motions.

We are often completely convinced of these dramas in the moment. We identify with our role and live studiously by its guidelines, until we are challenged and forced to reconsider our approach. Until this time, it can seem almost impossible to accept our lives, much less to take responsibility for them.

We often feel so full of thoughts, emotions, and impulses. We have a whole story full of things we do want and things we don't. The things we want are easy to accept but come along with things we don't. We learn these preferences through experience and example. For the most part, ever since we were born, we have been conditioned to behave in certain ways, conditioned to feel certain responses and conditioned to interpret our situation as we do.

To understand this a bit better, just look at the joy and wonder with which a young child meets the world. The natural human is, emotionally, just like this young child. But over time we get hurt, we get trained, we learn from others around us how we need to be in society. How we should feel, and what is possible.

Slowly, our lives become squeezed into appropriate channels. The joy gets edged out, along with the genius, and we learn to be effective units of the social machine.

Conditioning and Acceptance

As counterintuitive as it may sound, acceptance is the key to overcoming conditioning. It is the key to inner freedom.

Our conditioning is emotionally driven. On a gut level, we learn to veer away from things that brought us pain in the past. And straight into the reaction that we've learned, the behavior that meets our internalized expectations. Push the button, and observe a specific action in response. In order to overcome this automatic reactive tendency, we have to be willing to accept the feeling, to let it in and allow ourselves to process it.

A life guided by conditioned behavior, governed by conditioned emotional response, is a life lived unconsciously. When living like a mimic, trying to cultivate an external impression that fits what we think we need, we often feel unfulfilled. This is an uncomfortable state of being, so the first thing we do is justify our action, situation, history, and perception. We generate a backstory that makes it easier for us to accept our life, a story that we can inhabit rather than a less than ideal situation. We compare ourselves to others along the way, trying to follow this example and that, all in the hopes that it will eventually lead us to happiness and fulfillment.

All of this happens unconsciously, instinctively. So, at first, it can be challenging to see that this is what we have been doing. No one really wants to accept that they've been living their life according to someone else's needs and standards. It's a hard realization that we've been trying to earn acceptance, earn validation, earn self-worth, by following the models laid out before us. Even harder when we come to see that these things cannot be earned. The only way to earn worth or acceptance is to give them to ourselves.

Here's the key: if we only understand our lives at a surface level, we can spend all of our time and energy seeking validation, and never get anywhere. It's a bottomless pit. No matter how much effort we put in to seek acceptance from others, to seek validation of our worth, no one else can give this to us. It is up to each person to learn how to accept themselves, to give themselves permission in their own life, and to recognize the worth in themselves that they would like others to see. It starts within.

We often act as if we will eventually get to some better place in life, so long as we stay the course. Eventually we'll slog through the trials and get to the promised land. But forcing ourselves blindly onward never really works. We don't get to where we want by following the route to a different destination.

The logical extension of the "until then" game projects another life altogether, one where, so long as we have followed the rules laid out for us, we will always be happy and have everything we want, forever and ever. Maybe this is the case, and maybe it's not. But to live our entire lives in a way that is unfulfilling to us, all based on the promise of something different after our lives are over, this can lead people to act unreasonably, harmfully to themselves and others.

This is your life. Right here. No one is coming to save you. It's on you to determine your own course in life. And, more than that, this is a gift. A blessing. We have a life with which to feel, create, connect.

This moment, each moment, is so rich with life and sensation, that if we were to be fully present to it, we would have no space for regrets or fears for the future. And, no matter what we've lost, there is always a way forward. It's always worth it to start again from zero. It's ok to be exactly who and how we are. We get to choose where we go from here.

Deserving Life

Human beings are extremely complicated. We all have different voices within us, different needs. We have layers of awareness within ourselves, layers of being. The conscious mind is afforded only a glimpse of this depth. The journey of coming to know oneself involves looking within, often to be surprised at what we find.

One curious quality of the human experience is that we tend to live the life that we feel we deserve. Even when we have opportunities to improve our life situation, we will tend to unconsciously sabotage or overlook these opportunities unless we feel we deserve them. And, no matter how much we try consciously, we will strive unconsciously to remain within the limits we feel (deep down) are appropriate for us.

We unconsciously limit ourselves in part because we judge ourselves. We unconsciously take on the responsibility of punishing ourselves. We hold guilt, shame, and perceived shortcomings in our secret hearts, protecting ourselves from the intensity and discomfort they engender.

But, while this intensity is active in the background, it has a formative influence on our perceptions and decisions. Our unconscious emotions shape the life that we create for ourselves. Only once we are able to make peace with an emotional charge can we move on from the life situations that reflect it.

To make healthy use of this human tendency, we can learn to feel like we deserve the life we want. And, in order to do this, we must practice honest self-review and learn to accept what we find in the process. Emotional, not intellectual acceptance.

This is a process of allowing ourselves to feel our feelings, instead of running from them. Of allowing ourselves to *arrive*, to catch up to where we are right now. We learn to breathe with these feelings, to sit with them until we create a bit more space around them. Feeling our feelings leads to self-acceptance and to the sense of deserving the life we want.

It's ok to be who we are, to feel as we feel, even if others don't understand. We are, each of us, on a personal journey of life and experience. There is no one right way to play the game of life. We all make mistakes, and these mistakes teach us how to become the person we want to be, how to live a life that works for us.

Everything that we have experienced has the capacity to strengthen and teach us, so long as we are able to open to the lessons on offer. We are free to choose as we will, and to experience the consequences of these choices. We are free to customize our consequences with intentional choice.

Acceptance, Surrender, and Grace

The first step of acceptance is one of the hardest trials we can face. We build armor throughout our lives, protecting ourselves from the fear that we are not good enough, that we are not loved, or accepted, that we cannot be who we are without being judged and ostracized. Protecting ourselves from the fact that on some level, deep down, we don't even know who we truly are.

Over time, we forget that it's armor. It becomes our *self*, the only one we may ever know for years. And, when the pressures of life hit just right and crack that armor, it can feel as if our sanity, our very life, is at stake.

If we face this point unprepared, without a clear understanding of the nature of the battle, we can easily self-destruct. We could act out, raging against the unfairness, the pain, the cruelty or casual indifference of it all. Our sense of self shatters, and for a time, we are left adrift, unsure where we're going and what we're doing, unsure of how to structure our being amidst the chaos of life.

But this is not simply a bump in the road. It's a crucial part of our maturation and growth, a pressure that inspires the developing human to begin living life on their own terms, to find their purpose and align their lives with it.

Ego Death and Rebirth

Our self, our ego, is a subpersonality. It's a tool that we have created unconsciously, a story that helps us to orient within our life's journey. Our story of self tells us what is important to us, how we must be, what we can accept, and what we must reject, what we must fight or defend ourselves from.

When we come to these breaking points, the ego fears for its survival. For good reason, as our whole sense of self dies when we let go of old and outlived stories of self. The ego shatters. And since this is the only part we may know of ourselves, we tend to resist the experience as if it meant death for us.

It takes very little time for the ego to regrow. We soon make sense of our situation again and generate a new story of self that fits our new understanding. If we are able to be present to this transition and see it for the gift that it is, then we fast-track our personal growth and emotional healing.

The process is as follows: Our ego shatters under sufficient stress and we go through an intense period where everything within comes up for review. If we are able to surrender to this experience, really allow ourselves to feel it and process it, we then gain perspective on our needs and feelings, on how we have spent our time and what we truly care about.

And then we continue taking action, ideally informed by these experiences to act more fully in alignment with our real values and needs. In the process, we quickly regrow our story of self based on our current needs and understandings.

Acceptance and Surrender

It is natural, even healthy, to struggle against the challenges of life. When the struggle is within, against challenging thoughts and emotions, we often take action in the outer world to make the feelings go away. Again, this is perfectly natural. In a healthy state, our emotions help us to tune in to our needs and give us the energy to act towards the fulfillment of these needs.

However, sometimes we just need to feel things. Sometimes it's not about doing something to change the feeling or make it go away. In these moments, the most powerful move we can make is to surrender.

It's important to remember that surrender, in this case, is not losing. When we surrender to our feelings, to our awareness, to everything that is happening in our lives, our minds, and our bodies right now, we stop trying to resist it. We stop trying to run from it.

When we surrender to our now, just as it is, we finally allow ourselves to arrive, mentally and emotionally. It doesn't mean that we stop striving, stop taking action in our lives. It just means that we take that action with a clearer view of the playing field. When we surrender, we stop fighting who we are, where we are. And all of that effort – all of that attention and will – can be shifted to growing, consciously experiencing, and making the best use of the situation at hand.

A true moment of acceptance, complete acceptance, is a powerful experience and one that can reshape our lives around it. Acceptance on this level is surrender, just as it is peace, grace. It brings us in contact with a still, quiet space within. This stillness permits awareness, a wider and deeper consciousness of ourselves, of our situation, and of how we navigate this experience.

From this stillness, we can look upon the world and see the things to be grateful about. We can see the blessings we have right now and work from there. Surrender leads us to a space of inner freedom. In this space, we let go of a tension that we didn't even realize we'd been holding, and our entire experience of the world shifts in response.

My Emotions are My Own

Here is a powerful insight on the road to acceptance. Each of us lives within our own bubble of perception and story. Within that bubble, everything that we see, everything that we feel, is us.

When we have challenging emotions about another person or about a situation in our lives, this is all internal. These things come up for us even before we come into interaction with that person or situation, and they prime us to interact in certain ways.

Let's say that we were to hear something that hurt our feelings. It's not the words themselves that hurt. It's our reaction to these words. The way we interpret them, the way we react emotionally to this interpretation.

So, every time we judge something that we see, every time we react emotionally to any perception, it is because we link this outer sense experience with our inner story and emotional charge. Internal charge, the sort that shifts and matures as we grow.

So, let's say that someone made you feel angry. This anger may be utterly reasonable from your point of view. And yet, this person has no more power over you than you give them. It is not the other person that makes us angry. The other acts or speaks. We perceive this action or these words. We interpret this in a way that evokes emotion. We then tend to associate the other person with this emotion, sidestepping our accountability for our own emotional reactions.

No matter how justified our reaction, there was a choice involved. We participated in interpreting the situation, and our emotions responded to this interpretation. Often, we move from stimulus to unconscious emotional reaction without ever realizing it's happened.

When what we see moves us to unconscious reaction, we are not free. We are like a puppet on a string. Even more, we are brilliant at justifying our unconscious responses, generating a backstory that makes our actions reasonable. So, we might behave utterly predictably, much like a machine, and we will still believe that we are exercising freedom. We respond reflexively, and then use our intellect to justify this response.

Again, no matter how much we may wish to convince ourselves that our response is reasonable or justified, if we are moved to unconscious reaction, then in that moment we are not free. We are not, at that moment, conscious and intentional in our response. We respond according to our programming.

Our emotions are our own. When we respond emotionally to something in the outer world, it's because our perception of the outer world lines up with a specific inner emotional charge. No one can *make* you feel anything (without your participation). And when we do get triggered, it's always about us, about what the situation *means* to us.

So, for example, say you saw a behavior in another that just rubbed you the wrong way. Unless this individual's behavior directly impacts your physical situation, then your reaction is connected to your stories around that person, that behavior. We get triggered because of our relationship (internally) with that trigger, not because the outer world forces us to respond in a particular way.

The key here is that **any time we stand in resistance to the world, we're actually standing in resistance to ourselves**, to our own thoughts and emotions. Resistance on this level is a very young reaction, like a two-year old saying "No!" It doesn't help the situation in the outer world. Resistance simply pushes the thought or feeling away from the conscious mind, away from where we can work with it.

When we tense up, our energy becomes fixed instead of fluid. We feel any change, any new energy coming our way, as a challenge or a pressure. Fixed energy cannot flow with the changes of life. Acceptance drops resistance, allowing us to flow and adapt to our situation. We can feel resistance in the body, often as a heaviness or contraction. Similarly, acceptance often shows up in the body as a relaxation, a release. Inwardly, this can feel like a sense of expansion or flow.

The Diagnostic Mirror

We do not see things as they are, we see things as we are.

- Anais Nin

Another extremely helpful concept in coming to know ourselves is the *diagnostic mirror of the world*. We can use our perception of the world as a mirror, as a means to tune in to things hidden from the conscious mind.

By this point, it should be clear that a good bit of healing and growth involves bringing unconscious patterns, charge, and stories into the light of consciousness. While our patterns are unconscious, they are not up for critical review. They shape our perceptions, trigger specific emotional responses, and condition our reactions, all below the threshold of conscious awareness.

If we can't see something, we can't work with it. And, if we're unconscious of something, then by definition, we can't see it. So, the question is: how do we bring these subconscious patterns into our conscious awareness so that we can begin to work with them? How can we bring them up to where we can see them?

In psychotherapy, there is a test used to shed light on unconscious patterns: the Rorschach test. More commonly known as the inkblot test, the patient is shown random black and white images, just like you might get from blotting the paper with ink and then folding the page. The images formed in this way are random, yet they usually suggest a specific image to the mind of the patient.

Whatever is perceived in the inkblot is likely to be a charged aspect of the patient's inner world. The patient may not even know it at the time, but their interpretation of these random images is primed by their network of existing story and charge.

We'd all like to think that our perception of the world is beyond doubt. We saw *this* happen, so we know for a fact that it happened and that it meant what we thought it meant. The challenge is that our perceptions are far more biased than we'd like to admit.

Every human being has a tendency for both selective perception and projection. Without realizing it, we cherry-pick our sense impressions looking for previous patterns, for the things we've come to expect.

Everything we perceive in the outer world is interpreted through our network of story and given emphasis by our internal emotional charge. This means that anything we react to strongly in the outer world is a hint, a symbol of unconscious charge within. And, any patterns we observe in our experience of the outer world are influenced, at least in part, by how we unconsciously prime ourselves to meet the world.

This means that the world is our Rorschach test. As far as our perception goes, the world is a magic mirror that reflects our whole being. Not just the things we're conscious of. Our entire experience of the world is tuned to the charge and story we carry within.

So, any time you notice a recurring pattern, or when you notice yourself getting triggered by something you see, it's time to ask some questions: What is it in me that makes this so triggering? Why is this happening again? How have I participated in creating these patterns in my life? Before I react to what I see out there, let me take a look at what's happening on my side of the street.

This is a massively liberating reframe for our experiences. Instead of playing the victim, standing in resistance to the unfair or less than ideal situations handed to us, we can look at what is actually in our power. We can take accountability for our experience of life right now. We can review our experiences and feel out the unconscious charge within.

As soon as we become aware of a pattern or a bit of unprocessed charge, we have the opportunity to feel the stuck feelings and create space around them. Once we have begun to process these feelings, we are in a much better position to respond, rather than react. We begin to bring the light of awareness to things that were previously out of our view.

This is a breakdown of shadow work, the use of our perception of the world as feedback to tune in to unconscious content. In principle, it's fairly simple. In practice, we are ridiculously clever at hiding things from ourselves and seeing what we want (or simply expect) to see.

The first step is to learn the language of our emotions. The next is to humble ourselves, again and again, as we encounter stories and feelings that we thought we'd outgrown and those that we were never aware of to begin with.

Shadow work is one of the most important things that we can do to move towards empowerment and actual freedom. While we are unaware of our unconscious patterns, they completely dominate our lives. They call all the shots from behind the curtain.

Old charge and story can colonize our inner world to such an extent that there's very little cognitive space left for present moment awareness. As we tune in to these patterns and begin to address them, we free up our inner space. And, interestingly enough, as we address these unconscious patterns, we tend to notice that our lives in the outer world shift as well, often in interesting and unexpected ways.

A Celebration of Life

Shadow work is work. Sometimes exhausting work. It's not really sustainable to focus on unearthing old patterns 100% of the time. The good thing is that we can alternate between shadow work and celebration.

Shadow work is a negative practice. It focuses on tuning in to what's there so that it can be released and purged. The other half of this practice is celebration. Celebration is a positive practice, one that aims to bring something specific to the table. In this case, gratitude, appreciation, and presence.

When we adopt a frame of celebration, we intentionally tune in to all the things we are perceiving right now, all the things that we are blessed enough to be able to feel, experience, and enjoy.

Each moment is so rich, so full, that if we were to be completely present to it, we'd have no space left for fears, worries, regrets, or wallowing. There are times to take action, and times to review our experiences to deepen our understanding. For all other times, we have the opportunity to truly savor our experience.

The more that we can make savoring a habit, the more deeply it will transform our lives. When we cultivate an attitude of celebration, we often encounter more practical, tangible things to celebrate. Gratitude inspires abundance.

Just think about it. What if your internal baseline was set on savoring the experiences of the present moment? Even the small, silly, mundane pleasures offered by life? The feel of the water on your skin, the taste or smell of food, the beauty of the natural world? This is an inner orientation that meets life as a blessing. It's a beautiful alternative to the worry, distraction, and drama that can fill our inner space so completely.

A mindset of celebration orients us towards both contentment and creative engagement with life. With this inner orientation, it's far easier to enjoy our life as it is rather than looking to the next thing or dwelling on the last. Also, when we relax and open to what is around us, we are far more able to enjoy it and play. To dance with the moment.

That may not seem all that important, but from this artistic mindset, we are far better at learning, creating, performing. Celebration helps us to return to our natural state as artists and children, where we are fully alive to the world, free, engaged, and inspired. Celebration is also deeply helpful in bringing healing and growth into our moment of experience. As children, we get too caught up in the moment to give the past too much power. As artists, we can use creative expression to channel our feelings into something beautiful.

When we direct this feeling of celebration outwards, it can come across as a sense of warmth. We can engage with the other, or with the situation, joyfully, with presence and an appreciation for the experience itself.

Warmth is a key energy for growing things in our life. For growing healthy connections with others, growing plants, learning new skills (growing in knowledge and ability), practicing self-care (growing a healthy body). The list goes on. When we bring warmth to these things, we encourage them to grow strong and healthy.

Acceptance and Non-Attachment

This is a very challenging concept at first, and a pitfall along the path of growth and healing, especially for those who have delved into Eastern philosophy and practices. The practice of non-attachment is aimed at cultivating inner freedom.

When we are attached to specific people, things, or situations, then we cannot feel comfortable without having these things in our experience. We assign these things excessive value in the inner world, value above other things in our experience.

To get a clearer view of this, think about addiction. When deep in the throes of addiction, a person can give up everything and everyone in their lives, just to pursue their drug, or whatever they may be addicted to. Our attachment to specific things or people is of exactly the same quality, though not always experienced to the same degree. We tend to exalt certain ideas, feelings, and bits of sense experience, while marginalizing others.

Attachment places us in resistance to the changes of the world. It leads us to cling to certain things and to control the situation to make sure that we will continue to have these things. When the world moves in a different direction, this clinging can cause us to act destructively, to compromise our values or needs.

Since our perception is influenced by this attachment and the associated emotional charge, we will justify our attachments to no end. We convince ourselves that we have no choice, blind ourselves to the detrimental impact of these perceived needs and their attendant behaviors. All this as our attachments form the container of our lives and tighten around us.

The Problem with Detaching

Often, when attempting to move beyond our attachments, we begin by distancing ourselves from these things. We learn to detach, sometimes aggressively, from whatever in our lives we're attached to. But there's a problem with this.

Our attachments are a big part of the human experience. We have certain people, situations, things, that we value, enjoy, and love having in our lives. When we move into a place of detachment from these things, we distance ourselves from the experiences that make life worth living. Who wants to walk through the world untouched by the beauty and enjoyment that surrounds them?

Life is both a blessing to be savored and a classroom in which to learn freedom. But it can be tricky to enjoy life without getting attached to these enjoyments, a bit like having your cake and eating it too. So the question becomes, how do we find a balance between enjoyment of the world and freedom from our attachments?

The key is that there is a difference between non-attachment and detachment. In an ideal state, we can be open to all of the experiences that life has to offer. And, once an experience has played out, we can let it go and allow the next experience to flow in.

In a state of perfect presence, we could savor each sunset as if it was the first we'd ever seen. We could greet the beauty and uniqueness of every experience with grace and gratitude. And we can, indeed, learn to be alive to each moment of experience. But this is far easier said than done.

One challenge to this comes when something that we really like comes along. And then, like everything, the experience ends and we are left without it once again. If we really enjoyed the experience, we may be tempted to roll back the film and go for a repeat. We will, at the very least, be drawn to experiencing this pleasure again.

While this is natural, it can easily lead to dependence, to a need for some experience or sense impression to be repeated for us to be at peace. We can become attached to these things, driven to feel, seek, acquire, consume, and conquer.

The human condition is one of intense preferences for various sense experiences, emotions, and ideas. We are all, for lack of a better word, addicted to certain enjoyments, thoughts, and situations.

Whatever the object of the addiction, the mechanism is the same in our inner experience. Our pursuit of this experience, the form this pursuit takes for us, colonizes our attention, emotion, and story. We become driven by the things we desire and the things we run from. In either case, it is our attachment to this object or behavior that curtails our freedom. We have invested our power in it in the form of emotional charge.

Seen from this perspective, it is natural to assume that our problems will be solved if we simply get rid of the attachment. If we find more disturbing than reaffirming connections in our lives, we may be tempted to detach from these uncomfortable emotions as a means of inner escape.

However, this form of detachment distances us consciously from our experience. It is a subtle form of resistance to our life, to unpleasant emotions and challenging reactions. On an energetic level, it's like creating a wall and keeping all of the mundane or unacceptable aspects of the world outside of this bubble of awareness.

Whenever we are in resistance to life, we are in resistance to ourselves. Everything that we experience is us. It is *our* sense impressions, our emotions, our sense of meaning, and our story frameworks that we perceive.

As we learn to accept ourselves, we also learn to accept the emotions that come up within us. We learn to accept certain feelings and qualities within us, to sit with them instead of needing to change them. We learn to accept others more deeply, recognizing that our triggers are often more about us than them. On an energetic level, this is about opening up, about allowing these things in rather than blocking them out.

Non-Attachment, Rather than Detachment

This brings us to the practice of non-attachment. In simple terms, non-attachment leaves us free to allow every sense impression, every feeling and situation in, and then learn not to hold on to it. To let it in, feel it, let it go, and be present to each moment as it shifts.

This is incredibly difficult, a practice for a lifetime. It is also more liberating than can be explained. One key here is to truly celebrate each and every aspect of our experience. Each sense impression, each emotion, each thought, each breath. The more we can exalt all aspects of our experience equally, the more we are free from excessive attachment to any one thing.

An addiction to one thing can be overcome by making that thing equal in charge or value to all other aspects of our experience. In detachment, we do this by distancing ourselves from our network of emotional charge, from our feelings about the things we perceive. This works quickly to free one from unconscious reaction, but is counterproductive in the long run, a holding action rather than a solution.

In non-attachment, on the other hand, we strive to attune to positive charge, intense appreciation, in every aspect of life. In enjoying each thing intensely, equally, we are better able to be present to the blessings of the moment, to get the absolute best out of the situation at hand. This is an around-the-corner style of thinking, but it leaves one free to enjoy the pleasures of life while pursuing a life of intention and consciousness.

Acceptance vs Passivity

Sometimes we feel that we cannot accept what we see in the world, that it would be wrong to accept it. When it comes to things like the evils and cruelty that we perpetrate upon one another, the injustices or losses that we encounter along the path, acceptance can seem impossible. Indeed, it would be counterproductive to our health, as individuals and as societies, to passively submit to these pains, losses, and hardships.

But here's the thing. To accept, on this level, does not mean to passively submit. Acceptance is, psychologically, allowing ourselves to see and feel what's happening. Any forward action benefits from a clear view of the playing field. We can accept that this is our life, right here. This is what's happening. This is how we feel about it. And, if it's something that we feel strongly about, acceptance gives us space to see how best to act upon that feeling.

At first, in our conditioned, unaware state, we are moved to unconscious reaction. Later, we learn to overcome this instinctive reaction. We learn to create space around the feeling so that we are not forced to react to it, so that we are no longer triggered into action without having a conscious choice in the matter.

At this point in our growth, it can be tempting to act like the monk in the cave, unaffected by the affairs of life. In the process, we can become passive in the face of life's challenges. But this is not the end of the journey.

The Right Use of Will

In these moments, it is helpful to remember that we are a point of agency in the world. Each of us is responsible for our own lives. We are the stewards of our bodies and the space we hold. And we are stewards of our experience.

This life is, at its core, a journey of consciousness. Each experience in this life, each action taken to tend the body or establish a foundation in the outer world, is an opportunity to be awake to our experience, to purposefully engage with it. Each mundane thing is an opportunity to take action informed by our growing understanding. A chance to open to the blessings of the moment. To act, with consciousness and intention, creating consequences with open eyes.

We have a (potential) choice in how we respond to all situations. We have a choice in what we champion, what we create, what we support, and in the impressions we leave upon the world. We are connected to every aspect of life that we experience, responsible for how we interact with these things within our bubble of influence.

We each have will, vision, voice, awareness, and feeling. We are a force in the world, a part of the life of the planet. We are always taking action, so long as we are alive. We each have the responsibility (to ourselves) to be a force that we believe in, within the context of our own lives.

The key is to take action in a way that truly reflects our values, in a way that we choose, intend, and fully align with.

To put it in as clear terms as possible, if we walk by and see that a helpless person is getting mistreated, acceptance does not require us to simply walk on. To walk on is to passively submit to the situation we encounter. To take no action to correct imbalances that are within our rightful power is to shirk our responsibility to the world. We all have to stand up for what we believe in.

In acceptance, we allow ourselves to see what is taking place. We allow ourselves to feel the emotions it engenders. And then we choose how to best respond, given what we have seen and how we feel about it. Acceptance supports *right action*, well considered action. It does not absolve us of the responsibility to act within the context of our lives.

Forgiveness and Redemption

No one goes through their life without making mistakes, without suffering loss and pain, without taking actions that leave us feeling guilt and remorse. And, especially when we look back upon some particularly shameful mistake, we can find it hard to accept.

It can feel wrong to simply make peace with our misaligned behavior in the past. We use this lack of acceptance, this disgust or shame, to guide us in future actions, to make sure that we don't make the same mistakes we have in the past. This is an important step in self-awareness and growth, but it doesn't end there.

After we have felt, fully and deeply, our remorse for past mistakes, we are best served by coming to terms with them. We can either learn from the past or carry it with us like a yoke around our necks. After we have felt the lesson, after we have made sense of why and how we made that mistake, we are best served by learning to forgive ourselves. This allows us to drop the weight of shame and guilt. We can then step forward with a clear understanding of the impact we would like to have on the world and the values we would like to uphold.

This is extremely difficult. Often, our self-judgment hides within us, behind justifications and blind spots. Sometimes we don't truly want to let go of shame or guilt, perhaps because we are afraid that we'll repeat the same mistakes again, or because the consequences of our past mistakes live on in our current moment. How could we forgive ourselves, when they are still gone, when we've messed up something precious? How could we forgive ourselves for acts that we cannot now condone?

Again, the answer is that there is a difference between condoning past behavior and accepting that these things have happened. We can accept that this is where we are. These are the things that have happened, these are the things we've done. This is where we move forward from.

Forgiveness gives us the space to move forward. Redemption then comes by doing all that we can to rectify the mistakes of the past, and by making it a priority to address the reaction patterns and behaviors that led us to the mistake.

In forgiving ourselves, we transform old pain into current lessons. The things we regret, the things we are guilty about or those we find shameful, they help to make us aware of the things we truly care about. They show us the values that we would like to champion in our lives.

Informed by these lessons, we can move forward and take action in the world. We can redeem ourselves in our own eyes by dedicating our actions, from this moment onward, to serving the values we once betrayed. Our past shame becomes a sacred wound, an inner drive that clarifies our purpose and moves us to channel this energy into something worthwhile.

The Sacred Wound

The sacred wound is a powerful concept for true healing and authenticity. Each of us, along the journey of life, encounters pain, loss, death, and cruelty. These challenges are some of the biggest blocks to our practice of acceptance, and rightly so. If we feel moved in reaction to these things, then it would be foolish to ignore them or to suppress these feelings.

It is a gift to be sensitive to injustice or cruelty visited upon others. And, in a strange way, it is a gift to experience pain and learn to keep living, to keep growing and feeling. In order to accept these things, we have to figure out what we can do with this energy and how we can best take action in response to these feelings.

One excellent way to deal with stuck pain or shame is to ask ourselves what it has to teach us. Every experience has its lesson, its piece of gold. We can ask ourselves what value this pain clarifies. Why does it hurt? The pain shows us that something is truly important to us, something that we really care about. What is it? At the core, in terms of our personal journey, what value or feeling in this situation makes it meaningful to us?

Our sacred wound is never about what other people do. It's about what we ourselves do. It's not about changing the situation in the outer world. Our lessons tell us how we would like to show up in the world, not how the world must be.

We cannot change the past. The only thing we can control is our response to the situations we face. What we can do is strive to know ourselves well enough to know what is truly important to us, and then make certain to act upon it. Each time we do, we become part of something larger than ourselves, a dynamic force in service of those things we truly value.

Remember that the goal of acceptance, from this perspective, is not to cut us off from our challenging feelings. Instead, acceptance allows us to engage passionately with life, without that passion crippling us or driving us unconscious.

Acceptance, when it comes to the sacred wound, transforms pain into strength and sensitivity into wisdom. Rather than cutting off our feelings and suppressing our pain, we can let it all in and feel it. We can make peace with it, becoming more fully alive, more capable of expressing all that we are.

All this may sound too good to be true. It's not. It's work. The hardest work we can do within our lives. That said, it's harder not to do it. We carry around our past one way or another. It is both exhausting and futile to try to escape it. The only other option – the only option that has traction in the long run – is to make peace with ourselves.

Self-Parenting

It is possible that there are some people out there in the world who have had an extremely healthy upbringing, with strong, loving, supportive parenting. But this is far more likely to be the exception than the rule.

We all learn lessons from our childhood, lessons on how to handle our feelings, how to navigate life's challenges. We pick up most of these lessons before we are even aware that we're learning. We unconsciously adopt the habits and strategies of our parents, often without realizing that there is a choice involved. And this training carries through into our adult lives. *Our parenting teaches us how to meet ourselves and others.*

When we begin the journey of self-acceptance in earnest, we often encounter a huge load of old, unprocessed emotion and story. Things that we'd suppressed in the past now come up for review and release. To handle these challenges without going straight back into suppression, it's helpful to have some tools and an empowering perspective.

This is where the idea of self-parenting comes in. With self-parenting, we learn to meet ourselves in a healthy and constructive way. We learn to hold a safe space for ourselves and respect the things that come up in that space.

Imagine for a moment that the space within is a physical space. When you have a challenging thought or feeling come up from within, imagine that thought or feeling as a voice within, as a person in this inner space. It is as if a young part of ourselves is coming up to be seen, nurtured, comforted.

We often reflexively identify with these voices when they come up. We feel like the hurt voice or the old stuck story is *us*, as if it is our *self* that is experiencing this challenge. Instead, we could view ourselves as the observer, as the one within who hears this young part of ourselves and rises up to comfort them.

For the readers with some parenting experience, just think of a time when your child was crying and upset. The child is not going to respond well to being screamed at. "Shut up! I've had enough of that!"

Just think of a time when we were dealt with in this way. This treatment invalidates our emotions and experience. It makes us feel as if our reaction is wrong, not allowed, as if it will cause us to be rejected or abandoned.

When we were in such a situation, what we really needed was love. We needed patience and space. We need to feel as if it is ok for us to feel as we do so that we can process these feelings and move forward naturally, without suppression.

When learning to self-parent, we often come face to face with many unhealthy strategies. We may speak harshly, unkindly, and judgmentally to ourselves in our inner space. We may feel it weak or wrong to have certain feelings and chastise the child within when it reveals these feelings.

It's important to remember that our emotions are messages, often pointing us to things overlooked by our conscious understanding. They come up for a reason. No matter how much we might like to deny our feelings or needs or to try to make them go away, it is far healthier to acknowledge them.

In learning healthy self-parenting, we learn to be both firm and gentle with ourselves. First gentle, to meet that hurt, sensitive voice that's coming up from within. And then firm, taking responsibility for that feeling and for our actions moving forward, for the feelings that those actions will engender.

We take responsibility for our own self-care, making sure that our needs are met. We learn patience and allow ourselves to make slow, steady, sustainable progress towards an intentional life. In healthy self-parenting, we learn to practice the highest degree of compassion and self-love without allowing ourselves to become complacent in our lives.

No One is an Island

"Our lives are not our own. From womb to tomb, we are bound to others. Past and present. And by each crime and every kindness, we birth our future."

- Quoted from *Cloud Atlas*

In some very fundamental ways, we are each one of us alone, each the sole inhabitant of our own psychological universe. At the same time, we are inextricably bound to those around us. We share a planet with all other humans, with all living things on the globe. We breathe the same air, drink the same water. We are part of the same living ecology, the same energy and biomass circulating through the entire network of living beings, all impacting one another, all impacted by one another.

This is not hyperbole or idealism. We are practically, physically linked with all other beings on the planet. We are culturally, psychologically linked with all of the human beings that we encounter, and with those that they encounter, until the widening spiral encompasses us all.

We are interrelated with all beings, mutually interdependent with them. All harm or imbalance we put out in the world, physical or emotional, comes back to us. Directly or indirectly, we are influenced in turn by every impact we have upon the world around us.

This fundamental interrelatedness of all beings is the practical foundation of morality.

We are part of a living world, coexisting with many other beings. It is natural for each of these beings to act in their own interests. In fact, it's the only way it can work.

That said, in a healthy ecology, we collaborate with the beings with whom we share space. In order to have the space to act in the fulfillment of our own interests, we must grant the same space to others. Collaboration can create strong sustainable systems. Domination and power struggles create conflict.

Whether we want to or not, we share this living journey with other beings. If we act without consideration or disrespect the other beings we encounter, we will create unnecessary strife and hardship. For ourselves as well as for others.

It may not be immediately apparent. We may get what we want in the moment, or we may be distanced enough to remain ignorant of the direct consequences. But we will face those consequences in some way in our own life, in the medium of our own experience.

For healthy collaboration, we must respect other beings. We must see in them the same life and experience we perceive in ourselves. The same value and right to exist. We can then act with consideration of that life in the best way we understand and are able to.

Healthy Selfishness

Human beings are very complicated. There are times when we act selfishly, completely ignorant of the impact we have on one another. There are other times when we are so driven by some noble purpose that we give more than we can afford to those we care about. In these cases, no matter how good our intentions, we set ourselves up for a challenge.

Here's the thing: we are each responsible for the fulfillment of our own needs. Physical and emotional. When we come into relationship – any kind of relationship – with others, we pool resources and work together for the fulfillment of our needs. Sometimes, we share with one another to meet social or emotional needs, sometimes we share more deeply, learning to fulfill our physical needs together. Often, this sharing becomes unequal.

Just think of the relationship between parent and child. The parent is responsible for the fulfillment of the child's needs, until the point where the child can fulfill their needs on their own. It is healthy for the parent to prioritize the child's needs over their own. That said, the parent is a person as well, with their own needs and limits.

No one can sustainably support someone else without taking care of themselves. But sometimes, we can feel as if it is somehow wrong or irresponsible to take time for ourselves or give back to ourselves. If we believe that our role is to take care of others, it can seem selfish to focus on our own needs.

This is the path to codependence. When we over-give to others and neglect our own needs, we often have unconscious expectations that these others will make sure our needs are fulfilled in return. Since these expectations are unconscious, they're often not communicated well, and a person who believes their needs to be selfish will tend to mask those needs.

This is grounds for resentment. The one who gives too much may find themselves unmet, their needs unfulfilled on some level. They may feel as if the other doesn't care about them, as if they don't see them.

And how could they? The over-giver is not communicating their needs and may not even feel comfortable expressing those needs to themselves. We are each responsible for meeting our own needs, first and foremost because we are the ones that feel them.

No one else understands what we feel and need the way that we do. So how could someone else champion that need for us? Especially without clear communication. All too often, we're left with misunderstanding, second guessing, and needless conflict.

The key to bringing this situation into balance is healthy selfishness. Remember that if you don't make it a priority to meet your physical, emotional, and social needs, then you will need to be supported by others much sooner. It's much harder to be a caregiver when you need a caretaker yourself.

Step one, admit our needs. To ourselves at least. If it seems reasonable, we can admit these needs to those close to us as well. This will give them an idea of where we are and how they can show up in support of us, so that they don't have to guess.

Step two for healthy selfishness is to take some time for yourself. It could be no more than five minutes, but we all need it. Enough time to let things settle, to make some space within.

When we give ourselves this time, we are better able to show up for those we care for. So, take some time each day, each week, to catch your breath and feel alive. To listen to what's coming up so that you don't leave your needs unmet.

Step three is to give yourself permission to fulfill those needs. We might know that we are hungry but feel that it's not the right time or that we shouldn't eat now. Or that we need sleep, or activity, or any number of things. When we become aware of a particular need, it's important to give ourselves permission to act upon it, and then make use of that permission.

It is the work of a lifetime to distinguish between needs and wants. It's a deeply personal aspect of life's journey and one that goes beyond the scope of this conversation. For the moment, simply remember that you are the steward of your own needs, and that you are in a better situation to help others when your own needs are met.

The Healing Power of Human Connection

It's said in some circles that "You're only as sick as your secrets." When we hold shame and guilt in our heart, when we conceal it from the world, we grow it in the darkness. Over time, hiding bits of ourselves takes more and more effort. It distorts our entire way of relating to others, our whole way of being.

When we keep bits of ourselves hidden, we are practicing the opposite of self-acceptance. We are contracting around our sensitive points. We do this to protect ourselves, and it is helpful in extreme situations. However, this form of self-distortion is damaging in the long term. It is an unsustainable approach to life.

There is a power in confession, in sharing our thoughts and unburdening a heavy heart. Sometimes the things we're feeling need to come out. They need to be expressed. The act of expression is itself cathartic, an opportunity to release the pressure of a long-held thought or emotion.

Often, we are taught that it is weak to show emotion, to express vulnerability. And, if we're just falling apart and wallowing in tears when we need to take action, then emotion is a weakness in that moment. However, it is a measure of personal strength to be honest with ourselves about how we're actually feeling.

Connected closely with this is the courage to express our true feelings honestly and vulnerably. In the act of sharing or confession, we strengthen our capacity for both self-honesty and courageous self-expression. We allow ourselves to see ourselves and allow ourselves to be seen by others. We stop hiding.

Another benefit of this experience is a bit of drama. Human beings learn by example. We play out our stories, feeling them and learning from the feelings. When we share our challenging thoughts and deep, powerful feelings with another, the other shows us how we will be received. This example shows us how to receive these thoughts when they arise from within.

When what we share is met in a safe, nonjudgmental space, a space of acceptance, we are shown how to meet our own thoughts and feelings in this way. The example offered by the other person gives us a model. It shows us how to self-parent in a healthy way and how to navigate these hard spaces when we encounter them.

It's hard. Our habits go deep, and we tend to reflexively judge so many things without being fully aware of it. We can keep ourselves silent for fear of how we will be received long after the situation justifies it. And, so long as we keep it all within, we can remain in these spaces, stuck on the same lessons, for years or even decades.

By sharing in a safe space, with someone we trust, we can learn to look at our guilt and pain. We can begin to forgive ourselves, to release old, stuck patterns and continue to grow.

There are two situations which should be mentioned at this point. One: sometimes we don't have people around who we can really share with. Sometimes, we need to express ourselves, and there's no one who can receive what we have to say in a healthy way, or who can listen without reacting defensively or taking things personally.

In these cases, it's better that we share in other ways. Journaling is good for clarifying our thoughts. However, for the purpose of expression, we might try opening up to our dog, or cat, or plant, or fish, or tree. It's not quite the same as sharing with another human being, but it can be more fulfilling than it seems when expression is dearly needed.

The other notable exception is in dealing with those who have a constant supply of drama on tap for any who lend an ear. This form of offloading is not the same as confession. It is a process of unburdening, but in these instances, it is used as a surrogate for inner processing. It takes effort to show up for people, to offer presence in the face of drama and intense emotion. It is important for each person to know their limits.

If you find yourself constantly sharing your drama with those around you, you may wish to make some more time in your schedule each day, each week, to be quiet and let these things settle within. Perhaps make it a point to take regular walks in nature to decompress.

It can be difficult to make space for these things with our busy modern schedules. But when we take time to clear our thoughts and feelings, the quality of our relating improves more than we might expect. We come from a different space in our sharing and create more space for the other person in the interaction. It's amazing how much difference a little shift like this can make.

If you often find yourself on the other side, constantly lending an ear to others and acting as a crisis counselor for their troubles, consider the value of healthy selfishness. Each person is equally important. There's only one of you, and you know your needs better than anyone else can. If you push yourself past your limits, you won't be able to show up for others in the way you'd prefer. Ideally, we can give what's right for us, respecting our own needs just as much as we respect those of the other in the interaction.

Conscious Relating

A human life is formed around relationships. We each have a relationship with our parents, family, loved ones, children, friends, colleagues, etc. We are social creatures, and the ties between creatures, the points of interaction between them, are relationships.

We relate with others when we stand next to them in line, or when we greet other drivers on the road. We relate with others when we share space, or collaborate, or communicate. Each interaction is a relating, a contact between two beings.

Our relating doesn't stop at human beings. Each one of us has a relationship with our bodies. Each of us has a relationship with food, with water, with breath. We all have some form of relationship with time, with abundance, and with other life conditions. We all have a relationship with challenge, and with pain, and with purpose.

We relate with the earth as we walk upon it, and we relate with the air as it enters our lungs and fills our bodies with vitality. We strive to relate consciously not because the other being is conscious, but because every interaction is an opportunity to be present to our lives. To recognize and honor the living web that we all share and depend upon. Every interaction is an opportunity to show up as the person we want to be.

Always a New World

> "No man ever steps in the same river twice, for it's not the same river and he's not the same man."
>
> - Greek Philosopher Heraclitus

One of the biggest assets to conscious relating, to remaining present and open in our interactions with others, comes from knowing that every moment is fresh, new. This is a brand-new moment. It's never happened before.

This person that you see in front of you, perhaps you've seen them a million times before. Perhaps you've seen them every day of your life, or of theirs. At this moment, they are a new person. Whatever has happened before between you and this individual, all of that is done and gone. Our past interaction has exactly as much power over this moment as we give it.

We are all growing, learning, changing, every moment of our lives. Sometimes this change happens slowly, so slowly that we don't even realize it's happening. Sometimes we go through massive shifts or experience life challenges that leave a clear mark upon us and shape our lives from that point forward. In all this, the only constant is change.

We are not the same person today as we were yesterday. And the person that we're interacting with is not the same person they were yesterday. If we act as if they are the person we remember, the one we expect, then we're interacting with a mental script. The more closely we look at that script, the more we see what we expect of them. And the less we actually see the other person.

Over time, our closest and most cherished relationships can become distant pantomimes of real connection. We can find ourselves going through the motions, having argument after argument because we're not tuned in to the person we're relating with.

No matter how well another person knows us, it feels different when they are present and engaged, when they are really able to see and hear us. When others relate with us consciously, when they are present and open, when they are patient and create space for us, we feel it. We respond to it, even if we're not consciously aware of it.

When met with presence, we tend to relax, to let ourselves open up and be seen. When we are able to hold space in this way for others, they have the opportunity to receive it in this same way.

In relating, there's no guarantee of how the other will take what we have to offer. That said, it is powerful to hold an accepting and non-judgemental space and to be fully present with those we interact with. It helps to sidestep all kinds of conflict and guides us toward healthy resolutions.

Heart-Centered Relating

Human beings process the world around them in many ways simultaneously. Our mind processes the world in certain ways and tunes in to certain details. The mind is good at making stories, at helping us to see where we stand in relation to the world.

Our body processes the world in certain, unique ways as well. It keeps us tuned in to our physical needs and drives us to act upon these needs. It keeps us safe, vital, and engaged with our physical life.

Our heart, our emotional nature, processes things in yet another way, one that is difficult to describe. Our emotions come from a place beyond the conscious mind. They arise unbidden, often tuned in to aspects of our experience that we are not consciously aware of.

Our emotions are a subtle, beautifully calibrated compass which reflects the condition of the inner being. They inform us when our boundaries have been crossed, when we have unmet needs, and when we need to take action to protect ourselves. Although they speak a different language than the mind or body, the feedback they offer is priceless.

One beautiful feature of our emotional nature is that it can cut through a maze of story to tell if something is right for us, or if it is not. The mind loves story. It loves to make sense of things, to describe details in terms of concepts and their relation to us.

So, when someone comes along with an appealing story, the mind is tempted to go along. Perhaps the mind engages with the story by believing it, perhaps by rejecting it, but either way, the temptation is to engage mentally, to try to relate to the story in conceptual terms. While this is a beautiful tool and an approach that has its place, there is a much more direct path available to us.

When we rely predominantly on mental processing, it can feel as if our attention is centered in our head, behind our eyes. If we are able to tune in to that center, to the root of our attention, we can shift it to the heart. This can be done by paying attention to these spaces in your body and intending the shift. We can envision and feel the base of our attention moving down from behind the eyes to the center of our chest. Feel our being centered in our heart.

From this space, we are able to perceive both the ideas that enter our minds and how our body subtly reacts to these ideas. We tune in to emotional and visceral feedback, keeping our ideas grounded and in connection with our lived experience.

When our attention is centered in the heart, we are easily able to distinguish honesty from deception, and we get an almost physical sense of when ideas or choices are right or wrong for us.

Heart-centered attention also tends to be more present. Ideas come in, but they are diminished in importance. Words and the emotions beneath the words become equally loud to our perception. Heart-centered relating helps us to drop out of story and open up to what is actually happening in the interaction.

The first person that benefits when we begin practicing heart-centered communication is ourselves. We often relate to ourselves in a very unconscious way throughout our lives, tuned in to stories – ideas, memories, and anticipations – over what we feel, what we need, what we truly value.

When we make it a practice to become more conscious of ourselves in the moment, our entire experience of life changes. We begin to understand who we are, what we want, and how we create our lives with our choices and feelings. We make space for ourselves.

Once we are able to hold space for ourselves, we get a personal, experiential understanding of what it means to hold space for others. The greatest gift we can offer to others is to help them feel seen, met, and valued. To help them feel accepted, rather than judged. To help them feel appreciated, understood.

At a fundamental level, each one of us is alone, the sole inhabitant of our psychological universe. Whenever we are able to reach from one universe to another, to make contact with another being, it is precious. When we are met in this way, it can feel like a miracle. We can strive to bring this same gift to each person that we connect with throughout our days and our lives.

Tips for Conscious Relating

Conscious relating is a practice of a lifetime. Every moment, we are tempted to go unconscious and slip into old patterns. Every moment, we are given the opportunity to remain present to the person in front of us, to the relating of that moment.

Our unconscious patterns are *unconscious*, hiding out in our blind spots. So, when we slip into old patterns, we're not likely to notice that we have done so. We must use shadow work alongside this practice, looking at the world as feedback for our unconscious patterns. This will help us to distinguish between projection and the things we actually see and experience in our relating.

Human beings are extremely complicated, so conscious relating is never easy. We cannot ever know the other completely. We can't fully figure them out and then go on automatic. But we can make it a priority to be aware of what we are thinking and feeling, and to express ourselves openly and honestly. We can keep our eyes open in the moment, striving to be present to the other person – as they are, *right now*.

We can *own* our feelings. No one has any more power over our emotional space than we give them. We often unconsciously give others power over our emotions. We hang our sense of wellbeing upon their acceptance, or approval, or understanding. When we get triggered, it's easy to point fingers at the person that triggered us. But, when it comes right down to it, that person just touched upon the emotional charge that we have been carrying around within us, likely for some time.

Our emotions are *our* reaction to the event. You can't make me angry, but I can respond in anger to things that I perceive in connection with you. When I take ownership of my emotions, I take my power back. I can communicate clearly: when *this* happened, I had *this* feeling come up within me. This brings clarity and creates a container around the communication. It helps us to express what we need to express without moving into blame or defensiveness.

Sometimes challenges come up when we interact with others. Ruptures. Arguments. Differences of opinion. Times where we get hurt and withdraw, or lose our temper and push the other away. This is not comfortable, but it is natural. Crises come up between people as they grow, as they learn to express their needs, honor their boundaries, or explore new facets of themselves.

Sometimes crises have nothing to do with what's happening right now (on the surface, anyway). They're just an expression of old stories that have outlived their usefulness to us. And, since many of these stories are unconscious, we can be left wondering why we always have challenging interactions with a particular person, or why the same patterns keep showing up in our friendships or partnerships.

When these issues come up, there is massive potential for healing. If you remain conscious throughout the blow up, if you can step back and tune in to what you're actually feeling and what you need, then you have the opportunity to see yourself more deeply. And when you respond openly and lovingly, validating the emotional experience of the other while safeguarding your own boundaries, then these ruptures can lead to even stronger, healthier connections.

When we can consciously navigate a rupture, we first grow internally. We then bring this growth into how we relate to others. This alone has the potential to transform one's life. It's a new challenge every time, each conflict a unique maze of vested interests and emotional charge. Navigating past a rupture in a healthy way is rarely easy, but each time we maintain presence throughout the challenge, it's liberating, empowering, and meaningful for both parties.

Boundaries and Sovereignty

As we learn to relate consciously, we begin to become conscious of our boundaries. We all have a body, and we are all responsible for the stewardship and tending of that body. If someone wishes to touch us or do something to our body without our consent, then we have every right to take action to prevent this from happening. The right we have to determine what happens with our own body is a boundary, one that we are charged with safeguarding so long as we are stewards of this body.

We have boundaries in the emotional space as well, places that we draw the line with people. We may take all manner of abuse without question, but when this abuse crosses our boundary, we react. We may withdraw, or run, or fight, or speak up, or take action. Each of these approaches is used for the same purpose: to safeguard our emotional boundaries.

We have other subtler boundaries connected with our sense of self, and still other boundaries to protect the relationships and situations that are important to us. To safeguard the things we are invested in.

When we relate consciously with ourselves, we learn to listen to our boundaries, to feel them out. We learn what we are open to, truly, authentically, and we learn how to speak up for ourselves when the situation veers off course for us.

At the same time, we learn that the other people we interact with have all of the same rights, the same valid experiences and preferences, that we would like others to respect in ourselves. We all have the right to safeguard our boundaries. And, if we are to enjoy this right, we have the responsibility to meet others in a way that allows them to honor their own boundaries.

This way of relating leads to more lessons, more pieces of gold, than perhaps any other. Interacting honestly and vulnerably with others shines a light in the darkness and offers new insights into our own nature.

The key here is that we are all sovereign beings, all rulers of our personal psychological universe. We choose this life, one decision at a time. We choose our inner response to the situation, though often unconsciously. We choose our outer response to the situation, taking action in the way that makes the most sense to us.

We are free to support one another or to impede one another. In this shared space, we can best safeguard our own sovereignty by honoring that of those we interact with.

ACCEPTANCE &
ACCOUNTABILITY PRACTICES

As you explore the following practices, remember that they fall into three categories. The first class is a reframe for the moment. They help *right now*.

The second class of practices is helpful when something challenging comes up and you have the time to deal with it. They are the middle-range practices. These includes ritual, ceremony, prayer, guided visualization, any formalization of our intent for a concrete purpose.

The third class of practices is intended for deep training, for going to the core of the issue and renegotiating our relationship with some aspect of our experience. They work slowly but evoke powerful transformations over time.

Practice 1: The Temple and the Host

One of the most helpful frames I have encountered for relating with our inner space is to envision our being as a temple. From time to time, thoughts come up. These thoughts are visitors at the temple. Emotions come up. These emotions are visitors at the temple. Sometimes we have stories come up. These stories, with all their history, all their emotional charge, and all their association with outer situations, are visitors at the temple within.

Often, when we have strong feelings or loud thoughts come up, we identify with them. It's *me* thinking this, feeling this. As long as we identify with the thought or feeling, it is our master. It's calling the shots.

If we are able to see ourselves instead as the keeper of the temple, then we can see these thoughts and feelings as temporary guests of the space we hold within. We get a bit of distance from these sweeping thoughts and make some space around these intense feelings. And we gain just a bit more clarity around how these things influence our perception.

Clarity helps us to see our choice, and choice is the gateway to both freedom and purpose. In the living moment, in the now, each time we become aware of our inner space, each time we identify with the host, rather than the guest, we win. We reclaim just a little bit of personal power. We actualize just a little bit of our freedom.

By being a kind and gracious host of our temple, we can learn to self-parent healthily. We can allow our thoughts and feelings to come up, allow them to be seen and processed, and allow them to move on when their time is done.

In hosting our temple, we learn to be firm and loving keepers of the inner space, tending the temple by devoting our attention to it and inviting those visitors which are supportive of our life experience. We learn to honor all that arises from within while remembering our role as the one who chooses.

Inner Bell and Inner Compass

While acting as the host of our inner space, it's helpful to center our attention in the heart, in the center of our chest. This helps to balance our attention between the things we're thinking and the things we're feeling. It also helps to keep us tuned in to the body, to stay grounded and connected to our physical experience.

There are two gifts that we gain access to when we center our attention in the heart: the **Inner Bell** and the **Inner Compass**. Our bodies react subtly to everything we experience, just as our minds react to whatever we pay attention to. When we center our attention in the heart, we can strengthen the communication between the two. The **Inner Bell** is the first gift, a simple, direct communication between the body and mind.

Your body can feel out the things that are true or right for you, just as it can feel out danger, deception, or misalignment, all those things that are not right for you. If you are relaxed, tuned in to the reactions of the body while also listening to the mind, it can be hard to miss.

When you hear something that is true for you, or powerful or resonant with you, your body responds, often with a sense of expansion or lift. And, when you encounter something that's not right for you, the body responds to this as well, often with a sense of constriction, heaviness, or *stuckness* in some area of the body.

When we learn to listen to the body as well as the mind, we'll notice that these moments of the inner bell pop up in response to things we see, hear, feel, and think about.

When we feel that drop or sense of constriction, that's our inner "no." It tells us that something in the situation is not right for us. And, when we feel a sense of lift or expansion, that's our inner "yes." It tells us that there's something in the situation that does work for us.

Listen for your inner bell as you engage with others, as you navigate through your daily experience. Notice what it points out and pay attention to what this shows you about your own needs and perceptions.

When we learn to ask ourselves questions and listen to the body for the answers, we learn how to transform the Inner Bell into an **Inner Compass**.

All parts of our being are in communication with one another, every moment of our lives. When we become conscious of this communication, it's almost as if we get an extra sense. We can sit quietly, ask ourselves a question, and listen with the body for the answer. We can review possible choices and listen to the feelings that come up in connection with them.

Each person's relationship with their own inner bell is unique. We are all on our own journey, and we each tune our connection to the world in different ways. So, it is a personal practice to tune in to our Inner Bell and establish a dialogue with ourselves. There is no one right way to do it, though we will need practice to distinguish between the things we want to believe and those our body is truly responding to. This is an art of discernment, and yet another practice of a lifetime.

Entering into a new form of communication between mind and body is like beginning a relationship. At first, the pairing is awkward and there's loads of second guessing. But before too long a rhythm is established and we start working together smoothly.

In this case, you are learning to trust your visceral feedback. So, test it out. Listen, and confirm, again and again, until you have dialed in your body's messaging. This can be a constant, reliable guide and an invaluable tool for those who take the time to nurture it.

Celebration and Warmth

In a very real way, life is a collection of moments. Not all of the moments are pleasant, not all are spent in the way that we would choose if we had unlimited resources and no consequences. But all of these moments are ours to spend. They are all ours to experience.

In each moment, we can tune in to the things that make that instant of life worth experiencing. We can place ourselves in the way of beauty, opening up to the color and life of this very moment, whatever might be on offer. When we greet every sensation, every feeling, thought, and emotion, with pleasure and enjoyment, we cultivate an attitude of celebration. We learn how to savor our lives and make this attitude of savoring our baseline awareness.

Savoring, in this context, is a kind of open-eyed meditation where we focus on truly appreciating what we experience right now. Single-mindedly and with complete absorption. Celebration is a way of being where we practice savoring our experience in every moment we can.

Our emotional response is a matter of habit. Habitual placement of attention, habitual interpretation, habitual reaction. Each time we react, we train ourselves to react this way in the future. Each time we pay attention to what's around us, we are training ourselves to pay attention in that way. By training ourselves to savor every moment we can, we make celebration our habitual response.

So much of life is how we respond to it. The same things could happen in a day, and depending on where we stand in relation to them and how we respond to them, we could have a terrible day, or a wonderful one. With the life practice of celebration, we strive in each moment to open to the unique blessings in this moment of experience. We open up to the things that make the day worthwhile, even in the face of challenge or pain.

We could very easily do the alternative, focusing on all of the challenges we face, all the fears, or minor irritations, or unsettled thoughts, feeding these things with our attention. And we often learn to do just this without realizing it.

The downside of this approach is that anything we put our attention on grows larger in our inner experience. **Energy flows where attention goes**. When we unconsciously feed the challenging aspects of life with the energy of our attention, then they become more challenging in our inner experience. That said, we can also do the opposite. We can use the energy of our attention consciously to cultivate the relationship we would like to have with our lives and our moment of experience.

Our attention is a powerful force, both in our own lives and in the lives of those upon whom we spend that attention. In fact, one of the simplest and most powerful techniques available to us is warmth. **Warmth** is a natural form of support that we can provide to others, a form of celebration directed outwards towards a friend or loved one.

Wherever we offer warmth in our lives, we encourage growth and healthy connection. We can offer kindness, compassion, and presence to people in our lives, or to pets, or to plants. We can also offer warmth to our bodies, to our artistic endeavors or career, to any aspect of our lives that we would like to grow.

Practice 2: Releasing Old Patterns

One of the most challenging aspects of acceptance is learning to forgive, to let go of what has come before so that we have clear space to move forward.

Sometimes we have old pains and challenging stories connected with people or situations in our lives. Sometimes we have guilt and shame that can seem impossible to move past. Perhaps it defines us in some way, and we wouldn't know who we are without it. Perhaps these stories, these dynamics, are so natural and familiar that we don't know how to move past them. We may not even know they're there.

No matter why these stories and ideas are stuck in our minds, our hearts, and our fields, there comes a time when we have to face them in order to continue growing. Just think of a time when you have had an argument with a loved one. Sometimes the feeling of this argument lingers with us. We might have challenging feelings come up again and again when we encounter this loved one, all based in an argument that's done and gone.

In order to heal this rupture and move forward, we have to let go. After addressing all of the practical things that came up from the rupture, the next step is forgiveness.

Forgiveness is a way to wash the emotional space clean so that we can start fresh. And it's hard. Whether connected to ourselves, another person, or a situation in our lives, it can seem as if these old feelings and the interaction patterns that come with them are non-negotiable. It can feel as if that's just how life is for us and we don't have a choice in the matter.

The good news is that we do have a choice, at least potentially. We have old emotions, old stories, and old habits in relating that make this choice for us when we can't see them. This is how we get stuck in cycles of depression, or toxic relationships, or unhealthy self-talk. It's a matter of engrained emotional habits, built up in the background over time.

In order to reverse this process and renegotiate our relationships, we must see the issue clearly and exercise intent within ourselves. Forgiveness is a form of surrender, of releasing our old resistance. The process is to feel the hurt, truly allow ourselves to process it, and then let it go. To clear the emotional space and make way for something new.

Threads of Charge

In order to truly have a choice, we first have to be able to see and feel the things within us. We have to be open to meeting, rather than running from, our pain, fear, guilt, shame, anger, grief.

These points of emotional charge are connected to our stories, linked to our ideas about people, about life situations and aspects of our experience. It's almost as if there is a thread of feeling, of history and expectation, between one's self and the idea, the mental representation of that object of experience.

That sounds complicated, so let's take a step back. Let's view the inner space as the temple, and ourselves as the host of this temple. It's almost as if this host, the one who observes and the ones who chooses, stands in the center of the temple. When a visitor enters the temple, when a story comes in with its charge and its history, the host feels it, just like we feel it when a person enters the room.

Imagine that you have had previous issues with a person, and you know that you're about to run into them again. It's likely that your memory of this person, the memory of your past encounters, will visit your temple.

With that memory comes certain feelings, whatever emotion characterized your last interaction, and an overview of the charge you carry around this person. And, along with that come certain expectations, anticipations, projections, things that we think are likely to happen. All based on things that, from our perspective, we have every right to expect. And all of this happens within, before we even see the individual in question.

All of this history, all of this charge and expectation, could be described as a thread between the self (the watcher at the center of the temple) and the other, whether it is a person, an aspect of ourselves, or an aspect of our lives. On a basic psychological level, all of human experience could be described in terms of these threads between self and object, between the watcher and whatever is being viewed.

Each thread has a feeling connected with it, a gestalt overview of our history with the object. This feeling, on a physical level, is a point of specific muscular tension or contraction. We tense up physically just as we tense up emotionally and mentally, preparing ourselves for the coming challenge. But that tension can do just as much harm as good. It can prime us to relate to others counterproductively, or in ways that are misaligned with our values.

Whatever energy characterizes that thread, whatever story and feeling we have under the surface, it will come through in our relating with that individual. Even if we don't want it to. Even if we don't see it. Even if we could have had an otherwise pleasant connection with this person. The feeling and story we have on that thread will set the scene for our interaction with that person in the outer world before either side ever speaks a word. The emotional tone sets the dynamic of the interaction.

Often, it's important to look at the things that come up. The issues that show up between people can point out where our boundaries are sloppy, where we center our wellbeing in the other person rather than ourselves, and when we're interacting with a mental script instead of a living being.

After all this has been addressed, it's important to be able to let go of the dynamic linked with this thread. Otherwise, it can feel as if we're locked into a role, playing out old stories that have outlived their usefulness to us.

So, the question is: how do we clear this dynamic? How can we release the charge we have around a person, situation, or an aspect of ourselves? How can we forgive and move forward with open eyes and a clear playing field?

Techniques for Releasing Old Patterns

In the end, all technique for work in the inner space comes down to two things: **emotion and intention**. All techniques, prayers, rituals, visualizations, meditations, mantras, etc. are ways of focusing emotion and intention. They are a means to tap into a specific emotion and symbolically exert intent in our inner space.

There are no magic words, no magic formulae or prescriptions, which work from the outside. All of these things operate internally, by focusing our perception, concentrating our will, and tapping into specific emotional charge. So, all of the techniques that follow are methods of envisioning an inner change, and *intending* for that change to happen.

Cutting Cords & Forgiveness

The idea of cutting cords is relatively simple. Sometimes those threads of connection that we have with others do more harm than good. Perhaps they come along with a history of dysfunctional relating, or unhealthy expectations, or unreasonable pressures.

Sometimes we have old stories and old ways of being that cause us to play out the same patterns again and again. In these instances, a big part of learning the lesson and breaking the cycle is learning to cut the cord.

To begin this practice, enter a meditative state, a journey state. Intentionally, in your inner space, visualize the thread of connection between yourself and the other. Feel it, letting any emotions or stories come up in connection with it.

Ask yourself what these feelings and stories have taught you. Ask yourself if you are ready to let these things go. And, if the answer is yes, then envision yourself cutting the cord. Simply visualize the action and listen within, paying attention to any shifts in emotion or tension. And, when you're ready, bring yourself back up to engage with the outer world.

It's helpful to note that cutting a cord of unhealthy connection is not the same thing as cutting a person out of your life. By cutting the cord, it's as if we clear our side of the street. We let go of the old emotions and ideas we have around a person or situation. We strive to surrender these old feelings and open up to forgiveness. In cutting the cord, we express to our inner being a willingness to drop our old charge so that we can move forward unburdened.

Sometimes, we move on from the person or situation when we cut the cord. Other times, we find that our interaction with that person or situation changes significantly. Each situation is unique. What they all share is that the change happens from the inside out. We can stop creating the same patterns in the outer world only once we address their source in the inner world.

Clearing the Vibration

For some, the image of cutting the cords that connect us can seem aggressive or violent. After all, we are connected to all of our experience, to everything that shares space with us directly or indirectly. In a way, our fields are filled with these lines of connection between ourselves and every other being in creation.

On a psychological level, all of the thoughts, feelings, and sense impressions that enter our awareness are ours. We get more out of integrating all aspects of ourselves than we do from trying to cut feelings away.

If this perspective resonates with you, then you may wish to clear old charge more intuitively. Each bit of unprocessed emotional charge could be perceived as a sense of contraction, as a bit of tension held in our field. If we can tune in to this tension, we can allow ourselves to feel it, process it, and release it.

Sometimes it helps to envision this charge sent down through our bodies and deep into the earth. Breathe it down, relax, and let the tension flow out. As you do, view the thread as it changes. Watch and feel as the old charge flows out of the thread. Observe the new feeling and qualities that it takes on. This whole process takes place on the physical level as a movement from contraction to expansion.

Just as in the technique for cutting cords, this is best done in a meditative state. Also, remember that there is a difference between suppressing our thoughts and feelings and actually processing them. It's always helpful to listen to what our feelings and stories have to teach us. It's also helpful to make space within to actually feel these things, rather than simply trying to make them go away.

This practice is beautiful because it is physical, organic, and direct. It helps to cultivate inner awareness and a clear understanding of what's happening inside you at any given moment. Even and especially when triggered. And it offers excellent practice in the art of surrender. Releasing the old charge physically and emotionally, truly letting go, is an act of surrender.

As it becomes natural to note contraction and intentionally move into expansion, you will notice benefits in every aspect of your life. This is simple, quick, and feeling-based, so it becomes a huge asset for self-awareness and conscious self-regulation.

Remember that visualization is just a way to formalize our intent for ourselves. This means that you can get as creative as you want with it. You might, for example, envision circuit boards embedded in these threads that characterize the charge and story of that thread. You could then visualize removing the old, faulty board and replacing it with a fresh one. It really doesn't matter what image you use, so long as it resonates with you.

Techniques for Self-Acceptance

Some of our deepest acceptance work is directed not outward toward others, but inward toward ourselves. Before we can truly see another, love another, before we can authentically care, we have to learn how to see, love, and care about ourselves. And, since our stories of self protect us from uncomfortable thoughts and perceptions, it can be hard to tune in to those places where we are in resistance to ourselves, to the blind spots that hide our most sensitive areas.

In order to see ourselves truly, we often have to let things in that we've been trying to protect ourselves from, usually unconsciously. We have to slow down, look at ourselves, and let things come up. And then accept what we find. Forgive ourselves for whatever comes up and listen to what it has to teach us. That's really the long and short of it.

The hard part is that we often resist this in one subtle way after another. So, the techniques that follow help us to direct our attention towards ourselves, towards our story of self and the stuck charge within. They help us to get present, listen, and healthily process what comes to our attention.

Mirror Work & Ho'oponopono

Mirror work can be extremely powerful. Just think about how you look into the mirror. Are you looking for certain details? Imagining how you will appear to others? Are you judging what you see, or maybe preemptively judging what you think others will see? What comes up for you when you look in the mirror?

In order to do mirror work, find a place where you can have some privacy, some space and a bit of quiet time. Position yourself in front of a mirror and look at yourself. You may notice that you home in on certain details, notice this, notice that. That's alright. Just bring the attention back to your whole image. Take it all in and notice any feelings or stories that come up. Breathe, feel, see, and just let yourself be in this space. Stay here for as long as you like or as you have time for.

Another practice which can be combined with this is the Ho'oponopono. This is a Hawaiian tradition in origin, but it's very simple, very human. As you look in the mirror, as you see yourself, as you feel things come up, say the following:

"I'm sorry, please forgive me, thank you, I love you."

Repeat this statement like a mantra while viewing yourself in the mirror. With this, we're speaking to ourselves, acknowledging the old pains and feelings, acknowledging our part in the creation of those feelings. And with it, we're holding ourselves gently, warmly, and with compassion.

The Ho'oponopono simply helps us to stick with the feeling, rather than run from it. And it helps us to process this feeling and release it naturally, healthily, rather than tensing around it.

EFT (Emotional Freedom Therapy)

Emotional Freedom Therapy is a therapeutic modality specifically intended for clearing old emotions and the stories that carry them. This modality is extremely helpful, and a full description extends beyond the scope of this conversation. However, there are a few takeaways which are useful for our purposes.

The first takeaway is that our stuck emotions can be dealt with physically, through the medium of the body. The second takeaway is a mantra, a phrase we repeat to ourselves:

"Even though I feel _____, I deeply love and respect myself."

The technique itself is pretty simple. When you find yourself triggered, when you're dealing with a powerful story and charge, take a little space and tune in to your body. Ask yourself where you feel this emotion in your body. Begin tapping this area gently. Identify the emotion and give it a name: I feel _____. Follow this with the phrase: Even though I feel _____, I deeply love and respect myself.

As you tap and speak, you may notice that the feeling shifts places in your body. If it does, shift with it. Tap in the new area and continue repeating the phrase.

Keep with it, tapping to keep your awareness in your body, speaking to program a new way of meeting this feeling. And, as you do, begin to slide the tapping in towards the heart. Stay with the feeling, breathing, repeating the phrase, until you are tapping lightly at the heart and you feel like the pressure has been released around the feeling.

Having a physical technique to clear old emotion is extremely helpful. It encourages us to keep aware of the body and its subtle, constant feedback. It also sidesteps the tendency of the mind to try and run the show. Mind is great for many things, but it doesn't clear feelings. Body is a much more direct route for that. Just remember to be patient with the process and breathe.

Practice 3: The Story of Your Life

So much of the way we experience the world comes from our stories about it. Our stories show us how to interpret raw sense data into meaning. They give us context, history. Our stories about ourselves help us to understand what we want, what we need, what we are capable of. Our stories about the world help us to understand the stage upon which our lives are unfolding. Where we come from and where we're going.

Our stories, the specific way that we interpret events and situations, lead to specific emotional responses and reaction patterns. From *this* perspective, *this* is what we have to do. But we often forget that each story is just one way of making sense of the world.

Stories are mental models, always incomplete and imperfect. The map is not the territory. And two maps of the same territory may not look alike at all. We can look back upon the things we've experienced and learn new things, make new stories. Not false stories. Lessons that were always there in potential but went unseen in the moment.

When we learn new lessons, we can review past experiences and find new meaning in them. They then generate new emotions. Our entire perception transforms as we learn new things, as we grow and clear old stories, transform old charge. We deepen our understanding of ourselves and how our choices create our lives.

One of our closest and most cherished stories is the Story of Our Life. This is the story which forms our ego, our personal history and the role we currently inhabit.

Often, we experience life like a child, nose pressed to the glass. We react to things instinctively, often before we're even fully aware of them. We experience things and make sense of them (generate stories) before we have an opportunity to critically review these experiences.

If we do take the time to delve deeply into our history and learn new lessons, we gain a hitherto unimagined sense of scope and clarity. The following practice is an introduction to recapitulation, a Toltec technique for reviewing and transforming our life history.

Introduction to Recapitulation

Many things look different in hindsight. Recapitulation is a process of looking back upon the things we have experienced in the past. We step back and observe the story that we made about these things, our personal history. In the process, we tend to see that there was more going on than we saw in the moment.

Recapitulation shows us that the way we understood our experience at the time is just one way it can be understood. It shows us that we have a choice in how we make meaning.

Before we can see how our stories influence our perception, they look like the whole world to us. And, if we keep moving, always focused on the next thing, then we never have time to review our experiences, to process, clarify, refine, and learn what we can from what we've experienced. If we take a bit of time and make a bit of space to look back upon recent events, we often see them in a new light.

Recapitulation is a creative process of renegotiating our stories, our understanding of ourselves, our purpose, and our life history. It is a powerful process, and we will come back to it in the next module to explore it in greater depth. For now, we can set the stage for recapitulation by honestly reviewing our lives, to ourselves. By making it a practice to create space for reflection, and by breathing through what comes up.

There is a word that entered the English language from the writings of the legendary sci-fi author Robert Heinlein. This word is "grok." To grok, in the best terms we have available, is to understand a situation in full. Not just our little part of it. Not just the immediate emotional reaction, the initial interpretation.

Every experience we have shapes us, forges us into the person we're becoming. When we create space to review our lives, we allow ourselves to see it from a greater scope. We move ever so slightly towards grokking the situation, and our lives.

Sometimes, the feelings that we get when reviewing our experiences are so intense, they can be hard to handle. If this is the case, it's helpful to *step back*. In your inner space, instead of imagining yourself in the situation, see yourself watching the situation from the outside. You might even imagine yourself in a movie theater watching the events unfold on screen. Play it through in your mind, and notice the emotions that come up. If that's still too intense, step back again. You could watch yourself in the movie theater, watching yourself on screen.

Each time you step back, it distances you from the emotion, just slightly. Just enough to let it play out without reaction. Run it through in your mind again, releasing a bit of charge each time. When that becomes manageable, step forward again.

Eventually, the goal is to envision yourself having the experience, right in the middle of the action. Notice the emotions that come up in the process. Ask yourself what they have to teach you. Ask yourself what gifts are hidden in the challenge. How can this help you to grow?

As human beings, it's important for us to be able to find meaning in pain and loss. When we learn to see each challenge as a gift, as an opportunity to reclaim our power or become aware of our blind spots, we have a constructive frame that we can apply to any challenging situation. This perspective is massively helpful in transforming hardship into strength and pain into wisdom.

Cave of Shadows

This is an exciting technique to share. It is the first that we have come to which is a true shamanic journey. In shamanism, **imagination is used as a faculty of perception**. We journey in the inner spaces through meditation and visualization. In a process similar to free association, we allow ourselves to speak to ourselves.

The process is as follows: Step into your inner space with a specific intention, visualize the space, and listen. Be open to receive anything you have to learn. Sometimes we speak with a voice within, sometimes simply with the space itself. In any case, we use the visualized inner space as an interface to access unconscious wisdom, skill, and story. The journey state helps us to access deeper parts of our being, things that can be challenging to contact in our normal waking state.

In time, you may wish to craft a place of power in your inner space, a space in nature where you feel comfortable, at peace, clear, and strong. For the purpose of this exercise, however, we have a specific destination in mind: the cave of shadows. To better understand this destination, consider the following story:

Once upon a time, there was a young brave who ran away from his shadow. At first, this was great fun. But over time, he found that he was only half a man without his shadow. In order to once again become whole, he had to find his shadow and be reunited with it. But to find it, he had to go into a dark cave where only shadows lived.

Fearing for his very life, the young man entered the cave and was immediately swarmed by shadows. All of his doubts, fears, all of his points of shame and guilt, anger and deep grief, all of the pain inside him responded to the shadows. All of it whispered for him to go back, that he was no match for them. That he was nothing more than pain, that it would eat him alive and there would be nothing left.

The young man cowered near the mouth of the cave, paralyzed with fear, unable to go forward, and unable to retreat. But he remembered the teachings of his elders, and became still, and breathed. He noticed that the shadows did nothing more than whisper. The only power they had over him was the power he gave them.

All the power the shadows had over the young man came from his pain. And he saw that if he was able to face his pain like a warrior, without running or flinching away, then the shadows had no more hold on him.

The young man stood strong, then. He knew himself and his purpose, and the shadows could not touch him, all but one. His personal shadow, the pain that forged him and gave him purpose. He called out his secret name and took ownership of his shadow, and it returned to his heel.

This is not the end of the story. The young man's shadow was still loose, held on by the slimmest of threads. But, seeing the young man battle the shadows so fiercely, Moon Woman came to his aid. She sewed his shadow back firmly with gossamer strands of moonlight.

From that day forward, the young brave was no longer afraid of his shadow, and as he grew, he became known as one of the wisest and most courageous warriors of the tribe.

The Practice

To enter the cave of shadows, first set an intention. Be clear with yourself about the issue you would like to explore, the feeling that you are challenged by. Know what you would like to use the journey to work on. Then, go into a journey state.

In a light meditative state, we are relaxed and aware, slightly more tuned in to the body than during waking consciousness. This is a helpful mindset for flow state, conscious communication, engaged learning, and many other high-performance tasks. As we slow down and relax further, our inner vision often becomes more vivid and takes on the responsive quality of dreams. This is the journey state.

It is different to navigate this space than to work with waking consciousness. The journey state requires a light touch. Relax and tune in to the inner space. Let the image become clearer and more detailed as you tune in to it. Instead of forcing or overcontrolling the visualization, set the intention, and then visualize yourself going through the journey. In the process, try to remain open to anything we see along the path, anything that pops up or speaks to you in this inner space.

After entering the journey state, envision a physical setting, ideally in nature. Just let the picture build slowly, one little detail at a time, or however it wants to present itself to you.

Once you have a sense of this space, begin walking. Let the path lead you to the mouth of a cave. This is a place where the shadows live, where you can confront your fears, old stories, and misaligned aspects of yourself. This is a place where you can meet with your old pain and learn something new, where you can transform it from a challenge to a strength. In this space, you can come face to face with current triggers and listen to the self-awareness they offer.

Enter this cave, knowing that you are the one who observes, the one who chooses. Meet your shadow. Meet your challenge and let it show you its story. When it becomes intense, get still and breathe. Let yourself see and feel the situation in full. Learn what you can.

See how you can continue breathing in the face of this challenge. See how the intensity changes, how the feeling shifts when you allow yourself to meet it. Feel the space around it.

Ask yourself how this challenge can help you to grow, to care, to give back, or just to make it through. Just form the question, and then listen within. You might notice a medley of images, may hear a voice, may just get a sense of the answer.

The answers we get in the journey state may look very different from those we get in normal consciousness, but they can be incredibly valuable. Often, a symbolic image can offer insight into your experience or a solution to a current problem, but it takes time to see the meaning of the symbol in mundane terms.

At this point, though, don't be overly concerned with diagnosis. Learning to feel, listen within, accept yourself, and tune in to a specific experience, all in your mind's eye, these are invaluable skills, each one required for the full blossoming of human potential.

When you feel ready, emerge once more from the cave of shadows. Deepen your breathing, let it speed up. Bring energy into the body with small, subtle movements. And, when you're ready, open your eyes.

You may wish to give yourself a few moments to get back into the flow of things. Also, with journey work, it's helpful to keep a journal of your experiences. We often get just as much from "unpacking" the experience afterwards as we do in the moment. Journey work helps us to tap into unconscious content. It's always necessary to review this dreamlike content to see how it fits with our personal lived experience.

Our journeys are tools for insight and self-knowledge and to facilitate growth and healing. But they speak to us in symbolic language that can be challenging to connect with our daily lives. Journey work is most helpful when we pass all that arises, all insight presented to us, through a screen of discernment.

We will discuss the art of discernment more fully in a later module. For now, remember that no stories are true. They are personal (subjective) navigation tools, not accurate accounts of objective reality. Vision work offers symbolic stories that can yield fresh perspective, through metaphor, on our personal journey and what it means to us.

Final Words on Acceptance and Accountability

We have covered a wealth of techniques and stories in this section. We have begun to explore in depth how we can work with our inner space. We now have a description of this inner space in terms of story and charge, and an understanding of how our stories can lead to specific emotions and life experiences.

At the core of it all is the heart, the feeling sense. Once we begin to learn acceptance, we can then bear accountability. And, once we can bear accountability, we can then begin to cultivate freedom. Freedom from emotional chains to specific types of experience, freedom to move forward and generate new consequences, consciously and intentionally.

These lessons set the stage for real transformation, but you can *know* all of this and still be miserable. The key is to put it into practice. Every moment you are alive is an opportunity to be conscious, aware. To attune to your world as you intend and in a way that aligns with your values.

Every time we're triggered, we can take ownership of our feelings, process old emotions, and become aware of our blind spots. We can take time each day to make space and listen within. We can remain conscious of where we place our attention and learn to listen to the subtle language of our emotions and our body. Every moment is an opportunity to make these perspectives and practices more natural, more reflexive.

In the sections past, we have explored the ability to slow your biorhythms and enter a meditative state. We have explored the nature of emotions and the language they speak. We have explored the creative power of attention. And we have a model of the human experience which explains how attention, story, and charge filter our sense experience and make it meaningful.

We now have a clear picture of the inner human experience in archetypal human terms: Rhythm and Sense, Charge, Story Shell (Including Sense of Self), and Attention.

All of the work to this point has been to get clear of conditioned patterns, to live consciously, intentionally, and to make peace with ourselves. It's been about getting to zero.

Until we can accept ourselves and become accountable for our lives, we're handicapped. We live unconsciously, reactively. All manner of stories and habits colonize our will, our inner space. We are wild, untrained, and at war with ourselves.

Once we come to a place of acceptance of ourselves, true acceptance of our world right now and of our place in that world, the landscape changes completely. Up until now, we've been focused on basic navigation. Surviving the world. Using the natural gifts and equipment all humans were born with to relate with our experience in ways that help us get by, and little more. From this point forward, we begin the work of individuation.

None of us are cookie-cutter people. We all have our own gifts, our own stories, our own passions and values. As we move forward into an exploration of personal power, we must consider how we would like to apply that power. And, once we accept ourselves, we can begin to use that power with open eyes, consciously and aligned with things we truly value.

MODULE 5 - RECLAIMING PERSONAL POWER

Introduction to Reclaiming Personal Power

In the last four modules, we have discussed the nature of the human experience from its foundations up. We began with rhythm, which is connected to our heart rate, breath, and brainwave frequency. The exercises in this first module offered tools and techniques to shift your frequency with intention. We also had the opportunity to practice slowing our frequency to enter the meditative or journey state.

Next, we explored charge and the language of the emotions. No matter what we want to do or we mean to do, if we don't know how to handle our emotions when they come up, then our intentions will fall flat. If we don't understand how to listen to their messages and process them, we will be in conflict with ourselves. The second module offered guidance on tuning in to the emotions and making space to process what comes up in healthy ways.

In the third section, we explored presence and attention. We began to look more closely at the field of the senses and the stories that we use to establish context. We also began exploring the story of self, the conceptual identity that we first grow unconsciously. The tools covered in this module help us to become aware of our attention and our stories, and to work consciously with these aspects of human experience.

Finally, in the fourth section, we began to explore how to make peace with ourselves, with our life as it is now. This is essential for clearing the field of old emotions and stories so that we can move forward with intention and without fighting ourselves at every turn. Acceptance and accountability are keys to happiness and to living a purposeful life on our own terms.

Up to this point, the journey looks very similar for all people. From this point on, we focus on individuation. This means that from here on in, each person is blazing a unique trail of intention through their own lives.

Each person is different, so each person will want to spend their time on and devote their creative energy to different things. Your ideal life may not look the same as the next person's. Each person will explore this aspect of the journey in their own way. That said, everyone can benefit from some understanding of personal power, what it looks like, how it can be lost, and how it can be reclaimed.

In this section, we'll explore the nature of intention. Our intention is an expression of our personal power, our will. It is the means we use to make choices in life. And each choice that we make influences the experiences we have moving forward. Our personal power is the creative force that we use to grow, to build things in life, and to navigate through our daily lives.

Although each person will wish to use their creative energy in unique ways, we can all benefit from understanding certain aspects of the use of will. So, as you go through the following section, ask yourself a few questions:

What would I like to experience in my life?

What would I like to use my will to create, or serve, or support?

What changes would I like to make in my life?

What blocks me from making these changes?

How can I grow past these obstacles?

Each of these questions is linked to our use of personal power. Will. Creative energy. Our personal power is key to living a life of freedom, intention, and purpose. It is the means to inspire consciousness and promote healing, both in ourselves and in others.

As poetic as this description is, it's still a bit vague. So, what is personal power, in simple, human terms? And how can we access this personal power for the benefit of our lives and the lives of others?

What is personal power?

Personal power is the power to choose our response to life. It is the power to act in ways that we hope will build the future we would like to build. The power to live a vital, worthwhile, intentional life, vibrant, present, and passionate, right now, and in each moment.

Personal power is the ability to choose, to create, to navigate through our conscious experience, to make meaning intentionally and bring order to our environment.

Every word, every act, every choice we make creates our future. What kind of future would you like to create for yourself? Whatever your answer, the key to moving in that direction is your will, your personal power.

What does personal power look like?

Often, the word power is used in connection with things like money, or political authority, or leverage, or physical force. All of these things are forms of power, for sure. In a way, though, these are forms of "power over." Money and politics are part of the social game we play, part of how we exert influence in the collective narrative of society. But personal power is deeper, more fundamental.

Personal power is the will to make a change, to make a decision and follow through. After we figure out what we want, it is our personal power which determines whether we can act in ways that lead to this desire.

When we live in the ways that others have laid out for us, we invest our personal power in their dreams and their stories. And we create a life along the lines of those stories. As we reclaim our personal power, we can begin to create our lives in our own way, whatever that looks like.

Personal power comes in many forms. Some of the most fundamental forms are intention and will. At the functional level, personal power is the capacity to make an active choice, a decision followed by action, energy. Often, we give this energy in the form of time, or effort, or attention, or money, or other resources. Sometimes our personal power is expressed in terms of voice, or knowledge, or the exchange of story, or the application of skill.

Regardless of the form, all *personal power is creative energy*. This energy has an impact on the world, on how our lives unfold. It shapes our future.

We have used our personal power to create this moment, in subtle, sweeping ways. Personal power is the key to living a purposeful, intentional life. It's a gift that allows us to live our lives on our own terms in a way that truly works for us. In order to actualize this gift, we will need to understand the creative impact of our choices.

Although our personal power is *potentially* ours to spend as we choose, we must reclaim that power before we can consciously devote it to a specific outcome. If you've ever quit a habit, you've seen firsthand how our choices can be so colonized by our habits that they don't feel like choices. In these instances, we have lost personal power to that habit. We must reclaim this power before we can make a different choice.

The process of reclaiming our personal power is long and slow, and it requires both a willingness to see ourselves and a humility for what we find. It requires consistent application of discipline, combined with gentleness and patience for our slow progress.

Consistency is more important than intensity when it comes to major life transformations. Slow and steady wins the race. Slow, consistent growth is sustainable and builds momentum quicker than you might expect.

When we begin the process of reclaiming our personal power, we have to learn about many things. We have to learn about healthy boundaries, so that we do not impose our will upon others or allow others to impose unhealthily upon us. We discover our personal values, the things we truly care for and believe in, the things that truly matter to us. We begin to discover our voice, and with it, we learn authenticity.

Reclaiming personal power is a lifelong journey. It is not likely that any of us will complete it in our lifetimes, if such a thing is even possible. There will always be blind spots and room for massive growth. We are not likely to run out of opportunities to see things within ourselves that we didn't expect, and to humble ourselves in the face of them. But that's alright. Every step we take in that direction helps us to see ourselves and our lives more clearly, to actualize our choice and freedom.

Let's make the most of the journey. And a little tip for the journey ahead: sometimes it's all about asking ourselves the right question. Try this one: "How much better can it get?" Asking ourselves questions like this can prime us to see opportunities and blessings in the world. They bring hope and positivity, both which are essential when facing the challenge of reclaiming our will and using it with integrity.

The Dream of the Three Attentions

"We don't see the world as it is, we see it as we are."

– Anais Nin

At this point, I would like to acknowledge the work of Don Miguel Ruiz. In *The Fifth Agreement*, he tells a story about the dream of the three attentions. This is an allegorical account of the growth of consciousness. In other words, it helps us to understand how our relation to our inner world is central to our growth, and how that relationship changes as we walk the path.

This story begins in the forest, in a space full of trees. This is the forest of the inner world. Each tree within this forest is a story, a perspective. Each tree offers a unique vantage point, a unique view on the whole landscape. In fact, we could spend our whole lives viewing the forest from one tree, and there would still be more to see. Nuances, details, changes. A whole world – a whole universe – exists within each perspective.

The First Attention

We enter this forest as a small creature, low and close to the ground. We begin our journey through the forest with the first attention, and the animal used to symbolize this phase of our growth is the snake. In terms of human experience, the role we play in the dream of the first attention is that of the victim.

To the victim, the world is a very big, very scary place. When we play this role, we don't know how we got into the situation we're in. It's not our fault. We didn't choose it. And we often feel that it's unfair.

In fact, the main function of the victim is to blame. The victim identifies their pain or unhappiness with an external condition, one that they do not have the power to change. Unfortunately, this mindset leaves them stuck, first unable to conceive a change, to conceive that the world could be anything other than what it is right now. And later, unable to believe in their power to make a change.

Like the snake, in this phase of the journey we tend to be reactive. The victim is prompted to take action by fear, motivated to avoid undesirable feelings and stay within their safe, comfortable space. At this point in our development, we tend to take action only when life pushes us to. Also like the snake, when we play the victim, we tend to see the world from very close, only aware of what's right in front of us.

If you've played the victim, or seen one in action, you'll likely have noticed that they respond only when the situation is right on top of them. And often grudgingly then, unhappy about having their comfort intruded on by the inevitable changes and challenges of life.

It's not fun to be a victim. When we play this role, we tend to take everything personally, which often hurts and leads to misunderstanding and conflict. When we play the victim, it doesn't feel like we're playing. It feels like we don't have a choice, like this is just what's happening. Without knowing it, we are stuck in one tree, one way of viewing the world, and can't see that this tree is not the whole world.

The image of the serpent has another lesson for us, though. Just as the snake can shed its skin, we can shed our old stories, our old limitations. We can shed our justifications, excuses, and other points of power loss. Whatever we're doing that doesn't work for us, we have the capacity to do differently. As soon as we turn the blame game around and see what we've done to get here, we can begin to see how to move in the direction we want.

For those in the dream of the first attention, the key to moving forward is accountability. Accountability starts when we stop blaming others for our lives and take it upon ourselves to begin building a future we want. It's a big journey, in part because no one is working with a clear playing field. We all have forces, either outside or within us, that we have to overcome. A massive part of growth is learning how to meet these unique personal challenges with integrity.

It's possible that your life situation was decided by those more powerful than you, or that you just got dealt a random hand by the universe. No matter how we got to this point, it's down to us to decide how we move forward. There's no one else to blame for how we respond to the world. It's up to each one of us to do what we can with what we've got. We are all, at a fundamental level, accountable for our journey through life.

This can be a terrible thing to hear if you're really attached to the role of the victim. Much of that role is supported by a story of someone to blame. Once you stop blaming others for your situation and for your feelings, you're not really a victim anymore. You may very well be beholden to other people or situations in life. But you're only a victim if you sit back and passively submit.

On a psychological level, the victim is disempowered. They do not believe that they have the capacity to make a change, take action, or attempt to improve the situation. When we accept that it was our actions that led us here, then we know our actions can move us forward as well. That's the key. Accountability is the first step out of victimhood, the first step towards reclaiming our personal power.

The Second Attention

With accountability, we move into the dream of the second attention, the dream of the warrior. This phase of the journey is symbolized by the jaguar, a skilled climber and patient stalker. And, the entire work of the warrior, the entire journey of the second attention, is a process of waking up. We learn how to stalk ourselves, how to identify points of power loss and reclaim that power.

The perspective of the jaguar is a bit wider than that of the snake. The jaguar can explore the forest and find trees that are good for hunting. They know that if one perch yields poor success, they can seek out another perch from which to hunt. The jaguar is skilled at leaping out of the tree and climbing another.

Remember that in the inner forest, all of these trees are stories, perspectives of the world. And each tree offers its own vantage point, a perspective which we could easily mistake for being the entire world. The image of the jaguar teaches us to pay attention to the stories we use to make sense of things. It teaches us to pay attention to where we have traveled in the forest, knowing that it looks different from each vantage point. Each tree offers a different way of interacting with the forest.

In human terms, this part of the journey is dedicated to shadow work. Whenever we find ourselves in a situation we don't like, it's an opportunity to look at our perspective, our stories. There is something that we have done to navigate us to this situation, some story or belief or perspective which framed our choices and led us to this moment. Shadow work involves recognizing that subconscious choices led to this point and using feedback from the outer world to help tune in to these stories, to lift and shift them.

To bring the metaphor home, imagine you're in a situation that you don't like. The victim submits grudgingly to the situation, complaining about it but doing nothing to change it. The warrior looks at their own perspective and choices, looks at how they helped to bring this situation into being. And they strive to reclaim their power from the situation.

Just as the jaguar will give up a perch that offers poor success, the warrior will take note of stories, expectations, or beliefs that act as obstacles to the desired outcome or state of being. The warrior learns how to meet these stories and renegotiate their relationship with them. This process involves making space for different ways of perceiving and relating to the world. In the dream of the second attention, the warrior enters an empowered, intentional relationship with their inner world.

Let's bring this even closer to home. Just consider a habit that you would like to overcome. Maybe you've been a smoker, or a drinker, or an unhealthy eater. It can be hard to shift habits, especially long-term ones. It's almost as if they build up momentum and carve tracks in our minds. These are points of power loss, areas in which we have to reclaim our personal power before we have an authentic choice about how to use it. Before we reclaim this power, the habit chooses for us.

The dream of the second attention is devoted entirely to stalking our points of power loss and learning how to reclaim that power. Like many of the things we've covered, this is a lifelong practice. It's relatively easy to get lazy and let an unhealthy habit or story colonize our will. So, it will require constant attention, steady effort, and self-honesty to continue freeing up our power. We need vigilance to keep making conscious choices, rather than slipping into old, unconscious ones.

The dream of the second attention teaches us how to live an intentional life and how to extend this intention into every aspect of our experience. As we do this, our journey shifts slowly and imperceptibly from the second attention to the third attention. This happens as we come to know ourselves more fully, as we become clear about our values and learn to dedicate the whole of our lives to these values. As we learn what we truly care about and reclaim the inner power to actually do something about it.

The Third Attention

The dream of the third attention is also known as the dream of the artist or the master. At this point, we have reclaimed enough clarity and will to make real choices, to begin building something intentional with our lives. The animal associated with the third attention is the eagle, a bird that soars above the forest, both fully at home in the sky and able to roost in any tree. The eagle symbolizes the vision and freedom that we have earned by reaching this phase of the journey.

We are all different, unique. We are all on our own journey through life. What we all share is that we were given the blessing of life. We all have a choice about what we will do with this blessing. Each day, each choice, creates the future. Each act creates consequences.

When we blame others for our lives, we live relatively unaware of the creative power of our choices, stuck in loops and steadily creating consequences that we don't want. At some point in the journey, we lose the comfort of ignorance and we have to make real choices.

There's no one right way to live your life. And no one else can tell you what you truly value, or how to live your life aligned with those values. That's for each of us to discover for ourselves. The journey we have taken up to this point gives us the power to see more clearly and to take action with intention. In order to use this power with integrity, we now have to go on a journey to discover what we serve.

We make our lives meaningful by contributing to or connecting with something larger than our bodies, larger than our personal identity. I personally value three things above all others in my life: freedom, power, and purpose. I strive to support consciousness in the body, in the form of power, in the mind, in the form of freedom, and in the heart, in the form of purpose, for myself and for all beings. This is what I serve, the goalpost that I use to evaluate every choice I make, every word.

Your own relationship with your values is likely to be different from mine. You have your own journey, your own history, and your own pain points. When you understand your values clearly and in depth, you can both act in alignment with these values and communicate them more effectively. This leads to a life led on your own terms, accountable to yourself, and with the potential of serving something meaningful.

Imagine, for a moment, knowing what you want, what you care about, clearly enough to see whether your actions support or contradict these values. Imagine really knowing what you believe, what you believe in, in personal, compelling terms.

What would you create with your life, if you could?

What do you want to create with your life, now that you know you can?

How can you make your life meaningful and fulfilling, rich with vitality and deep, abiding happiness?

What values do you serve?

Traps for Personal Power

Energy flows where attention goes.

Attention is one of the most powerful tools we have access to. The attention, like the breath, can be directed consciously. Each moment throughout the day, we spend our attention on something. And whatever we place our attention on influences our experience of that moment. Our attention leads both our perception and our will.

Anything we want to accomplish requires energy. Put another way, when we want to make something happen, we have to dedicate energy to that outcome. It may be in the form of time, or physical effort, or money, but all of that begins with attention.

Energy directs change. Energy can be used to build or destroy, to initiate and govern specific changes. Whatever we want to create in our lives, energy makes it happen.

Attention directs and focuses the energy of our consciousness and will. When we reach out and pick up a cup, it is the attention that initiates and guides the physical action. When we accomplish a goal, it is because we have paid attention to that outcome and to the steps required to accomplish it.

We use stories, habits, and routines to structure our attention over time, throughout the course of our days or lives. These stories, habits, and routines form energetic loops, circular tracks of attention. These circular paths are holding patterns that establish regularity and security in our lives. They protect us from the chaos of the world and from the uncomfortable thoughts and feelings within.

Holding patterns help us to establish a specific kind of order in our lives, a specific structure. The order of the known and the familiar. And these loops work for us for a time, otherwise we would never have developed them to begin with. But sometimes, they can become so strong that it feels like we cannot make a different choice. In these moments, our habits, stories, and routines can become traps for personal power. They can lock our creative energy into outcomes based on old decisions, choices no longer relevant to our lives.

Anything that requires our focus, our attention, our continuous effort – anything that we feel we have no choice around – is a trap for our personal power.

Habits, Routines, and Loops

Just think back to how you have spent the day, the week, the year. If you're like most people, from the moment you wake up in the morning to when you are in bed trying to sleep, your attention is pulled to one thing after another.

We send the attention down similar tracks, over and over, and we form habits. When these habits are arranged in sequence, they create routines. Now we make coffee, now we get dressed, now we drive to work... on and on it goes. Each moment, the attention has somewhere to go.

There is nothing wrong with these habits and routines. We form habits and routines to give our attention familiar, structured tracks to follow. And, when our routines and habits work for us, they will help us devote attention to those things which keep us healthy and happy, aligned with fulfillment and meaning.

The challenge comes when our routines and habits are misaligned with our needs and values. We build up our habits and routines unconsciously at first. Our habitual behavioral patterns give a sense of safety and certainty. They create order out of our lives, give us comfortable places to focus our attention. But, once we are ready to grow and experience something different, our habits become traps.

Our habits are one way to maintain control over our lives. With our routines, we know exactly what's coming, exactly what's going to happen. Again, we've written a mental script for the day, the hour, the year. We have a plan, and it's awesome if the plan manages our energy to accomplish our needs. Often, though, our unconscious habits and stories demand more and more energy from us while giving less and less back.

Human beings need change at a fundamental level. We change when we grow, and we only feel fulfilled while in a state of growth. When our habits and routines become very strong, we stagnate. Life can seem like it's stuck on instant replay. Even if we don't like our daily grind, it can be frustrating when we are forced to change plans. Essentially, we tend to go more and more on automatic, disengaging from our lives and just staying the course.

No matter how comfortable our habits, on a long enough timeline, they will feel like a trap. It can feel like we don't have a choice; we have to keep the hamster wheel going. It can feel as if we can't get off of the wheel, like we're stuck with the current situation and can't put our attention on other things. We end up feeling like we hardly have enough energy to keep things going as it is, and if we were to let go, then everything would fall apart.

Sometimes this is true. Sometimes we arrange our lives in such a fashion that if we were to step back, things would fall apart. But if these patterns prevent us from taking care of our own needs, they are unsustainable in the long run.

If our habits don't give us time to process our experiences, space to give back to the body and to do things we truly care about, then we won't be able to keep the wheel going forever. No matter how much we want to, and no matter how much we feel we have no choice.

The "Until Then" Game

How many of you out there have spent days, maybe weeks or years, living for something that hasn't happened yet? We could spend decades plugging away for an imagined future that never comes. The carrot on the stick that keeps us moving with the promise of fulfillment and never actually delivers.

When we're living on automatic, stuck in cycles that fulfill our physical needs but leave our deeper needs unmet, we tend to retreat into fantasy, often without realizing that we're doing it. Just think of the person who grinds away at their corporate job, climbing the ladder of conventional success. They often have an image of how that success, that imagined future, will leave them fulfilled. Even as the meaningful relationships in their lives wither from neglect.

In these cases, our imagined future becomes more real to us than what is actually happening in our lives. In extreme cases, we can let all the things that truly matter to us slide while we go all out for a finish line that doesn't really exist. We begin living more and more in our heads – in our story about the situation – than present to how the situation feels and the impact that it has on our lives.

I like to call this the "until then" game. My life will finally feel good when ____. When I get that next promotion. When I finally lose those ten pounds. When I get a girlfriend or boyfriend. When the kids are grown. When things finally settle down. When I retire. Whenever this thing happens in the future, then I'll finally be able to start living my life.

If this sounds like you, here's some bad news. That moment, even if it comes, is just another moment. Just like this moment. And, if you don't know how to be alive in this moment, then you won't know how to be alive in that imagined one. Don't worry. There's good news too: you don't have to wait to start living your life.

After all, what are we really waiting for? Some fundamental difference in how we experience life, all based on some twist of fate in the outer world? Whether our imagined outcome ever comes to pass or not, we are alive *now*. Choosing *now*. Investing our attention *now*. Building our lives, our connections, our stories and our meaning, *right now*.

Waiting for Godot

When we are unaware and reactive in the placement of our attention, we get scattered. Ineffectual. Our lives get stuck in certain patterns, certain types of experience. In a way, this approach to life is instinctive, animalistic. It's great for addressing the next thing. But when we respond instinctively, it's also easy to waste our energy, to spend time and effort in ways that accomplish little to nothing in our lives.

One of my favorite images for this is from a play by Samuel Beckett: *Waiting for Godot*. In this play, there are two men in a clearing, having a conversation and waiting for someone (named Godot) to arrive. There are only two things in this clearing: a rock, and a tree. The two men spend the entire play going from rock to tree, tree to rock, and Godot never shows up.

What struck me about this is that it's very much like we often live our lives. Moving towards the next thing in front of us, waiting for... for what? Permission? The right time? For something that, quite often, never actually happens. Life always offers the next thing, the next task, the next issue. There's always something to take care of. And, in the words of John Lennon, "Life is what happens when we're making other plans."

There is no "right time" in life. The right time to start living our lives intentionally is now. The only right time to look at the gift of our life, to choose how we would like to spend it and what we would like to create with it, the only right time for that is *now*. No one is coming to rescue us. No outer situation which will somehow make things magically work, happily ever after. Everything we experience happens now, every decision, every action.

As you look back over the last hour, the last day, the last month, year, think about where your energy has gone. Look at what you have spent it on. Consider where you have placed your attention, and consider what it has produced, what it has built, strengthened, created. What have you been serving? In your body, in your mind, heart, and in the outer world? Are you simply passing time, or are you living life as the blessing that it is, creating, growing, savoring?

So, the next question: how do we get out of these cycles? How can we get our power back? How can we get to a place where we have a real choice, where life feels meaningful? And is it even possible to do that and support ourselves at the same time? Are we doomed to a pointless hamster wheel where the only escape is death?

Just to pull us back from the edge of hyperbole, I'll offer a bit of reassurance. There is hope. Life is right here, for each of us, just waiting for us to arrive and get back in the driver's seat. We can use our attention, our energy, our will, to build and grow things in our lives, things that are meaningful to us. Right now.

Each moment, we are given a choice as to where to put our attention. Each moment, we have the opportunity to place our attention on things that truly matter to us, on things that are life-affirming and aligned with our values.

Attention and Addiction

Addiction is a major issue in today's society. But more than that, addiction is part of the human condition. It is an intensification of our tendency to become attached to things in our experience. In moderation, attachment can be enjoyable. Just consider your favorite meal or an activity that you truly enjoy. It is beautiful to savor life's pleasures and accept this experience for the blessing that it is.

The challenge comes when we become reliant upon that meal, that activity, in order to feel comfortable. When we cannot be at peace unless we have *this*, or when things in the outer world are set just *this* way, then we have a recipe for future crisis.

When we are addicted to something, it seems as if we don't have a choice. Whatever we're addicted to has the power of a need in our inner experience. We have lost our personal power in that area of our lives. Our addiction commands our attention and our response.

The tricky thing here is that anything can act like an addiction. Any habit or attachment that commands our attention also infringes upon our personal power. We can be addicted, for example, to drama, or to fear, or to chasing, or buying, or image, or many other things, just as we can be addicted to tobacco, alcohol, or prescription drugs.

All of these addictions are points of power loss. They are places where we do not have an active choice. We have to reclaim our power from this addiction in order to truly make a different choice. That's hard, every time. In order to make the shift, we have to be able to see the loop, see the triggers, and react differently when the triggers happen. Consistently, over time, as we program new habits.

When we're in the trenches of life, it's easy to get caught up in what we're doing and lose clarity. We have the things we have to do, the things we like to do, the things we're accustomed to doing. We have the things that pop up along the path, the curveballs life throws at us. With so much momentum built up and so many things going on, it can be hard to see where we are truly making choices and which choices will move us in the direction we'd like to go.

A small tip for future consideration: Watch out for energy sinks. Energy sinks are activities that take energy without giving anything in return. For example, sitting and watching television, or playing video games, or drinking, all of these things can take more than they give. Some people can also act as energy sinks in our experience. Energy sinks often feel good in the moment but do not positively contribute to our needs or values.

We can go hours, years, decades, spending our attention in this way and accomplish very little. Sometimes it's enjoyable to spend time and attention in these ways, and if what we're doing is working for us, awesome.

In the end, there's no one right way for every human being to live. That said, we all have a need to live our lives in a way that means something to us, in a way that builds, or creates, or grows, or explores something we believe in. On a long-enough timeline, all energy sinks begin to pale when compared to meaningful action and meaningful connection.

The question then becomes a practical one. How can we step out of this addictive lifestyle? How can we spend energy in our lives as we choose right now, rather than in ways that were chosen long ago?

Addiction vs. Meditation

> "The Fremen were supreme in that quality the ancients called "spannungsbogen" – which is the self-imposed delay between desire for a thing and the act of reaching out to grasp that thing."
>
> —Frank Herbert, *Dune*

Whether we're addicted to a drug, or drama, or a routine, or money, the result is the same in the inner world. As soon as we think of it, or we've been triggered, or we have an opportunity to engage with it, we feel an impulse to do so. Impulse, reaction. Just like a button being pushed.

All throughout our days, we have things that draw our attention and move us to reaction. These are hooks for our attention and triggers for our emotions. When we get triggered, we feel an inner push to action. When we think of something, or notice something, or get an urge from within, we move in response to it.

Each time we have an urge to reach out and grab something, we have an opportunity to reclaim just a little bit of personal power. To reconsider placing our attention and will in that direction. This is how habits are changed. One step at a time, over and over until new habits are formed.

This can be hard, especially at first. Crazy hard. Our long-term habits can colonize our inner space so thoroughly that it doesn't feel like we actually have a choice. But, as with all things, with practice, we get better at noticing the impulses and responding as we choose. We learn to be vigilant with ourselves, to keep our eyes open to our loops and the way they shape our lives. And slowly, we regain a bit more choice.

In a strange way, meditation and addiction are polar opposites. Addiction trains us to come running when the bell rings. Meditation teaches us to notice the bell, and let it pass. Anytime we can slow down, breathe, and create a bit of space around what we're feeling, we have more choice. More freedom.

When we meditate, we practice slowing down, allowing thoughts and feelings to come up and allowing them to pass. We will have things come up, urges and impulses, and we will have the opportunity to practice presence when they do. Instead of launching into action, or story, or emotional triggers, we have the opportunity to stand in our center.

We don't actually have to meditate in order to practice this. The key is consciousness. When the impulse occurs, notice it. Notice that you are making a choice, in where you put your attention, in how you engage emotionally, in what actions you take in response. Notice, and strive to make the choices you would truly like to make. And, when it comes to letting go of old habits, strive to starve them of your attention, replacing them with healthier focal points.

Boundaries

A boundary is a line that divides one thing from another. When it comes to physical space, most people are familiar with property lines. These boundaries determine the physical space under our care and stewardship. We manage the property within our boundaries, and we have a right to speak up when others use that space in ways that we are not comfortable with. In this case, the right use of our power, the right exercise of our will, is determined by the boundary of the property line.

We have boundaries in personal relationships as well. These are imaginary lines or limits that determine what we're ok with, what we're open to, and what we'll accept. Some people think that boundaries are unkind or selfish. These people tend to become enmeshed with those they interact with, without clear boundaries between their feelings and needs and those of the other person. Others have boundaries so excessive that they cut themselves off from others and impose their will upon those they interact with.

Unhealthy boundaries are a major point of personal power loss. Poor boundaries lead to resentment and conflict, codependency and control issues. On the other hand, healthy boundaries will tend to lead to healthy relationships. We all have limits, and at some point, these limits will be violated. We begin learning our boundaries when we learn how to be aware of our needs and speak up for ourselves.

There are two things required for establishment of healthier boundaries: self-awareness and communication. We have to be able to notice when our boundaries have been crossed, and we have to be able to communicate those limits in a healthy, constructive way.

Our boundaries are living, shifting things, renegotiated with each interaction. Healthy boundaries require us to be present to our own needs and feelings, capable of sitting with those feelings to gain clarity, and capable of speaking up for ourselves. When we respect both our own boundaries and those of others, our relationships transform, often in ways we didn't expect.

For the most part, people violate others' boundaries unintentionally, just as we allow our own to be violated unintentionally. This often happens because we are not clear with ourselves about our needs or feelings, or because we do not feel empowered to speak up or take action regarding our needs or feelings.

Put simply, most people don't have a clear understanding of healthy boundaries. Because of this, we often see dysfunctional relationships that don't work for either party.

Each person deserves boundaries around:

1. Their physical body, physical space, and physical needs.
2. Their emotional needs, being heard and validated.
3. Their time, as we all have a limited amount of time to commit.
4. Their sexuality, in terms of consent, preferences, privacy.
5. Their intellect, in terms of respect for ideas and curiosity.
6. Their property, in terms of money and material goods.

As we become more aware of our own boundaries, we also begin to notice others'. This is absolutely essential. If we don't respect others' boundaries, then they will not tend to respect our own. As we learn our boundaries, we also begin to learn our needs and to distinguish between needs, preferences, and habits.

When we gain clarity around these things, we can communicate them to others. We can give our loved ones the opportunity to show up for us in the relationship. And, right alongside that, we become better at showing up for those we care about.

Respect and Sovereignty

People often resist when we begin to develop healthier boundaries. Some of this is because we are initially clumsy in the enforcement of our boundaries, still overcoming our own defensiveness. Some of it may come from the fact that others have become accustomed to our unhealthy boundaries, especially when they benefit from the situation.

When we first begin to honor our boundaries, we also begin to renegotiate our interactions with others in our lives. It's important to remember that all healthy interactions are mutual. They are based on a foundation of respect and consideration for one another's needs and feelings. If we want others to respect our own boundaries, it's important that we respect theirs. Living in this way teaches us integrity and inspires trust in those we relate with.

Respect is the number one key to move into healthier relationships and a happier life overall. When we respect our own needs and boundaries, we take on the responsibility of making sure those needs are met and that those boundaries are not violated. We learn to speak up for ourselves.

When we also respect the other person that we're interacting with, we view them as a being, just as we are. We strive to treat them with the same consideration for their needs and boundaries that we would like to receive from them. And we learn how to communicate our needs without veering into defensiveness or unnecessary aggression. This approach can help to heal ruptures and form strong bonds.

A key concept here is sovereignty. We are all sovereign of our inner world, of our world of meaning and emotion. No one influences this world without our consent and participation. We are free to make meaning in the way that suits us, to spend our attention in the way we choose. We are free to create consequences in our lives as we see fit.

At the same time, we share this journey with others. Our actions impact everyone we share a home with, share a close relationship with, share space with, anyone we teach and influence. When we come together in collaboration, we make agreements with one another as to how we will pool our time and resources, and around how we will relate emotionally, intellectually, and practically. We establish agreements and boundaries to support this mutual interaction.

These agreements are, for the most part, made unconsciously. They're made for the purpose of shared survival and shared wellbeing. A healthy family or tribe will support the physical wellbeing of all within it while still leaving room for individual growth and expression.

In order to establish this, each person must take responsibility for voicing their own boundaries and needs in a healthy way. Also, each person must take it upon themselves to honor the needs and boundaries of others to the best of their ability.

None of us exists within a blank canvas. We are social creatures, part of a living ecology. Everything that we do in the world is done in this medium, this context. We are growing alongside others, sharing space in the garden of life.

The right use of our power is towards the fulfillment of our needs within our healthy boundaries. This benefits massively from an equal respect for our own sovereignty and for that of others we share space with. A conscious use of our personal power teaches us to take responsibility for our journey and create as we will, while remaining considerate of the impact of our actions on others. It teaches us to form a healthy, balanced, and sustainable relationship with our world.

Passive, Aggressive, Assertive

When our boundaries are unhealthy, we often see-saw between passive and aggressive. We may say nothing when a boundary has been crossed, bottling up everything inside until… the dam finally breaks! When we have aggressive outbursts like this, we usually communicate in unhealthy and destructive ways. We create rifts that must be healed before we can return to smooth, healthy interaction.

The challenge is that we have to start finding our power before we can give ourselves permission to speak. We have to learn to be aware of our boundaries and have the courage to say something when they've been crossed. And ideally, when we do speak up, we will say something that actually reflects what's going on for us. When we do enforce our boundary, we also renegotiate it for future interactions.

When we are overly passive, we negotiate fuzzy boundaries that welcome people to ask too much. Fuzzy boundaries let our needs go unvoiced and unmet. But that situation can't last forever. When we first learn to speak up for ourselves, we often have to get over a massive hump of resistance from within. We might have to get a bit aggressive, mostly to overcome our internal timidity. And that's the first step.

Aggression can help us to enforce a boundary and push away uncomfortable thoughts, emotions, and people. But in order to have healthy boundaries, we have to take the next step. We have to move from aggressive to assertive.

Aggressive communication is defensive. It creates arguments. Assertive communication comes from confident, clear expression of our needs or boundaries. We can be assertive when we understand the boundary that has been crossed and when we can communicate it clearly with the hopes of overcoming the issue. When we can express our boundaries calmly, without fear or anticipation of conflict.

Sometimes things come up, and the best thing for us to do is step back. At least for a moment. Long enough for the pain or self-righteous defensiveness to ebb off so that we can get some clarity around the situation. And, once we can see what's coming up for us, we can then ask ourselves how best to move forward.

There are two sides to every interaction, and really winning means coming to a smooth, workable relationship with every person or situation in our lives. To this end, clarity is an invaluable ally. In learning to tune in to our boundaries and striving to respect others' perspectives, we start to notice how much of our lives, how much of our conflict with others, is a result of projection. We see what we expect to see in so many subtle ways.

So often, the conflict that we encounter with others is the same conflict that we're playing out inside. By striving to let go of our emotional momentum and open up to other perspectives, we can completely change the game. It can help us to let go of old stories and the dynamics that come with them.

Real, healthy communication gives us a mirror to see ourselves and come to terms with what we see. It helps us to see our stories in a new light and relate to them in healthier ways.

Values and Authentic Motivation

Take a moment and think back to a time when you were doing a task you love to do. Think about how it felt inside, the energy, warmth, and engagement with the moment. Remember how the task came out. How was the final product? If it's something less tangible, like music, how did it sound and feel as it was coming out?

Now think back to a task that you *didn't* really want to do. What did *that* feel like? A drudge perhaps? Or like you're only half there? What did the finished product look like? Good enough, maybe?

From the inside, there's just one difference between these two tasks. One, you wanted to do. The other you didn't. And because of this, one felt like a burden, and the other a joy.

Much of the time, it's like we force ourselves through life, driving through the uncomfortable spots with persistence and force of will. This works. Sometimes. For a little while. And it's a really important approach to have in our repertoire, but it's not the best life strategy.

Much of the situation at hand is what we make of it. In every moment, we choose where we put our attention, how we engage with that moment. Every moment we are alive is a blessing, on some level, in some way. And every task is an opportunity to learn and grow, on some level, in some way. When we put our attention on the things that make this moment worthwhile, life feels better.

This is not the same as ignoring our needs or shirking our duties and practical responsibilities. Each time we do a task required for the fulfillment of our needs, or to establish healthy connections with others, or to support our loved ones, each time is an opportunity. It's an opportunity to align our will with our moment, to be alive and engaged with what we're doing right Now.

Even when doing the dishes or folding the laundry, we can practice presence, grace, and economy of motion. We can cultivate consciousness and gratitude. Whatever means something to you, whatever you most care about, there is a way to connect with that in the moment, even in the most mundane of tasks. We can orient even the smallest details of our lives towards the service of our values, creating powerful meaning in the mundane.

Life becomes much easier when we learn to want what we have, rather than chasing what we don't have. But it doesn't stop there. As soon as we look for opportunities to learn, grow, and deepen, we find them. In ways that we didn't expect. Shifting from, "why am I even doing this?" to "how can I get the most growth out of this situation?"

is a massive transformation. It takes us from a survival mindset to one focused on thriving.

Authentic Motivation

What do you want? Why do you want it? What is the core feeling at the base of this desire? What emotion, experience, or story motivates it?

It's incredibly helpful for us to ask ourselves these questions, and then to answer ourselves as clearly as we can. This is a challenging process, in part because it takes work and honest questioning to come to know ourselves. The things we want, and our real motivations for wanting them, may not fit very well with how we'd like to see ourselves.

We often grow our desires and attachments unconsciously and we begin this process young, before our conscious memory. So, for example, we may have learned that when we have money and success, then we will be safe, or accepted, or loved. Perhaps we learn that we need to be attractive in order to be worthwhile, so every new outfit, pair of shoes, or shade of make-up catches our eye. Maybe that muscle car is what makes us cool by getting acceptance from our peers.

When they are stated outright, we can see that these desires are not quite aligned with our real motivation. True motivations are inner qualities, like worth, acceptance, and love. We are all motivated by safety as well, and it is important to make sure our physical needs are met.

That said, nothing we purchase or achieve can buy us acceptance, love, or worth. These inner qualities, our true motivations, are things that we have to give to ourselves. And they radiate outward from there, shining into our interactions, and reflecting from our words and deeds.

Everything we do, we choose to do, at least on some level. We don't have unlimited choices or unlimited resources. But we still have a choice every time. So, even when we do things that we don't want to do, there is some reason we have chosen to do it. Maybe we don't like the alternative. Maybe we don't see another option. But when it comes down to it, there is a reason we *want* to do it, given the situation we're working with.

Step one of authentic motivation is knowing that *we have chosen this moment*, this situation, on some level. This is what's happening right now. Step two is reviewing these choices consciously, assessing our true, inner motivations. Asking ourselves if this is the best way to address that inner need. Asking ourselves if it's what we truly want. Balancing it against the other things that we want. And then putting our energy where we really want it to go.

Each moment we can tune in to "want to" rather than "have to" is a win. When we know why we *want to do what we're doing right now,* we can show up for it. We can do it better and enjoy it more in the process. And, when we can ask ourselves what we want to do, rather than just what we have to do, we can finally start choosing instead of reacting.

Core Values

What are your values?
What drives you?
What are you passionate about?
What do you believe in?

After consistent, honest, and humble introspection, we start getting some real answers to these questions. It's very challenging, and sometimes it's easier to work with a partner who's on the same journey. When we begin asking ourselves why we want what we want, we often see loads of childish things that we thought we'd outgrown. But, on an unconscious level, they have been influencing all of our decisions, driving us in one direction or another for the bulk of our lives.

It can feel really exposed, sometimes humiliating, to see these childish desires and motivations. It's much easier to justify them, explain them, bypass them, or dress them up in more acceptable clothing. But this is the only way to really move on. We have to be willing to look at these things, to make space to feel and process the emotions around them, before we can make new choices. We can begin to get those childish parts of ourselves up to speed with our conscious mind, just by accepting them, owning them.

As we tune in to the desire behind the thing we want, the inner quality that motivates us, we come to find that this is a core value that we feel, It's something that matters to us, a quality that we want in our lives. And, once we can see it more clearly, we often find that this core value can be better served with a different approach.

In the examples above, acceptance, worth, and love were the core values. So, we may wish to be pretty because we want to feel loved and accepted. Or we may wish to have money because we value freedom, safety, and practicality. If we truly understand *why* we want something, if we understand the core value behind it, we often see that there are better ways to approach the goal.

When we understand our core values, our communication becomes much clearer and more powerful. Every human being is different, but we're all human. And, as such, we share some fundamental core values. If we speak in terms of these shared values, what we have to say will resonate more deeply with others.

From this perspective, clear self-knowledge, a deep and thorough understanding of one's core values, is the most powerful asset for a leader, for one who influences the hearts and minds of those around them.

Emotion & Intention

In the inner world, emotion can be described as charge, as a force that moves us and moves through us. Intention, in the inner world, could be described as a point of focus. In essence, everything we do, consciously or unconsciously, is given force by our emotions and focused by our intention.

It should be clarified at this point that we are not conscious of all of our intentions. There are times when our unconscious intentions are at odds with our conscious understanding. Each person builds their own unique maze in their minds, so it is up to each of us individually to explore that maze and figure out how to navigate it. But suffice it to say that humans often do things, quite intentionally, that our conscious minds have no awareness of.

Whatever intentions and emotions we hold, they will be reflected in the decisions we make, in when and how we take action, and in what we perceive and respond to. This is the underlying mechanism behind all prayer, ritual, visualization, inner work, magic. All processes of intentional inner change work in the medium of emotion and intention. All personal growth and healing involve clearing old emotion and intention, letting in fresh emotion and cultivating new intentions, more in line with our current needs.

Setting a clear intention can give deep meaning to an otherwise mundane act. On an inner, psychological level, it's not so much about what we do. It's about what it means to us, about the intentions that shape our actions. When we set an intention, we bring specific, consciously chosen meaning to the action, to the experience. We align with that meaning and prime ourselves to relate to the world in support of it.

For many, this may seem a bit abstract. But think about it this way: the next time you have a challenging task or experience ahead of you, set an intention. Set an intention as to how you would like to conduct yourself in that situation. You might even set a background intention to get as much growth, strength, and resilience as you can out of the major hurdles of life. And then pay attention to how this changes the quality of the experience.

This tiny shift in attitude can completely transform how we engage with the world. Setting an intention formalizes, to our inner self, how we would like to show up for our journey.

Reclaiming Our Power: The First Steps

We have, each of us, spent a lifetime cultivating the habits we now carry. We have habits in how we move our bodies, how we relate to others, how we respond emotionally to the situations we encounter. We have habitual stories that flesh out the context of our lives, explaining our life history and current situation to ourselves.

Our habits, and the thoughts that accompany them, continuously reiterate our view of the world. When they get big enough, they can look like the whole world. Reclaiming our power means, to a huge extent, reviewing our unconscious habits. Becoming conscious of them, so that we have a choice in that area of our lives. So that we can reclaim just a bit of freedom.

To this end, watch for your loops and your triggers. Map out the hooks that catch your attention. Our attention is like a tuner for our conscious experience. Whatever takes hold of your attention, forces it here or there, also relieves you of your freedom. Whether it's a habit, a story, or an individual, if this thing commands your attention, then you have given your personal power away to it.

Personal Power and Boundaries

Becoming aware of our needs and boundaries is essential for reclaiming our personal power. And becoming mindful of others' needs and boundaries is essential if we'd like to use our power in healthy, constructive ways. Each time we learn how to speak up for our needs and honor our boundaries, we reclaim just a little bit of our personal power. And, if we are present and conscious in our relating, we can learn to do this in a way that leads to smooth, healthy interactions with others.

We step into our power when we speak up for ourselves to others. And we do the same on an inner level when we are honest with ourselves. When we are clear and authentic with ourselves about what we want, what we feel we need, and why we feel we need it, we can stop running from ourselves and stop denying ourselves. We can gather in all of the scattered threads of our being and move forward with integrity.

We lose power when we act in ways we don't believe in, when we do things out of alignment with our values. In these cases, we have crossed our own inner boundaries, perhaps ones we didn't know we had. To reclaim that power, we must learn to be true to ourselves, whatever that looks like in our lives. We must learn to honor our own boundaries and take it upon ourselves to speak up or take action when these boundaries require it.

The journey to truly honoring our boundaries begins with taking accountability, with owning our lives and our situation, knowing that we choose, each day, each moment. Next, we have to figure out what we actually value, what we really want to choose. And do it. In the moment, where it really matters, and with an eye for the future we create with this choice.

Every time we act with integrity, every time we listen and respond with our whole beings, we train ourselves to do so in the future. And, in the process, we reclaim power from all the fears, doubts, and other obstacles that, in the past, have prevented us from having clear boundaries and living an intentional life aligned with our values.

Personal Power and Space

Another way that we can begin stepping into our power is to become conscious of our space. How do you hold the space around you? Do you shrink in, trying to take up as little space as possible? Do you bull (or stumble) through, unconscious of what's around you? Do you take center stage, trying to be in the middle of the action?

However you show up in your space is how you're likely to show up in life. Hold yourself, and the space around you, in a way that you really want to show up. Perhaps that's confident, poised, or calm. Perhaps it's engaged, joyful, or powerful. Whatever quality you want to bring to your life, hold that feeling in your body and in your space. Keep coming back to this, practicing it until it becomes natural. And remember, it's not about how it looks. The feeling is the key.

As a natural extension of this, we can start to tune in to how we keep our personal physical space, whether it is our room, our home, or our business. We can pay attention to that space, open it up, fill it with life, and make it work for us.

We feel the space around us, often unconsciously. The feeling in a space sets the tone for the interactions and activities that take place within it. It creates a container for specific types of actions, interactions, emotions, and dynamics. We can work with this by learning to consciously qualify the space we hold.

As we begin to take hold of our lives, we'll often start to get our house in order, from the inside out. First our breath, feelings, and attention. Then, learning our stories and making peace with ourselves. Then extending this into the life we're living, clearing and organizing the space around us, making it supportive of what we would like to do in that space. And it ripples outward from there, as we consciously create our lives and share our voice.

As we reclaim our personal power, our lives become steadily more intentional and streamlined towards our authentic values. This is reflected in any area of our life which benefits from our attention. We learn to feel this clarity and hold it in the space around us, on both tangible and subtle levels, and our action, words, and life situations shift to match.

Personal Power and Voice

On a fundamental human level, our power is linked to our voice. Our voice is a symbol of being heard, of our capacity to relate to others and express ourselves. A major aspect of reclaiming personal power is to find our voice, to discover our message and give ourselves permission to speak it.

When we open our mouths and speak up, we allow ourselves to be heard. This can leave us feeling exposed and vulnerable. That's completely understandable. It's the rare person who has not, at some point in their lives, felt rejected, unaccepted. Sometimes, we learn to hide ourselves, to stay quiet and keep a low profile. Other times we learn to shout from the rooftops. But if you listen closely to the shouting, you might notice an edge of desperation under the enthusiasm. Bravado based on insecurity.

We hide in subtle ways, and our voice, what we say, how we say it, whether and when we choose to speak, reflects how much we hide or how freely we express ourselves. But it can be very challenging to speak up, especially when we have a history of remaining silent. Even if we speak freely, we may not be inclined to express the things that really matter to us, those we feel sensitive or insecure about.

One practice which can help us to find our voice is singing. When we sing, we lift our voices and make a joyful noise, if we can. Because singing really puts us out there where we can be heard and seen. Each one of us experiences doubts and pain, each one of us has felt rejected, unworthy. And when we sing, all of those feelings tend to come up. This makes it an ideal practice for meeting those feelings, allowing them to be and to pass while we engage with the business of singing.

Some people have trouble with singing. You may feel like your voice isn't very good, or you may believe that you don't have a singing voice at all. The truth of it is that everyone's voice is different, and we can all sing sweetly if we know how to work with our own voice. Mostly if we allow it to flow without constricting or over-controlling.

But, if singing is too much at first, toning can work wonders. Toning is just lifting your voice, just like humming along with music. And, it's one of the gentlest ways to bring these feelings up, sit with them, and move past them, all while we're reclaiming our voice.

If you'd like to practice toning, you may want to try it in private first. Let yourself make some noise. Maybe it's a little impromptu melody, maybe just some sound. Whatever it is, let it come out and notice how it feels. Spend some time with it, making sounds for the joy of it, just as a child might. See how loud you can be. Make higher and lower tones, string them together, and through it all, pay attention to the feelings and thoughts that come up.

Are you keeping quiet? Even though no one's around? Does your throat feel tight? Are you focused on performance? Criticizing your voice? Does it feel good? Like your voice has been waiting for a chance to come out?

Toning helps us to open up. It is a way of allowing ourselves to be seen and heard. Each time we raise our voice, just make a sound and enjoy what comes out, we get a little bit more comfortable with it. Over time, we might start to feel comfortable toning even when others are around. Making sound just because it feels good and letting our voice carry.

Toning and singing also help on a practical physical level, in learning how to open your chest and throat, how to breathe so that the voice can be strong. On a psychological level, working with the voice means taking symbolic action to embrace our power. It may sound a bit silly, but these symbolic actions can be extremely transformative. Opening up our voice is like coming out of hiding. Lifting it up with song teaches us to express ourselves with confidence and grace.

What Do You Really Want?

It can be really challenging to figure out what we want. The little stuff is easy. Maybe we want to eat *this* for dinner, or we know that we want to have *that* personal item. Some basic things are easy as well; no one wants to be hungry or thirsty, freezing or overheating. Some things are fundamentally human. On some level, we all want security, growth, love, change, meaning, and creative expression.

Past that, it's all completely unique. Personal desires and values attuned to a unique personal journey. In simple terms, we all have to look within to decide what we really care about. All the things we seek in the outer world – money, possessions, status – are symbols of what we really want. They are symbols of inner qualities like acceptance, security, and worth.

It's important to take care of our practical needs. To pay the bills, put food on the table, build and run business, make things happen in the outer world. That said, anything we set our hands to in the outer world fares better when we understand our motivations for doing it. Any collaboration will work better if we understand the shared values that inspire the collective action.

Once we've addressed our immediate, pressing needs, and once we review our old habitual desires, something really special begins to happen. Our entire motivational structure begins to shift. We start to move from "have to" to "want to." This is a huge step in reclaiming our personal power, and it's a process.

At first, we may not feel motivated at all, especially if we've been goading ourselves through our lives like a reluctant bull. Soon, though, we'll find ourselves moved to show up in support of others around us. We begin to discover that everything that really means something to us comes in the form of connection, with ourselves, others, and our world.

At some point in our journey, if we're lucky, we discover that we want more than just the fulfillment of momentary pleasures, or the acquisition of material possessions, or the fulfillment of physical needs and desires.

At some point, we realize that we care. About something. It may present itself to us as Truth, or good, or kindness, or beauty. It might take the form of patriotism or ecological activism or social justice. It might just be about showing up for our loved ones each day. Whatever that is that we care about, that's something we value. It's something that can lift us out of our shell and brings us into meaningful contact with our world.

The Sacred Wound

Before we can even start to step into our power, we first have to come to a place of acceptance of ourselves and our lives. The biggest block to accepting our lives is pain. Each of us, at some point of the journey, will deal with loss and death. Each of us will deal with guilt and shame. Each of us will make mistakes that we regret.

We can make peace with many of these things over time. We can learn to find the good in them, or see how they have taught us, strengthened us. But there are some things that we simply can't make peace with. Maybe we've been hurt or betrayed or deceived, and we just can't move on from it. If this is the case, we may have encountered a sacred wound.

Consider the person who grew up on the streets, and then went on to serve at homeless shelters after their life turned around. Or the person who has mistreated a loved one and who uses this experience as a reminder and inner drive to never again treat a loved one in this fashion. The old pains, those we can't move on from, can drive us to step into service to the world. To help others who are on a similar journey to our own, those who are faced with similar pains, trials, and regrets.

When we encounter a sacred wound, we have the opportunity to find meaning in challenge, to turn our pain into strength. When we honestly face our pain again and again, we learn compassion. And, when we can act upon that compassion, again and again turning our personal challenge into support for others, we learn wisdom.

All of these things transform our lives slowly, by degrees. Eventually, we find that our wound has become a beacon of healing and growth, for ourselves and others. It has become a key part of our life's purpose.

The Petty Tyrant

Each day, we interact with someone who has power over us. This power may come in financial, practical terms, like the power an employer has over us. It may come in emotional terms, like the sword of guilt wielded by mothers the world over. Sometimes this power comes in intellectual terms, as when we give our critical understanding away to accept without question the thoughts and ideas of another.

These people have power over us because we have given that power to them. We give our power away to our employer by entering into an agreement, an exchange of our personal power for something we want or need, in this case, money to pay the bills. We might give our power away to our loved ones by modifying our behavior in the hopes of receiving approval or love, by taking their perception of us as our own.

We give power over our inner world to others all the time, just as others give their power away to us. We may do it because we feel we need approval, or acceptance, or security, or worth. In the end, on the level of personal power, it all amounts to the same thing. In the hopes of getting something we want or something we feel we need, we give away our power and attach our sense of wellbeing to someone or something in our outer world. And then we become beholden to that thing in our experience.

Often this is reasonable, even helpful. The exchange between employer and employee can work and can be necessary for our lives at the moment. We enter into this exchange willingly, for the most part, and it serves us to do so. With friends and loved ones, especially those we look up to or those that we would like to see us and accept us, it can be reasonable to give some portion of our power away to them. As children, we look up to our parents and we try to earn their love with our behavior. When young, we naturally give our power away to our parents.

Now consider the example of the child trying to earn the love of a parent so self-absorbed that they abuse the power that has been handed to them. How about when parents live vicariously through their children, or when they consistently use guilt to ensure that the child does what they ask? How about the employer that uses their financial leverage to violate their employees' time boundaries, or to manipulate them into the kind of behavior the employer desires?

Whenever we use our power in selfish ways, in ways that are inconsiderate of or disrespectful of others, we have become a petty tyrant. When someone wants or feels they need something from you, and you use that to get what you want, you are acting as a petty tyrant. Whenever, even for the best of intentions, we impose our will, our perspective, our approach, upon others, we are acting as petty tyrants.

This is incredibly common in the world of today. Many people are unaware of both their power and their boundaries. In this space, it is easy to impose our will upon others and allow others to impose their will upon us. We will tend to unconsciously violate boundaries and allow our own to be violated. When we are imbalanced like this, it's always both at once. We will have areas where we impose upon others, and areas where we have given our power away and allow others to impose upon us.

Any time you encounter a petty tyrant, remember compassion. A bully is a bully because of pain and insecurity. People who control others are often very afraid of what would happen if they didn't. The world feels very big and scary, and strategic use of power is one way to feel safe. At the same time, remember that this petty tyrant is giving you an opportunity.

Whenever we notice that someone has power over us, we have the opportunity to become aware of points of power loss. We gave this power to them. We may have given them the power to make us feel unworthy, unloved, unsafe, or unseen. To feel threatened or cornered.

We gave this power to them because we wanted something or were afraid of something. And, on some unconscious level, we decided that this person was a way – maybe the only way – to get what we want or avoid what we fear. So, for a time, we lost our center, trying to say, do, and be what the other wants.

Remember that no one has any more power over our inner world– the world of our thoughts, feelings, and will– than we give them. When we encounter someone who uses the power we give them in ways that don't work for us, it's time to take it back. Time to ask ourselves what we want from this person, why we want it, and if our approach to getting it is really working for us. Time to have faith in our capacity to fulfill our needs, even and especially when we let go of interactions that are not right for us.

Taking our power back from a petty tyrant can look like stepping away from a relationship or interaction that's not working for us. It can look like renegotiating boundaries in a current relationship, or learning to give ourselves the approval we were trying to get from others. Often, we take our power back with forgiveness, or when we are finally honest with ourselves or others.

Petty tyrants can sniff out weak points in our psyche, chinks in our armor. So, when trying to get our power back from an unhealthy interaction, we can expect the other to strike our blind spots, those things we are still learning to accept and make peace with.

This is a blessing! We're so good at hiding from ourselves that it's great to have some help finding these points of stuck pain and potential growth. Consciously and intentionally stepping into an interaction with a petty tyrant can be amazing for stimulating old pains, unconscious stories, and inner blocks.

However, this requires caution. Petty tyrants, whether they know what they're doing or not, tend to be champion button pushers, phenomenal at triggering people. We can go unconscious quickly when triggered. And in this case, going unconscious means doing the same thing that didn't work with this person before.

A final tip regarding petty tyrants: Inner freedom means having a choice. This choice becomes power when we use it to create things in our lives. The key to balancing power and freedom is purpose. Purpose is something we value, something that has meaning for us. Purpose is inspired from within like a seed, and blossoms outward into the world through our actions. Purpose, whatever form it takes, is service.

Petty tyrants do not understand this. They have their power, and they have a choice about how to use that power. But the highest principle that the petty tyrant understands is their own will. The highest logic the petty tyrant understands is their own justification, their personal narrative of the world. When we dedicate ourselves to something larger than ourselves, when we use our power to create something we believe in, it becomes the new center of our journey.

When you decide what you would like to do with this gift of life, what quality you would like to champion, then you gain a new compass. Regardless of others' opinions, you have a goal, something of value that you can approach with each moment, each decision, each conversation. This will not eliminate conflict with petty tyrants, but it will give you a source of strength and clarity that makes the leverage of a bully seem a lot less intimidating.

Perhaps even more important, by finding a sense of purpose and dedicating our lives to values and virtues we truly believe in, we can avoid becoming petty tyrants ourselves. For the average person, this question may not come up. If you don't know what you want to do, if you don't realize that every choice is an expression of power, then it may never occur to you that we need practical guidelines to use this power with integrity.

When we are clear about our core values and use every act, every word, to support these values, then the whole of our life becomes a coherent message. It begins to form a clear and powerful picture of the virtues that we feel and resonate with. Which virtues, what purpose, this is personal. We all have to find it – to feel it – ourselves, in personal terms. And then, in those same personal terms, we begin to learn how we can dedicate our lives to the values we've discovered within.

Meaning, Purpose, & Service

Meaning is massive in the inner world. We respond not to a situation, but to what that situation *means* to us. To make things more interesting, the meaning of a situation is personal, different for each person. We can also tune in to different meanings in an experience.

To see this more clearly, just consider something in your past, a point of pain and growth. In all likelihood, it means something different to you now than it did in the moment. Over time and with growth, we tend to align with new and deeper meanings, things we didn't see in the moment, but which stand out to us now. The same event in our personal history means *this* to us now instead of *that*.

We interpret the situations we experience. We then make meaning out of a sequence of images, definitions, or remembered experiences. Most of the time we interpret things unconsciously. In other words, we make meaning unconsciously. And, when we do that, it may not seem like we're *making meaning* at all. *This* is what happened, and of course I feel *this* way about it. We blend our stories and sense impressions without discrimination.

It is a massive step towards freedom – towards choice – when we can distinguish interpretation from actual sense experience. When we can tell the difference between what we actually perceived and how we personally interpreted and responded to it. This shows us how we make meaning in a situation, how we tend to selectively interpret bits of our experience.

Meaning becomes even more important when we look at our lives as a whole. On some level, past the part of us that just wants to survive, to be comfortable, to feel good, past all that is a part of each human being that wants their lives to be meaningful. We all, somewhere deep down, want our lives to matter.

The key to making our lives meaningful is to find a purpose, and dedicate all of our efforts, all of our being, to this purpose. Different religions and spiritual traditions offer this purpose in the form of a story, a concept. This is beautiful, helpful in many instances. But if we find our purpose in a story, the way to fulfill that purpose is to share that story with others. To give them the same meaning you have borrowed.

At the core, each of these stories is intended to inspire a feeling, a sense of connection with the world, a path to purposeful, healthy interaction with our world. The story helps to illustrate a value, but it is not the value itself. The next step of the journey, for each of us, is to align our lives with this value. Not with the story, but with the quality it is intended to foster. And we all do that in our own way.

No one can tell you what form your purpose will take. Each person is on their own unique journey, and each will come to their sense of purpose in personal terms, in the context of their lives. Borrowed meaning can only get you so far.

One thing common to all human beings, though, is that our purpose takes us out of ourselves. It lifts us beyond our personal interests and moves us to contribute meaningfully to the world around us. In whatever way resonates with us.

It's not uncommon for people to try to help the world even before they have found their purpose. And, while this is beautiful and virtuous in intention, until we have done work to make peace with ourselves and reclaim our power, it's just window dressing.

Our true purpose receives confirmation from within. If we wish others to see the good works that we do, then those works come (deep down) from a place of fear or desire, rather than from a place of conscious, intentional purpose aligned with personal values. Our true values guide us even when there are no witnesses and no rewards.

The best thing that we can offer the world is our conscious, healthy presence. We can also share many practical and tangible gifts with the world. But this sharing will have the most integrity and best impact when backed up by conscious, healthy presence.

So, the first step to standing in service in the highest and best way is to dedicate ourselves to our own healing and self-knowledge. Our life purpose grows naturally from this space, as we gain clarity around our values and regain the personal power to take action aligned with these values.

How do I know?

Here is one question I've heard many times: How do I find my purpose? How do I know that it is the right purpose?

The right purpose is the one you choose. At the same time, it is the one that calls to you, through your heart, through the experiences that you have had and what they mean to you.

Our purpose comes knocking through the things we care most about and would most like to offer the world. Through what we love, what we see as important, what we're passionate about. Our passion and purpose come to us through the pain that inspires us to care. This is where you will find your purpose, but it only becomes yours when you choose it.

RECLAIMING PERSONAL POWER: PRACTICES

Practice 1: Not Doing

Not doing is an extremely simple practice, in principle. And completely self-explanatory. This is the practice for reclaiming personal power in the first scope of time, in the now. And, if you've ever tried to quit a habit, you know it's much easier said than done.

Not doing is something that anyone can do, but to be practiced and successful at it, we must start with a strong foundation. In the moment, this means a foundation of mindfulness and presence. It also means we need some practice with shadow work, in exploring how our minds play with our experience and color it with charge.

In order to consistently practice not doing, we must also learn how to be aware of impulses when they come up within and learn to redirect those impulses in a healthy way. We must begin to self-parent, to host our inner temple and be aware of the visitors within, many of which are old stories, feelings, and patterns that are no longer in alignment with our lives.

The next step is to be on the lookout for points of personal power loss, hooks for the attention, triggers for the emotions. Look for the loops that give nothing back, the energy sinks that greedily drink up your time, money, attention, vitality.

Pick one. Just one. And starve it of your energy, of your attention and your will. Whatever habit, whatever emotional or behavioral reaction pattern you'd like to move past, sit with it. Feel it. Look within to understand what it's doing for you, why you have chosen this. Find your meaning in this experience or issue. Let yourself feel into it and create space around the feeling.

Next, get clear about what you would like to do with that energy. All that attention, energy, will, needs to go somewhere. What are you going to build with it? How are you going to use this newfound energy, this extremely uncomfortable inner pressure, to move your life in the direction you'd like to go?

Make no mistake. Not doing is hard work. It's taken years – sometimes decades – of meticulous cultivation to develop our habits as they are now. To train specific behavioral patterns and emotional reactions, specific patterns in interpretation and meaning-making. It will take a commitment to just as many years of hard work to make new, healthier patterns.

It is the rare person who can dedicate themselves to this level of growth without some crisis to prompt them. But the more we wholeheartedly dedicate ourselves to growth in each situation from the outset, the less severe the crisis when it hits.

Sustainable growth and transformation happen in baby steps. One teeny thing at a time. Consistency is more important than intensity. So, pick one thing, and practice not doing. Reclaim your power. And, when it comes time, pick another, and so on. Over time, the bubble of your conscious will expands. Almost imperceptibly, we start to move into a larger and more meaningful connection with the world.

Each time we are tempted to go into old patterns, old habits, triggers, we are also given an opportunity to practice not doing. This is a powerful tool in the arsenal of consciousness. Every time we're tempted and we overcome that temptation, we win. In that one moment, we have practiced not doing.

If we're aware that we are cultivating the power of not doing, then we become better at it over time. Stronger, more disciplined.

And our lives begin to shift in kind, coming into greater alignment with the lives we'd like to live.

Practice 2: Transformation

Change is one of the few constants of life. When we live and respond unconsciously, the change in our lives appears random from our perspective. Things just happen to us. However, as soon as we start to reclaim our power and make conscious choices, we get in the driver's seat. At this point, we begin to learn the art of transformation, the art of guiding the changes of our life in a direction that we would like to go.

Every moment, we die to who we were before, and we are reborn in who we are becoming. And, as we do, we can move forward with intention, aligned with our values. We can release old stories and patterns, gain clarity around our values, and learn to dedicate our lives to these values.

The challenge is that some old patterns don't want to let go. Or, to put it a bit differently, we don't know how to let go of them. Sometimes we need a little bit of help.

In the second scope of time, linear time, we can make use of processes, such as ritual, prayer, and guided visualization, to intentionally release old patterns and old conceptions of self.

In this section, we will cover two completely different processes. The first is a shamanic journey, a visualization in which we experience the death of the body and watch as it's reformed, as it's rebuilt, healthy, strong, and renewed. This is a symbolic inner process, a way of focusing our intention to shift from one state to another, to let go of old stories, old charge, and open to the new.

The second process is recapitulation. With the practice of recapitulation, we revisit our life history and learn how to see it, to *feel it*, and to interpret it in life-affirming, strengthening ways.

Death and Rebirth

Death is one of the most powerful aspects of the human experience. We all deal with it, in one way or another. And it's never easy.

We are all going to die someday. Well, unless something really unprecedented happens. Our bodies will wear down, if we're lucky to get that far. And we don't really have any solid consensus on what happens next. So, it can be frightening.

It hurts when a loved one dies. If they are very close to our heart, this can be a deep hurt that takes a long time to come back from. That's hard, and it's real.

Because we have so much pain and uncertainty and fear – so much charge – around death, we often avoid the subject, or find comforting stories to invest our belief in to ward off the fear. There's nothing wrong with this. It's natural and, in a way, beautiful. That said, there is a rare strength and power that can be found by confronting the inevitability of our own death.

When we know that our time will end, every moment matters. We look back upon our life and we reflect upon what we see. How do we feel about the life we've led? What matters to us, at the end? Who matters to us? Have we made a difference? What kind of difference? For whom? How has our life been felt by our family, by the world?

When we put ourselves in that position, even in our imagination, we come face to face with some honest reflection and some hard questions. And this is *good*. This is how we deepen into our experience. This is how we get to know who we are and what we care about.

We can't change the past. What's done is done. But we have a choice, in this moment and for all of the moments yet to come. We can apply whatever clarity comes to us in these times to everything we experience from here on in. Do what really matters to you. Make your time count, according to your own values and needs. And remember that our healthy, balanced, and vital relationship with our world is more important than our story of self.

Death and Rebirth: A Shamanic Journey

For this particular journey, you will want to have privacy and a quiet and relatively comfortable space. If you can manage it without falling asleep, I'd recommend laying down, relaxing, and preparing to go deep.

Begin by closing your eyes and entering the journey state. Count downwards and breathe. Relax the body with a body scan. Slow your rhythm until you feel light, relaxed, and the mind is almost beginning to drift.

At this point, envision moving down a tunnel. Breathe, and simply let yourself move forward along this tunnel toward the opening. See yourself coming to the opening, and then, step out into a space in nature. Look around and see this space. See it in all the detail that you can. Allow it to form in your mind's eye.

What does the ground look like? The vegetation? Is it night or day? Is it warm or cool? How does this space feel?

In the journey space, we are in partnership with our deep mind, consciously suggesting, and then listening as the subconscious responds. Watch as this inner space becomes more detailed, as it takes on solidity in your mind.

Find yourself a comfortable place to sit in meditation in this inner space. Find the space within where you would like to meet death. Envision yourself sitting and becoming settled in this space, preparing for the journey ahead. Feel the ground beneath you and take in the view ahead.

Now take yourself to a month before your death. Place yourself there in your mind, see what it feels like. What do you want to do before you die? Who would you like to see, to spend your time with? Is there anything that needs to be said, anything that needs to be done, any air to clear? See yourself doing these things in preparation for the journey ahead.

When you're ready, take yourself to the week before your death. Seven short days. What will you do with them? How will you spend this time? What does it feel like? What comes up for you? Pay attention to whatever thoughts or feelings have been waiting here for you. Let them in and breathe space around them.

See yourself a day before your final moments. The last hour. Place yourself there, feel it, and see what comes up for you. And breathe…

And now the time has come. See yourself once again in your settled place, where you have waited to meet death. Watch your own body from the outside as time passes, faster and faster. The body dries, shrinks, and crumbles into dust. The dust settles to the earth, enriching the soil and becoming new life. Linger here, bodiless in this space, a memory. Simply...letting...go.

When you feel ready, watch as a new body is formed. View each part as it takes shape, growing healthy and strong within your mind's eye. Stay with this and view each detail. See this new body take form and refine, finding your proportions, your features. And then envision yourself, your being, moving into this body, filling it with life and consciousness. Feel it, this new body. Slightly more aligned, a slightly better fit. Sit with this and let it come through in greater detail.

When you are ready, view yourself standing up in this new body, returning to the mouth of the tunnel. Walk down the tunnel, and as you do, begin to notice your body in the outer world.

As you get to the end of the tunnel, this newly formed inner body merges with your outer body, strengthening it, smoothing, aligning. Teaching your body how to grow stronger and healthier. Teaching you to hold a different feeling in the space around your body.

Feel this space, this new body, feel it in your own body. Pay attention, and commit that feeling to memory. Anchor it in your body and your feeling space.

When you are ready, slowly, slowly, begin to deepen the breath. Sometimes this feels like coming up from deep water. Let it happen smoothly and gradually, speeding your breath and frequency a bit at a time. Bring a bit of energy and slight motion to your limbs. Wiggle fingers and toes, and, when you're ready, rise.

You may wish to record this experience in your journal for future reference. It can be extremely powerful on several levels, and we can revisit the process in times of trial and great change.

Remember what you learned in this experience. What it felt like. What truly mattered to you, in the end. Remember that you can take action about the things that really matter to you *right Now*. And for all the Nows to come.

You have been given a blessing, a gift, a life. What will you do with it?

Recapitulation In Depth

What does your life mean to you? What is your purpose? How has each event in your life helped you to grow and fulfill this purpose?

We are building a legend, each of us. Day by day, choice by choice, story by story. With the meaning we discover in our experiences. With the meaning that inspires our action. We can craft a truly remarkable legend with our lives, each of us and each in our own way. We can live in a way that makes life rich and full, in a way that forges us into a powerful force.

The key to all of this is the story of our lives. Our personal history, just like all history, has more to do with how we link things together than with what actually happened. We learn to interpret the things of our past unconsciously, in the one way that suggested itself to us in the moment. But when we look back at things we have experienced in younger times, we see them from a different perspective. They mean something a little bit different now.

We garden the meaning in our minds, tending it with our attention. We can tune in to meanings that break us down, wear the past like a yoke around our necks and spiral into depression. Or we can tune in to the meanings that separate us from the world, that make us feel like we have to look out for ourselves. Or we can tune in to those things which make life worth living, to the blessings that we can enjoy and share with one another. Whatever we choose.

With the practice of recapitulation, we review our personal history, and we begin to write our legend consciously, intentionally. We begin to learn the mythical epic of our lives, our dramatic journey of discovery, healing, and growth. Recapitulation looks different for each one of us. But for each of us, it begins with telling ourselves our own story. And we have to be open, real, authentic, honest. Anywhere we go, we start from there.

It is incredibly powerful to practice this with a journal. Each week, maybe each day, write a bit of your own story. See it take shape on the page in front of you. Hear it all, without judgment if possible. These things happened to the person that you were, and they helped to form the person that you are. They are still helping to form that person. How will they help to shape the person you become?

Write honestly, looking back over each experience and seeing how it has crafted you, shaped your path through life. Every challenge offers a gift, every hardship a strength. Every pain, when we make peace with it, offers wisdom and compassion.

At first, we tend to interpret things in a way that emphasizes the pain or depicts us as a hero. Neither one is ideal. We are all just people. No one's perfect. We've all made mistakes. And we become stronger when we can be vulnerable, when we can own our mistakes and learn from them.

Remember not to self-censor. When recapitulating, it's important that we intend to be shown ourselves, as we are. And it's equally important that we look upon the things of the past with fresh eyes, first feeling the old challenges and emotions, opening up to process and release these things. And finally discovering how this old story fits into your legend. Seeing how it supports your purpose and your values, how it has helped you to learn and grow, to understand what really matters to you and do something about it.

With the practice of recapitulation, we come to see ourselves more deeply than ever before. We gain clarity about our life's journey. We begin to see how our current moment is part of the legend, both in what we offer to the world right now and in how this experience forges us for future moments.

Each day, with each choice, we write a little bit more of our legend. And one day, if we're lucky, we will look back and realize that our legend has become more powerful, more meaningful, than any of those little stories we used to cling to.

Practice 3: Stalking

Drawn from the Toltec tradition, stalking is a life practice of reclaiming personal power. The image of stalking is taken from the dream of the second attention, from the image of the jaguar. The jaguar is a patient hunter, seeking out the best perch and waiting for their prey to pass beneath. The jaguar will evaluate each tree in terms of its value as a hunting perch. If one perch offers poor results, the jaguar will abandon the tree and explore the forest for another.

When we practice the art of stalking, we learn to hunt ourselves. We practice vigilance, taking note of the stories, charge, and habits that enter our inner space. We watch, internally, as things come up for us and we are moved to reaction. We watch for our loops and holding patterns. We watch for hooks that catch our attention and triggers that send us unconscious.

Our points of power loss will tend to hide in our blind spots or behind strong stories and justifications. It's often easier to believe that we're powerless, especially if we're doing something that's out of alignment with our values. It's easier to say, "That's not my fault. I didn't have a choice."

The simple, hard truth is that we always have a choice. We always make that choice, though we may be unconscious of it in the moment. Our entire journey through life is guided by the choices we make. Whenever you encounter an area in which you do not feel you have a choice, you've found a place where you have lost your power, where you have given it away to someone or something.

Shadow work is an essential part of the art of stalking. In shadow work, we recognize that our unconscious stories and charge will have an impact upon what we experience in the outer world. And, rather than blaming things in the outer world for our inner condition, we turn the tables. We look for patterns in our life experience, in our interactions with others. And then we look within to determine what feelings and stories align with these experiences.

Real change begins within. If we have not addressed those aspects of the inner world which move us into *this* kind of interaction, or *this* kind of situation, then we will unconsciously repeat these patterns. We will continue to unconsciously craft situations in the outer world that bring us face-to-face with our issues until we make peace with those issues, release them, and move forward. And then, as if by magic, we begin to experience new situations in the outer world.

Thus far, stalking has been discussed in terms of ferreting out blockages and points of power loss. There is another aspect of stalking which is just as valuable. As we learn to let go of old stories, we must find new ones. New perspectives, new, more life-affirming ways of making sense of our experience. New stories that inspire us, guide our decisions, and help us navigate more effectively through future situations.

In a way, this aspect of stalking is similar to being a method actor. So much of who we have come to know as ourselves, in the early stages of our development, is a role. It's a set of physical, mental, and emotional habits that we have played for so long that they have become natural. Reflexive. And it's tempting to think that that's just how we are. But we have a choice here as well.

Remember that we have a choice as to how we will interpret the situations we experience, the stories that we use to make sense of them. We could make sense of our current challenge with stories about bad luck, or the world trying to break us down. We could look at the same experience and see that it teaches us, points out our blind spots and helps motivate us to make meaningful change.

Each of these perspectives is a story, a way of making sense of the world. And, in the forest of the inner experience, each of these stories is a different tree, a different vantage point from which to hunt and view the forest. In the process of stalking, we gain skill at navigating our own mind, at working artistically with our own meaning and perspective. We learn to link our view of the world with the tree, the story that we use to view it.

When we intentionally take on a perspective, we can then watch to see how this perspective primes us to engage with the world. What kind of interactions and situations result from this story? Is there another way for me to view this situation? One that might be more helpful in meeting the situation constructively? Was I expecting this outcome, deep down? Is it the outcome I would like, one which is aligned with my values? Can I learn to expect, or at least to be open to, something different?

A final word about stalking: it helps to set a goal and work towards it. When we're drifting, we can't really tell if our navigation is working as we need it to. But, when we set a goal, when we try to move forward each day towards the accomplishment of this goal, we start to see the things that get in our way.

When we strive to move towards a desired outcome, we encounter stories that run counter to this outcome, inner blocks and limiting perspectives. By setting an intention and following through in the outer world, we are shown all of the inner qualities that stand in our way. And, when we meet these qualities like a warrior, they become ladder rungs for growth. Each time we encounter an inner limitation and learn to overcome it, we reclaim just a little bit of our power.

MODULE 6 - STORY AND DISCERNMENT

Introduction to Story and Discernment

How do we know what is true, and what is not? How do we distinguish between the two?

Human beings, as a species, have access to more information now than at any other time in recorded history. Any question that comes to mind, we can look up the answer in moments with the computers we carry in our pockets. But even with these bewildering arrays of facts and stories, we are left just as confused as ever about the big questions: Why are we here? What is the meaning of life? What is good?

It's not as if we're lacking answers in this regard. The problem is that we have too many answers and they rarely agree with one another, at least on the surface.

So where do we look for Truth? Is it to be found in authority? In fact? In consensus? How do we know that what we believe or what we've learned is True?

The focus of this section is to provide tools and perspectives to cultivate strong, grounded discernment, to understand the landscape of the mind and be able to navigate through its labyrinthine corridors.

But to do this, we have to go to the beginning, to the very foundations of our perception, understanding, and knowledge.

A Psychological Universe

In order to bring some clarity into this maze of stories and ideas, let's approach it from a psychological angle. We all live in the center of our own personal world, our own psychological universe. We interpret everything that we experience in unique and personal ways.

To take it one step further, everything we experience in this life comes through the human machinery of the senses, through the medium of the body. On a psychological level, we all exist within a sphere of sense perception. We live in a bubble of the things we can see, hear, touch, taste, and smell. To top it off, we don't see what's really there in the world; we perceive only how it relates to us, how it impacts us.

To understand this, consider the fact that our eyes do not function like a window. More like a digital camera. We do not see the world as it is, directly, but rather through a complex translation matrix. Our sense organs take in information from our environment in a variety of ways, transform it into electrochemical impulses, and then deliver these impulses to the brain. The brain then decodes these impulses and helps us to interpret them in terms of an image of the world.

Everything that we see, hear, taste, smell, feel, is a translation. It's *our perception* of the object, not the object itself. This may sound like nitpicking, but it's more than that. When we understand that we do not see the world as it is, but only how it relates to us, we begin to perceive situations and events differently. We begin to see how we select and modify sense impressions to make our picture of reality.

The meaning that we attribute to external events, objects, or situations is relative. It means something to us, but this meaning comes because of our relation to the object or situation. A situation is not hard or easy, good or bad, in itself, but only in how it impacts us and others we care about. Every quality that we observe in the world is a matter of relation, the interaction between the observer and that which is observed.

To this we add stories, which are ways of looking at the details present in our sense perception and memory, linking them together in ways that have meaning. In ways that relate to us and show us how to deal with the world and navigate our experience. Our stories, including our memory, extend our mental model of the world to cover the portions not currently in our sense perception.

Story, from this perspective, describes all conceptual knowledge, all ways of attaching specific words and meanings to the things we perceive. Seen in this way, we can begin to understand the awesome creative power of the word.

The Word

When we have a word for something, we can represent it in our mental model of the world. We can then use this model to understand how to relate with the thing thus described. Words form the chaos of sense impressions into objects, specific and comprehensible collections of qualities. When we have a word for something, we can see it in the world around us.

One of the most often-heard examples of this is with the Inuit language. The Inuit, sometimes known as the Eskimo, are a collection of indigenous peoples native to the northern regions of Alaska, Canada, and Greenland. Their language is known for having many ways to describe specific snow conditions, qualities of falling and fallen snow, icy and snowy terrain.

In the process of learning about these different snow conditions, a young Inuit also learns what to expect from different types of terrain, how to travel through them, and what to watch for. Their words for snow prime their perception and their understanding, enabling them to safely navigate their surroundings. These words help the Inuit to look at the land, see these types of terrain, and know how to handle them.

All of the words that we learn, all of the ways that we come to understand the world and how it relates to us, work in the same way. Words help us to pick specific objects, specific collections of sense impressions, out of the kaleidoscopic delivery of raw sense data. Just imagine learning the names of different trees. All of a sudden, you will begin seeing these different types of trees, picking them out from the surrounding greenery.

By learning the words, structures, and ideas related to each tree, we prime our perception to notice and identify it. And when we do notice this tree, it primes our interpretation with all the other things we know about it. So, when we notice an oak tree, we may think of the word oak. We may have a subtle undertone of acorns, squirrels, of an oak we played in as a child. Whatever personal associations we have made with this idea in the past come up as an unconscious story, as a gestalt of feelings, ideas, and remembered imagery.

All of the information we have accumulated throughout our lives is woven together in a network of associations, stories linked to other stories to form a patchwork mental model of our entire universe. From a purely psychological perspective, absolutely everything that we know about things beyond our bubble of sense impression comes to us in the form of a story.

What we know about the past, about history, even our own history and memories, all that we have of the past is a story about things that have come before. Our understanding of the world, current events and what is happening on the planet right now, anything beyond what we sense in this moment has come to us through a story.

The same could be said for our investigations into the nature of the world. Science forms stories and then tests these stories against our experience. The goal of science is to continually refine our mental model, to find stories with better explaining power, those that help us to work constructively with our experience. In the end, they are still stories, useful ways of linking together things we have perceived and seeing how we stand in relation to them.

Stories, Truth, and Certainty

Stories are very powerful and very valuable. Each story has an impact on us. Each one shapes our perception, primes us to understand and respond to the world in specific ways. But stories are not True. Our idea of truth in an absolute sense, in a way that's objective, factual, and equally true for all people, is something very different from the explanatory power of our stories. Stories are relative and Truth is taken to be something impersonal, something more certain and Real than the relative.

This is one of the reasons that Truth is such a hotly debated topic. When we form stories to make sense of the world, these stories view the world from one specific angle, one specific perspective. And this is necessary; the vantage point is an essential part of the story. But here's the rub: the world could be viewed from any angle, and you'll get a different story. A *different and equally valid* story that also helps you to make sense of your world and navigate it effectively.

When we use stories to describe something extremely powerful, deeply meaningful or simply obvious to us, we call these stories true. The challenge is that the world looks different when viewed from another perspective, when explained with a different story.

Often, we are left with two people saying much the same thing, at the core, but unable to resolve their disagreements because they are saying it in different ways. They emphasize different aspects of the story, focus on different details, and we get an irreconcilable difference in perspective, an argument that cannot end upon the same terms it was begun. To find a resolution between two seemingly mutually exclusive perspectives, we must find a third which can accommodate the both.

When this approach is used to explain the physical world, we get science. Science teaches us to observe the world and generate stories about what we see and how it works. We then use experiments to test these stories. If these stories, which we call hypotheses, withstand many attempts to disprove them, then they are upgraded to the status of theory. Theories are tested stories with a strong ability to explain and anticipate the things we observe and interact with.

The scientific method is one of continual refinement, with the underlying assumption that our approximations of reality will come ever closer to what reality actually is. This works very well for understanding the outer world, the world of physical objects and materials. However, the underlying assumption of a single, fixed reality has, as yet, been no more than an obstacle in psychology and our approach to consciousness.

On the psychological level, each of us inhabits a subjective universe, and there is no guarantee that this universe matches up with the personal universe of another individual. For each of us, this subjective universe is fleshed out and characterized by our personal stories, by our personal experiences and how each situation relates to us personally.

To illustrate this, let's consider a brief story. Let's say that a lumberjack, naturalist, and artist went for a walk in the woods. Same walk, same woods, each person presented with all of the same sensory stimuli.

After they return from the walk, you ask them what they saw. The lumberjack may tell you about stands of woods that are ready for logging. Approximate value, access points, etc. The naturalist might have noticed the different species that come together to form the ecology of the area. They might tell you how certain species are more common in the low areas, others clustered around certain trees. The artist may have noticed the dappling of shade on the leaves, the million hues of green in the canopy.

All of these stories could be described as true, after a fashion. At the same time, none of these stories are complete. They are not Truth, in the sense that Truth is eternal, unchanging, and the same for all beings regardless of vantage point. They are not True in an absolute sense. However, these stories are all *functionally true*. They do what stories are supposed to do: they explain the world in terms we can understand and work with.

For the purpose of clarity, let us define absolute Truth as something which is certain, true for all observers at all times. From this perspective, it can be seen that very few things could be described as absolutely True. Absolute Truth is an impractical concept; everything we experience is relative.

All concrete knowledge comes from experience, so all of our concrete knowledge is relative. All of our abstract knowledge comes in the form of a story, which means that it's relative to our vantage point. None of it is True in an absolute sense.

The closest that we can come to truth in *concrete terms* is functional truth. Functional truths are things that we feel we can be reasonably certain of, even if they would look different from another perspective. They could also be described as conditional truths, as things which we hold to be true right now, and from our perspective. This has very little to do with absolute Truth.

Again, functional truths are stories which help us to refine our approach to the world, to be aware of and respond intelligently to the things they describe. They help us to function in specific circumstances.

Functional truths are both subjective and based (at their psychological core) upon assumptions. For example, it is a functional truth that the sun will rise tomorrow morning as it has risen each morning of my life. I can say this with confidence approaching certainty. Based on my personal, subjective memory of the sun rising each day, and based on my story about how the world works and my assumption that it will continue to work in the way I understand.

But there's still the chance that something different will happen. That the sun will rise tomorrow is so probable that it's almost certain, but it is not absolutely certain. It is a relative and functional truth rather than an absolute Truth.

Functional truths are necessary for learning. Each experience helps us to anticipate future situations, to assess the likelihood of encountering different experiences and the best approach for responding to them. From this we develop specific, concrete ways of perceiving the world.

For example, gravity is a functional truth. Gravity is a story used to explain observed phenomena. This story has been more successful than any previous stories to explain the phenomena of things falling and planets circling the sun without falling or flying away. It works, in all the ways we need it to, so we take it as a functional truth.

To recap, the value of functional truths – and of all stories – is their explanatory power, their ability to help us to see what's going on, understand it, and respond to it effectively. Stories are subject to a specific viewpoint, to a specific set of parameters, needs, and desires. Stories are helpful, and we could describe the most important and relevant of them as functional truths. But this does not mean that they are True for all people, or that they will be true for us the next time we look.

Time to cut the Gordian Knot: *Stories have no natural relationship with Truth.* The value of a story is how it helps us to understand and navigate our life, our conscious experience of life. Stories are not and can never be True. Helpful stories prime us to engage with the world in ways that help us to meet our needs, keep us safe, permit growth, and foster meaningful interaction with our world. A story is either useful or not; it is never True.

When stories are used to express something True, they do so poetically, metaphorically, like when the finger of a pointed hand is used to indicate the moon. The finger is not the moon; the finger is simply intended to draw one's attention to the moon. Again: stories are not about truth. They are about effective perception and response.

Here's the thing: when we talk about truth, what we're really after is certainty. We want to know for sure, if this thing is so, or if it isn't. Certainty brings clarity. What we are certain of, in our own minds, forms a foundation, a backdrop against which to evaluate any further information. With certainty, we lock down our mental model, say, this part is mapped out, I can relax around that now. I can use this fixed point to add to my collection of certain information, to build my picture of the world.

Inwardly, when we feel certain of something, we behave as if this thing is definite. *That* person could never do *this*, or *this* happened on *this* date, or I'm definitely going to fall if I jump off a bridge. These are all examples of things that a person could feel certain about, inwardly and to themselves.

From an outside perspective, we can see that these things have differing degrees of confidence. Although we may feel equally certain about each, there is no guarantee that things are a particular way simply because we feel certain about them.

We hold things to be certain because we have learned them from someone we trust, because we want to believe them, because we're emotionally or intellectually invested in that certainty. We hold things certain for psychological reasons, but when it comes down to it, little of this certainty is merited.

To make matters worse, if we never review our beliefs, our knowledge, and the things we have learned as facts, then our minds are filled with a mixture of accurate and inaccurate information. We have helpful and unhelpful stories and we have no immediate means of distinguishing between the two.

This leads to an inefficient mental space, plagued with cognitive overload and essentially operating at a bare minimum. Which, in itself, is nothing to be concerned about. But, when viewed against the awesome brilliance and creative ability of the human mind, it's an outright shame.

We are, each of us, geniuses. We have abilities at a far higher level than most of us have ever suspected. But we will be unable to realize these intellectual and creative abilities unless we review our knowledge and cultivate a conscious, healthy relationship with the wilderness within.

Right Speech and Metacognition

In order to tame this inner jungle of story, we must review all of our thoughts and beliefs, all of our knowledge, and assess the level of certainty of each bit of information. In the process, we must ask ourselves why we believe or know this thing, where we learned it, and how we have come to this certainty.

After all that is out of the way, we can ask how this story, perspective, or bit of information is relevant to us. We look at how the information would influence us and our thought patterns, if we were to believe it to be true and accord it certainty.

This is a Herculean task, a mental self-stalking and reclaiming of power that is every bit as challenging as our efforts to reclaim power in the outer world. Thankfully, the process itself is pretty straightforward: right speech.

Right speech could also be described as striving to be impeccable with your word. It is a powerful practice of consciousness to pay special attention to our words and to consider them carefully before we speak. With this practice, we cultivate awareness around our words and the thoughts behind them. We get a window of insight and influence into the workings of our stories.

In practicing right speech, each time we speak, we review beforehand. We ask ourselves, how do I know this? Am I speaking honestly? To the best of my knowledge? Am I passing along things I've heard without truly evaluating this information? Where did I hear it? Is it helpful, honest, or kind? When we strive to speak with accuracy, honesty, and precision, with kindness and integrity, it forces us to look ever deeper at each word and each thought.

When we make an effort at right speech, to speak as honestly as possible and to understand why we believe what we say, we cultivate consciousness around our spoken words. And it goes further. As we consider our words before we speak them, we cultivate consciousness around our thoughts. Instead of reflexively identifying with these thoughts, instead of believing them outright, we make a habit of reviewing and reconsidering them. This gives us a solid foundation for metacognition.

Metacognition is a practice of looking at how our mind works and adjusting, refining, and optimizing that function. Metacognition is thought about thought, or thought regarding the thinking process.

When we are aware of the thoughts that enter our mind, we can see how they prime us to relate to the world. We can see, if we look for it, the impact of each thought or story upon our performance, our perception, our emotion, our experience. And we can begin to seek out stories and perspectives that help us to deal with the things we experience in life.

Before we can see our thoughts with this level of clarity, it's as if we're responding instinctively, in a relatively fixed pattern. Once we begin to slow down and observe our thoughts before speaking or acting upon them, it's as if an entire world opens up. We begin to see that we often have thoughts that work against us and emotional reactions that sap our energy. Stories that create unnecessary obstacles to both perception and personal growth.

With right speech and metacognition, we begin to reclaim our power over the stories and thoughts that we have invested in. And, in the process, we begin to reclaim our freedom.

Fine-Tuning our Mental Model

Here is a massively helpful concept when it comes to information and certainty. First, remember that certainty is not Truth. We can be certain about things that we later find to be false. Certainty is an inner, psychological property. In our mental model, certainty is a fixed, solid point that later concepts can be built upon. Certainty has no relationship with what's happening in the world around us. It only describes what's happening inside, in our own thought processes.

Certainty is a sense of knowing something absolutely. *This* thing will definitely happen. *This* thing actually happened. The world is *this* way. That sort of thing. We want certainty because it helps us to have a clear picture of what's going on. So, as we learn things, we accumulate bits of information that we *feel certain* about. We will hold these things as true, using them as fixed points in our lens of story to make sense of our current experience.

Most of the things that we learn are helpful. They could be described as functionally true, as useful and valuable, since they serve us in some way. Some things that we learn cannot be described as functionally true. We all pick up bits of misquoted trivia, erroneous assumptions, and misinformation along the way. We tame the wilderness within by observing our thoughts, reexamining them, and *choosing* whether or not to engage with them.

In order to sift through our stories, it's helpful to understand how we become certain of things we learn. There are three conventional ways for an individual to come to certainty regarding a piece of information:

1. Repetition,
2. Reason, and
3. Authority.

With repetition, think of the sun coming up each morning. Because we have seen it ourselves, time and again, we can feel certain that the sun will rise again tomorrow.

Repetition of past events can provide high likelihood that the future will bring the same. But never *absolute certainty*. There's always the "x factor" that can come in and change the game. All fixed patterns are only fixed from our perspective; everything in the universe is in a constant state of flux. So whatever patterns we have observed are functional truths subject to unprecedented change.

With reason, we can look at all of the stories we have about the earth and its rotation – its relationship with the sun, our conception of our solar system – and see that it makes sense according to these stories for the sun to rise tomorrow. And it doesn't make sense in the context of these stories for something different to happen.

The challenge with reason is that it works by making a mental model. No matter how beautiful and in-depth this mental model, it is limited. The map is not the territory, and it always leaves things out. Sometimes important things.

With authority, we are certain of information because we trusted the person who told us. Just think of a young child for whom their parents form much of the world. What the parents teach the child is given, in the child's mind, a high degree of certainty. Dad says this is how it is, or mom said this is not good. We extend this authority to peers, teachers, employers, religious officials, politicians, scientists, etc., often trusting their words without critical review or thorough consideration.

The problem with certainty derived from authority is that humans are imperfect and they're not always honest. Even if someone has the best of intentions and speaks as honestly as they can, they got this information from somewhere as well. They may be repeating inaccurate information or they may have been mistaken in their own reasoning, observation, or assessment of the situation. Even if the perception is as accurate as humanly possible, no perspective is complete and comprehensive. There's always another way to see the situation.

So we have three ways of being certain about information: repetition, reason, and authority. And although these things can help us to *feel certain* about a specific piece of information, they cannot guarantee that the outer world will match our assessment. Put another way, *our feeling of certainty is no indication of the accuracy of the information*. No guarantee of Truth.

So, we cannot find Truth in stories or in certainty. How about facts? Facts are bits of information we have regarding the outer world. And, like any bit of information, we learn complex facts from others, through stories. Through that imperfect lens of heuristic cognition.

However, facts have an additional requirement: they are a matter of consensus. Not only can we check a fact (in some way that satisfies our reason), others can check it and agree upon it.

We could hold ourselves to nothing more than facts, if we wished to think with the greatest precision possible. However, if we were to do this, we would begin a journey of removing all personal qualities from our information, all relative qualities, and expressing this information in solely objective terms, in ways that others can check and come to a consensus upon.

Once upon a time it was a generally accepted fact that the Earth was flat. It was obvious to the senses, and you could easily find a crowd or a culture in agreement with this assessment. It was a fact. And yet, this fact has been overturned by other facts. The idea that the earth is flat, once accepted as a fact, was found to be no more True than any story we have.

Each fact is relative, an assessment based on common conclusions from a common perspective. All social facts share this: they come through the medium of stories and are only accepted as facts when they find a majority consensus, or when such could be found if evidence was presented.

Facts are practical. But they are not True. It is possible that our consensus is collectively developed in delusion or with a limited understanding of the situation. Facts are great for specific situations. They have an acceptable level of certainty to guide our actions through the world. But they are not True, in an absolute sense, any more than any other form of concrete knowledge.

So, if truth and fact are insufficient for our purposes, how do we determine the value of our stories? How can we tell if this is a story that we would like to use for our processing and interpretation? How can we tell which stories we would like to cultivate with our attention? For this, we need *discernment*.

The First Steps of Discernment

We have already laid a groundwork for the practice of discernment by looking more closely at how we perceive and interpret the world. We know that we perceive the world imperfectly through the translation matrix of the senses. We know that we understand the world imperfectly, that our stories form mental models or maps, and that the map is not the territory.

With all that said, what can any of us be truly certain of?

Descartes asked this very same question, and I like his answer: Cogito ergo sum. Je pense donc je suis. I think, therefore, I am.

This answer is often misunderstood. Descartes did not mean to say that his existence stemmed from thought, but rather that he can be certain of his own existence, since he's around to ask the question. Not to put too fine a point on it, this statement says nothing about what thought is. It says nothing about what "I" is. All it says is that I can be certain through my own experience, of my own existence.

I am. This is all that I can accord absolute certainty with guaranteed precision. It is the only statement I can make that I know to be definitely accurate. It is the only thing I know for certain. All else is in question.

I can't even know this about you. I can only truly be certain of my own existence. I know that I'm experiencing. I don't truly know what this experience is, what reality is. All I know for certain is that I am experiencing. I am Being.

It's the rare person who subjects their own thoughts to this degree of scrutiny. Those that do are forced to confront many half-truths, parroted bits of information, emotional conclusions at odds with our rational understanding, and the like. After facing down with these demons, if we make it through to solid ground, we do so without a number of props. No story is true, even the ones we want to believe. We know with certainty we are experiencing this moment. All else is in question.

The next level of certainty has to do with the immediate feedback of the senses. I am seeing *this*, feeling *this*, hearing *this*. I seem to be perceiving these things in connection with a body, with my body, which I claim ownership of because it seems to be a constant background of my experience.

I am not sure that my senses are reporting something in the outer world, that they are reporting this thing accurately, or even if an outer world actually exists. It might be no more than an illusion, but since it seems to be a persistent one, it behooves me to *act as if* it was real.

To *act as if* is a powerful technique. It can bring clarity and focus when we might otherwise be scattered and made ineffectual by doubt. And in order to *act as if*, we must understand that we don't really know. We don't know what is happening in the world, we don't know ourselves.

No matter how much we think we know, there's always more. So much more that our meager understanding pales in comparison. Lacking certainty, we make the best approximation of the situation, and then *act as if* this is what is happening, at least until a fuller picture presents itself.

We *act as if* when we assume that there is a world beyond the bubble of our senses. We cannot be truly certain of that world, or of anything that happens within it. But so long as the conditions persist, we can take them as a hypothesis as to the nature of our extended experience.

We may never have visited Baghdad, for example. But we have likely visited other cities and we have heard that Baghdad exists. We can *act as if* this city exists, we can use it as a (relatively) fixed point in our mental model of the world.

Things we have heard, seen, felt, things we have personally experienced, all of these have a higher degree of certainty than things we hear about from others. However, the way that we perceive these experiences and the way that we interpret them is still limited. Our memories often distort or completely rewrite these experiences without our awareness. And yet, even with all of this potential for distortion, what we have experienced personally is more solid, more sure to us, than any story we create or receive from others.

No thought or conclusion that we come to has any guarantee of (justifiable) certainty. Our memories are not certainly True. Our reason is not sufficient to guarantee certainty. Whatever authority has educated us is not beyond error. And nothing that has happened in the past can predict anything that happens in the future with absolute certainty. In purely intellectual terms, we cannot know the Truth, and we cannot be certain that what we do know is True.

As soon as we accept that we don't know, the mind opens.

As soon as we accept that we don't know, we can begin thinking again. We can reconsider our assumptions, bring fresh awareness into our stories. As soon as we question our ideas, our beliefs, our stories, we bring them into the light of scrutiny.

Many people fear doubt, but doubt is like a crucible that burns away those aspects of our knowledge which were not fully understood, not matured, not integrated with the rest of our understanding. Honest self-inquiry and a thorough review of even our most cherished beliefs will strengthen both our understanding and our faith, if we see it through.

When you truly understand why you believe what you believe, when you can communicate it clearly and embrace it with all of your being, it becomes powerful.

When we take the stories we have, roll them around, look at how they connect to one another, and see where we stand in relation to them, we develop eloquence. We learn how to thread our path through this maze of story, how to lead others to different points within it. With right speech and metacognition, we slowly transform our entire network of thought from an overgrown wilderness full of hazards to a welcoming forest crossed by game trails.

Remember that **the value of a story is the fruit it bears in our lives**. Questions of Truth and certainty lead us in circles. With stories, the only solid approach is a pragmatic one. If a story, a way of seeing the world, a way of seeing ourselves, is helpful to us, if it serves us in some way, then it has value. If this story does not serve us in some way, it does not have value to us. The Gordian knot is cut.

In reviewing our stories, our beliefs and ways of understanding the world, we challenge ourselves. We ask, how does this story serve me? What value does it serve? How does it help me to understand the things I encounter along the journey? How does it help me to navigate this journey in a way that works for me?

In the process of challenging ourselves in this way, we often become aware of things we value. We find stories that are precious to us for reasons we don't even fully understand. This is beautiful. This is how we grow.

Any lesson that truly has value to us helps us to deal with our daily lives. When we bring this lesson into the context of our personal journey, it can flower into personal knowledge and personal meaning. A person who knows their own mind in this way speaks with power and grace.

Borrowed Meaning and Personal Meaning

When we learn something from someone else, we borrow the meaning they give to us. So, let's say a child hears their mother say, "Don't touch the stove, it's hot." While the child accepts this as the case, it is *borrowed meaning*. It is helpful, as it helps the child to understand what is happening and navigate the hazard.

However, when the child forgets the warning and bumps into the stove, suddenly that borrowed meaning becomes *personal meaning*. The inner process might be something like this: I know that that stove will burn me if I touch it; I got burned before and didn't like it. And I'm going to remember that and be more careful around it this time.

Children operate primarily off of borrowed meaning. There is so much to learn, and the world is so big. Our society is so complex that it takes us many years of learning others' stories before we are prepared to take care of ourselves. Borrowed meaning is good for keeping society functioning smoothly. A culture of shared meaning gets everyone on the same page, all thinking about things and responding to them in similar ways. But borrowed meaning is of only limited value for individuation and personal growth.

At some point in our growth, borrowed meaning must give way to personal meaning. To carry this process to completion, we must go through a period of deconditioning where we re-evaluate every single aspect of our knowledge in the light of what we currently understand and of what we have experienced. Knowing even then that our knowledge is not complete. As we learn more we will come to see what we know now as limited, as the understanding of a child.

Stories have power. Power to help us to understand the world. Power to help us work with what we see there. Power to move hearts and minds. When we hold a story to be true without fully understanding it, our connection to that power is weak, tenuous.

When we come to understand this story in personal terms, it becomes personal meaning. The power of this story then becomes ours. We have reclaimed that bit of wisdom, that bit of alignment, we have internalized the lesson. We truly understand it. We can apply it in our lives and express it clearly to others. You can tell the difference between borrowed wisdom and personal wisdom; borrowed wisdom uses well-worn talking points and it comes out in words more often than actions.

Any lesson we truly learn will be learned in our own terms, through the medium of our own experiences. No matter how brilliant and beautiful the message we receive from another, it won't fully land until we understand it ourselves, in our own language. Once we learn a lesson fully, we can use it to guide our actions and we can express it in simple, human terms to others, in personal terms.

A Review

All that I can know with certainty is that *I am*. I am experiencing *this* right now. I don't know what *this* is, not with any certainty. But all that I have experienced has come through the medium of my senses. Therefore, what my senses report to me in this one moment is what is real to me right now. I do not know what real means, but I do know that the reports of the senses are as real as anything I've ever known. For all intents and purposes, *this one moment of sense experience is my functional Real.* All else is story.

The value of a story is the fruit it bears in my life. If a story helps me to understand the world and helps me to frame my actions so that I can handle the situations I encounter, then this story serves me. If a story does not serve me, then it has no place in my life. It has no real value to me.

No story is true, and all are relative. Each looks at the world from a different viewpoint, for a different purpose, with different needs and parameters. No story is, in itself, better than another. Different stories are good for different purposes.

To understand this better, remember the story of the lumberjack, the artist, and the naturalist. Each one will tell you about the forest in the terms they understand. The lumberjack's perspective, their frame story, will highlight the details we need to harvest the trees. The artist's perspective will highlight the beauty they encounter and the capacity to express this beauty. The naturalist will look at how the living things along the path work together and how they grow in relation to the earth.

Each of these stories primes us to relate with the world in a different way. In fact, each story is a tool that helps us to navigate specific aspects of our experience. Once we separate the ideas of story and Truth, we take a massive step towards clarity and discernment. Then, when we begin to notice the story we use to make sense of the world, we finally have a chance to choose. We can see if this story is helpful to us. And, if not, we can explore other ways of looking at the situation, other ways of understanding it and ourselves.

Choosing a story as a tool means that we can observe the outcome and use it as feedback to refine our approach. This is an entirely new level of mental engagement with our world, and it begins to open doors in our inner experience. We become our own authority for new thought, and our own testing ground for new stories and perspectives. We begin to dance with our perceptions and understanding, rather than being bound to fixed steps and patterns.

Meaning and Power

When we learn a story, we gain meaning. Say, for example, we learn the story of chemistry. We gain meaning regarding chemicals, elements, molecules, and atoms. We learn about the process of transformation. The meaning and value of this story is evident in the skill that it engenders, in the capacity to work with physical materials. This ability to work with materials is an expression of power which springs knowledge. A power that we access by assigning specific meaning to what we observe and interact with.

Every time we gain meaning from a story, we gain power to respond intelligently to the world. When we truly understand what we believe, when we have found personal meaning in it, we gain the power to live that belief and express it in compelling terms.

Meaning comes in relation, in how we relate this skill, this information, this field of knowledge, to the things we experience and interact with in the world. The more personal our relation to this knowledge and the more we can apply it in the context of our lives, the more powerful it becomes for us. The more powerful we become in our relation to it.

The mind of the average person is filled with information, many details at varying levels of certainty, unreviewed. Often we pick up stories from anywhere and everywhere, decide to invest in certain bits of information and suppress other bits. This makes the thought paths tangled and overgrown. The mental terrain becomes unfriendly and hard to navigate.

In these conditions, we operate primarily on borrowed meaning. We play on the surface of life, responding for the most part instinctively. Our words lack clarity and power and our thoughts are confused and scattered. We make reflexive associations between thoughts and stimuli, primarily influenced by advertising and the haphazard medley of emotionally charged stories we have accumulated. A human being living in this condition is experiencing a bare fraction of their potential. A tiny sliver of the power that is their birthright.

It is a job of a lifetime to review our stories and find clarity. There's always more to see, always blind spots that are illuminated by current challenges. It's a way of life. But the first benefit of this way of life is to be progressively released from the hostile actions of our own minds. Slowly, steadily, it builds momentum. We come to know ourselves more deeply. We question and doubt and move through these challenges to establish a more solid foundation. Ever so slowly, we bring forth reliable knowledge. We gain skill, power, and wisdom.

It takes time and work to develop discernment and shift from borrowed to personal meaning. But the process itself is fairly straightforward. We must cultivate awareness around our thoughts and words. Then we must cultivate vigilance and practice self-reflection.

Over time, we review all of what we think and believe, subjecting it to the light of consciousness, and then considering the foundations of this thought. Why do I think or believe this thing, and how does it serve me? When we make this degree of self-awareness a personal discipline, our thoughts become clear and focused, coherent and well-integrated.

Stories and the Strong Dreamer

So much of the container of our lives comes in the form of stories. Our entire perception of the world is projected from these stories, whether they be in the form of agreements or shared dreams. When someone has a very clear perspective, one which touches on our emotional charge and which our intellect finds compelling, we tend to take that dream on. We share this view of the world and align our actions and words with it.

Just think of a time when you encountered someone you respected. Someone with strong ideas who showed you a different way of looking at the world. When we share a strong perspective with others, it's as if we pull them into our dream. The strongest story becomes our view of the world, and we learn from this story what is important, what is possible, what is happening in the world, and what it all means.

Much of history can be interpreted in terms of the life of dreams, the survival of the fittest story. Each culture generates a dream of the world, and all people within this culture share this dream. When this culture comes in contact with another, the dreams interact. Sometimes they go to war with one another, and the people follow suit. Sometimes the dreams can coexist peacefully. And the people who subscribe to those dreams follow suit. For the unconscious masses, the story is the real master.

The same goes for individuals. A good leader has a strong vision of what needs to happen and how it can be done. A good leader inspires others with this vision, helps to give them direction and a way to act in unison. A good leader is a strong dreamer.

Those who are unconscious of the nature of their stories will find a strong dream compelling without truly understanding why. There's a power that comes with confidence and clear vision. It draws people in and gives them a shared focal point.

Remember that the entire world looks different from the vantage point of different stories or dreams. When you encounter a strong, compelling dream, take a step back. Check in with yourself. Ask, how does this perspective, story, dream, view of the world, how does it serve me? What would happen if I acted as if this was the truth?

How does it feel to me? Some stories are limiting. They say, *this* is the only right way. *This* is how you have to be. Other stories are expansive. These stories show that things are possible. They open the world to us.

All stories have their place, but as a general guideline, limiting stories *do not* support growth and individuation. They are good for regulating behavior and establishing control, both of which have their place. Expansive stories *do* support individuation and personal growth. They give us more choice, rather than less.

Practices in Story
& Discernment

The practices offered below give three approaches to the art of discernment, one suited to each scope of time. In the living now, in every moment that we can remember to do so, we practice right speech. Impeccability in our words.

For the second scope of time, we learn to see others' perspectives. We practice looking at the world through other eyes. In the process, we encounter unconscious assumptions and contrasts to our fixed ways of perceiving things, and we are given an opportunity to review those assumptions and explore a different perspective.

Over time, we tune in to our assumptions through self-reflection. We question all of our knowledge – our assumptions, beliefs, conclusions, and interpretations – knowing that our understanding is imperfect, that our perception is prone to error. We assess our stories in terms of how they serve us. Honestly, openly, and with a willingness to encounter many stories which we thought we'd outgrown years ago. If we can see it, we can work with it.

Practice 1: Right Speech

Right speech has been mentioned in the passages above, and it is one of the best methods for cultivating awareness around our thoughts. With the practice of right speech, we consider what we are about to say. We ask ourselves, how certain am I of what I'm about to share? Why am I certain of it? Where does that certainty come from?

Our words train our thoughts. When we slow down and pay attention to the words we use, we also learn to tune in to our thoughts and see them in greater detail. This leads to metacognition. We learn to see how we're thinking, and how that thought leads to specific experiences.

Right speech, or striving to be impeccable with our words, doesn't mean trying to be right all the time. It does mean trying to be honest. To say what we mean and mean what we say. Right speech means considering where we learned things, why we believe them, and how they serve us. It means considering these things before we decide to share our thoughts with others. It also means striving to speak from personal experience rather than repeating stories and reasoning from others.

Right speech is our practice for the first scope of time, for the living now. It is a practice that helps us to cultivate awareness of our words right now, and, as it becomes more natural, of our thoughts from one moment to the next. Practices for the first scope of time are important, because all of our decisions are made – and all our actions taken – in the living Now.

No matter how wonderful our intentions, if we aren't aware of what we're saying before we say it, if our thoughts are rumbling away in our blind spots, then we'll be moved to unconscious reaction. With the practice of right speech, we pay closer attention to what we say and think. We learn to notice our assumptions and question them, rather than jumping to conclusions. It's much like showing your work in math class. It was a pain, but it helped us to see our errors and avoid them in the future.

The power of this practice grows over time. As we become more conscious of our words and thoughts, we learn how to express them more clearly, in a way that lands with those who hear it. We become more tuned in to the people we interact with and less full of the next thing we want to say. It's a lifelong practice and one that's worth every moment.

Practice 2: See the Other Side

Each person perceives the world through their own perceptual frame. This perceptual frame could be called a *view of the world*. It is a story which shows us how we relate to the things we experience, what these things mean to us. And, while you're in it, it can look like the whole world.

Many arguments arise because people are unable to see the other person's perceptual frame. We can have a hard time seeing another person's view of the world, especially when we're not very aware of our own. When we do learn to see things from another person's point of view, it often points out surprising contrasts. When we interact deeply with others, they show us new ways of looking at the world and navigating what we find there.

Looking at things from others' perspectives can be a challenging practice. It requires us to drop our own perspective, just for a moment. To let go of the ideas and feelings we're invested in for long enough to feel what it's like to be in the other person's position.

This practice is helpful in understanding others better, and through reflection, coming to understand ourselves better as well. But it doesn't stop there. The mind is an organ of perception. We can learn to tune in to specific ideas, feelings, skills, and bodies of knowledge. But in order to do this, we first have to learn how to tune in to things intentionally. By working with others and tuning in to their perspective, we get practice at directing our attention and attuning to a specific focal point.

In order to do this, simply put yourself in the other person's shoes. Imagine what it feels like to be them in one moment, as vividly as possible, with the same life conditions, concerns, challenges, vested interests. See what life looks like from that perspective.

Try this with friends or loved ones, coworkers or associates. Try to tune in to the feeling and story of this individual, and look out upon life from that vantage point. Understand what motivates you in this space, what is desirable, what is challenging. Feel it, and let the feeling expand into a more tangible, embodied expression. And, when you speak to this person again, pay attention to how your actions and words will be felt from that vantage point.

This is a process of tuning in to a specific perspective or vantage point. Over time, this same process of tuning in can be used to get into flow state for high performance work like musical or martial proficiency. For a writer, this skill can be used in a way similar to channeling. Tune in to a specific thought or subject, and then let the ideas flow through catching them with words on the way out.

Tuning in is also extremely helpful when working a high-level mental challenge, as it helps us to access the intuitive leaps necessary for true innovation. And literally everything we do can be done better if we're in tune with the moment. We can learn to move with the dance of the world.

Every bit of this begins with learning to step back and tune in. To shift the center of our perspective, and create space so that we can listen within.

Practice 3: Discernment - How does this story serve me?

There are two elements to the practice of discernment. First, we must be able to distinguish between what we have perceived with our senses and how we have interpreted this sense information. Next, we must recognize that each story is a choice, and choose wisely.

The **Fair Witness** practice is an excellent way to make the first step. When we practice being a fair witness, we take on the role of a keen impartial observer of ourselves and the world.

To practice being a fair witness, remember that your emotions are your own. No one makes you angry or sad. But sometimes we notice anger, sadness, or fear coming up. We hear these words, or observe that someone has taken action, and then we have a feeling rise up within us. Break the two things apart. *This* happened. I felt *this* rise up within me.

When we decide that something we observe means *this*, we have interpreted it. We have modified our raw observations to provide a personal, relative assessment. This is natural. It's how we think and make sense of things.

The challenge comes when we don't realize we're doing it, when we're unable to distinguish between what we perceive and how we made sense of it. This causes us to jump to conclusions, leave important things unsaid, take things personally, and make unwarranted assumptions. Instead, you might try to slow down and show your work to yourself. Be a fair witness of your own experience first.

The next step is to evaluate our own stories, our way of making sense of the world, from a functional perspective. Regardless of whether or not they reflect our experience, stories that we invest our belief in appear true to us. And each story guides our actions in a specific way. Some stories make us more open minded. Others close us off. Some stories make things possible, while others show us that we shouldn't even try.

Whatever stories you use to make sense of the world, those stories shape and prime your perception to see things in the outer world that confirm them. We will tend to see things that line up with our unconscious expectations. Before we're aware of this, it's easy to fill our minds with stories that leave us locked-in to undesirable patterns, blind to other ways of working with our lives. Blind to the things that we're doing that aren't working for us.

Every belief, everything we learn, even every fact, if it is not in our physical presence at this moment, comes to us in the form of a story. And every story is just one way (of many) to validly interpret the world.

Every story is good for something, just like every tool is good for something. You wouldn't want to turn a screw with a hammer. So, remember to evaluate your stories, whenever you encounter them, as the tools they are.

It is possible to use a story without investing belief in it, if we remember that it's a tool rather than a Truth. If we understand that a particular story, a specific perspective or view of the world, supports a particular function, we can use this story for that function. We don't have to believe it's true, only useful. As we begin to relate to our perspective in this deeper and more nuanced way, we begin to see that we can change these perspectives out like lenses as needed.

MODULE 7 - WHO AM I?

Introduction to Consciousness

Who am I?
This is one of the deepest questions any of us can ask. It goes right to the heart of consciousness in terms we can all feel.

Are you your name? Your memories? Your history? Your family? Your culture? If all of these things were taken away from you, is there anything that would remain?

I'd like to open up our discussion of consciousness with a story about one of our culture heroes, a person you may never have even heard of: Da Mo.

Also known as Pu Ti Da Mo, or Bodhidharma, Da Mo is a figure in Chinese history and myth. He was said to have lived between 470 and 528 C.E., though accounts differ. It's also said that he was born and educated in India and migrated into China after experiencing his awakening. Da Mo is considered the 28th patriarch of Buddhism of the Indian traditions and the first patriarch of Chan Buddhism in China.

Da Mo is credited with bringing Chan Buddhism into China from India and with first teaching kung fu to the monks at ShaoLin temple. Both of these transmissions of culture have rippled across the world through history. Da Mo's teachings flowered first in Eastern spiritual and martial traditions, and later as the global community has benefited from Eastern practices. The Zen Buddhism of Japan sprouted from the roots of Chan Buddhism and has since become an established perspective in Buddhism.

Now that we have a bit of context, I'd like to share a story of Da Mo's experiences in China. Just one. There are loads of insightful and irreverently comical tales in the history of Zen, and in Da Mo's life in particular. This is one that highlights the core focus of his approach to consciousness:

Da Mo Meets the Emperor

Da Mo had been wandering the countryside for some time, doing what wandering monks tend to do. Helping when he saw that help was needed. Walking when the path called. Eating when hungry, sleeping when tired, and sharing consciousness with all he encountered.

Eventually, word of the wandering monk reached the Emperor. Emperor Liang Wu was a pious man, respectful of the Mandate of Heaven and wishing to be regarded well by the Divine judge. So he sent messengers to find Da Mo and bring him for an audience.

(Just as a bit of foreshadowing, this was the last time in legend that a patriarch of Buddha's teachings responded to an Imperial summons.)

So, the messengers returned with Da Mo and brought him before the Emperor. Where he waited with an entirely inappropriate smile for the Emperor to kick things off.

The Emperor, not to be put off balance, addressed him, "We are honored by your presence, wise teacher. Words of your deeds and teachings have reached us from far and wide. I would call upon this wisdom now."

"During my reign, I have constructed many temples and monasteries. I have required that many young men and women take service as monks and nuns. Enlighten me, honored teacher. What esteem do these actions give me in the eyes of the Divine?"

Da Mo paused for a moment to consider the Emperor's question, to shine the light of consciousness upon it and listen within to what arose. He then dutifully shared, "Absolutely none!" Again with that inappropriate smile.

"Hmmm." The Emperor's brows furrowed. *Da Mo's impertinence was challenging enough to handle when he wasn't speaking.* He began stroking his beard.

But the Emperor was a patient man and a person of strong intellect. He took time to think through Da Mo's response.

If building temples and recruiting monks and nuns didn't earn approval in the eyes of the Divine, then what would? What could he do that would gain merit in the eyes of the Divine? What is Good? What is that one thing which is good above all other things, which shows what good really is?

"So, tell me, *great* teacher, what is the First Principle?"

In the language the Emperor spoke, that was very much akin to asking "What is Good?" But the form of the question elevates one thing above all others. It confuses the Good with that which is better than anything else, desirable while other things are undesirable.

Da Mo once again reflected on the question. He paused and rolled it around, shining the light of awareness throughout it. And then returned to the Emperor with the height of clarity, "Nothing!" Still with that grin.

At this, the Emperor began to boil. His brows furrowed further, and his beard stroking started to include a bit of tugging. *No first principle? No Good? How can there even be a Divine if this is so? Either this conceals a wisdom that I cannot yet penetrate, or this man before me is a charlatan and raging jackass!*

And the legendary third question, "Then, who are you?"

In the Emperor's terms, 'what gives you the authority to speak on these matters?' But again, Da Mo took the question in and reflected in the most honest and real way he could. He considered it without precepts or assumptions to the best of his ability.

And he responded, "I don't know!" Huge grin now.

At this, the Emperor started to sputter. He had enough restraint to simply have Da Mo forcibly ejected from his presence, rather than summarily executed or incarcerated indefinitely. It was probably half luck and half superstitious fear that saved Da Mo's life that day.

Although the Emperor spent hours, and then days, and then years reflecting on Da Mo's words, he could not understand them. They seemed to attack everything that he held dear, to be the words of a madman rather than a sage.

But every once in a while, in the depths of meditation, in the quiet moments between activities, the thoughts would flash through his mind. What is right? What is good? Who am I? Little questions and doubts which, if followed, might threaten the Emperor's holy persona.

In the meeting between Da Mo and the Emperor, we see a clash of two very different perspectives. The Emperor has an empire to run. He is concerned with solid things, things we can see. What feeds people. What helps defend and expand the empire, and what helps quell disturbances within the borders.

Da Mo is a philosopher. He seeks Truth in his actions and words. Da Mo is a champion of the subjective, of the art and science of consciousness. The seeker of Truth questions all things. Those who seek to know themselves must continually question their long-held and reflexive beliefs, no matter how obviously true those beliefs may seem on the surface.

Da Mo's spiritual practice involved an intention to see clearly. Without assumptions or preconceived notions. Willing to question all things, even his own identity. Willing to admit uncertainty about an idea without moving into defensiveness. Da Mo understood that we are not our ideas, and we can change our ideas without dying, even our ideas about ourselves.

Da Mo's path is also about embracing all aspects of our experience. Everything that we are conscious of is an opportunity to be conscious. If we remember that *we are consciousness* and that this is all we really need, then we can let go of our attachment to specific conditions, objects, or situations. And we can greet all things as a blessing, finding gifts even in the challenges and crises.

This is an ideal. A guideline. To strive steadfastly to open to all aspects of our life and recognize the divinity within them. Perhaps we never complete it; perhaps we always have some resistance to aspects of our lives, to certain people or situations. And certainly it is important to honestly listen to things that come up, to honor those feelings and learn their language, rather than going into spiritual bypass. That said, the more that we are able to fully embrace our lives, the more aligned we can become with our joy and fulfillment in every moment of life.

Da Mo understood that our spiritual journey is an awakening of consciousness, and you don't awaken consciousness by gaining points. Whether those points are dollars in your bank account or the amount of temples you have had constructed in your empire, you can rack them up for life and remain unconscious, remain out of touch with yourself.

All of the real work happens within. The real change happens as we learn to be honest and real with ourselves. As we learn to listen to our feelings and process them healthily. And most of all, as we learn to show up, in the Now, for ourselves and what we care about.

When the Emperor asked about the first principle, Da Mo recognized that all aspects of our experience are perfect. All aspects of our experience are us, and to reject any of them would be to reject part of ourselves.

Nothing is supreme, elevated above all other things. We are all interconnected, every aspect of the world coming together to form a living system. Health comes from the balanced, healthy interaction of *all* parts of this system. And no one part of that system is supreme above all others.

So, *no thing* is sacred. No one thing is elevated above all other things. All things are good, right, in their own place. All things we encounter are part of our perception, part of our experience, and part of the living world that we interact with each day. Every bit of that is good. Right. Part of a living ecosystem. Sometimes things hurt, and yet those things that hurt often teach us lessons and train us for future situations.

There is potential value and potential good in each situation. We can align ourselves with this good, with this meaning and value, if we set out to do so. Every situation that we're in, no matter how challenging, has a lesson and a piece of gold to offer. If you think that one thing, one story, one perspective, one action, is right above all others, it puts you out of touch with your current moment.

When we face each current moment *as it is*, rather than *as you think it should be*, the landscape changes. We can move forward with an eye for the latent growth within each experience. We prime ourselves to handle each situation as capably, gracefully, and sustainably as possible.

The cultivation of consciousness is subjective. It's not an objective game, and it doesn't work on objective standards. So, no divine brownie points for monks, nuns, and temples because we don't achieve consciousness or earn it in some way from actions in the outer world. And no first principle, because *all* things cooperate to form the whole, and that's good. But what about the last question? Who are you? Who am I?

There's a Zen aphorism about this: If someone asks who you are, tell them your name. But if they ask who you *really are*, then answer with silence.

The Experience of Consciousness

"Who are you?" is one of those questions that can easily evoke defensiveness. And that's interesting. Because the only reason that this question itself might make us uncomfortable is if we have doubts as to who we are. This question is so powerful that it can be used as an exercise to tune in to the experience of consciousness itself.

Don't take my word for it. Try it out yourself. Find a bit of space to look within and ask yourself, "Who am I?"

The first things you're likely to encounter are all the stories you have about yourself. Your name, your history, your job, your family, all of the connections you have with the world around you. But even if you had a different name, a different history, a different configuration of connections to the outer world, there would still be some essential *you* beneath these things.

As we begin to see all of these things as stories, helpful but not True, we are encouraged to look deeper. I see this, I feel this, I am aware of perceiving this moment. I have a body which seems to me to be at the center of this bubble of sense experience and emotion.

At the same time, the reports of my senses fluctuate from moment to moment. I see different things, I hear different things. Now I am hungry, now I am thirsty, now I am tired. Over time, these things shift like a kaleidoscope image.

Even my body shifts in time. The face in the mirror looks very different from the one I saw ten years ago, twenty, fifty. With all of this, the only thing that remains constant in my experience is that "I Am."

My "I," my sense of consciousness, has a sense of persistence which cannot be accounted for by the outer world. Deeper than *this* situation, *this* feeling, *this* image, *this* condition, deeper than anything I see, feel, hear, or know, is the fact that "I am" experiencing. This is fundamental consciousness, which means that it is the psychological foundation of our experience.

Consciousness, Being, Isness, I Am. This is the rock at the foundation of every single human consciousness, the basis of all human experience. The I Am is tuned to the living Now. This means if we identify with the I Am, then we can be present and fulfilled in each moment.

When we can feel the *I Am* at the center of our being and make our home here, we have a source of strength and clarity that can never be taken away. We can base our sense of self on something solid, something that is fundamentally ours. We are complete in Being, and everything else is icing on the cake.

The Power of Consciousness

This sounds really poetic and metaphorical. But it's actually some of the most practical philosophy ever. I am not my job. I am not my history. I am not my name, or my family, or that one crappy mistake I made. I am not defined by what has come before. I am not defined by my current situation.

If anything, I am defined by my self, in the moment, by my actions and choices. And I'm making choices every moment, continuing to define myself with each action and emotion, each thought and breath.

I Am is the real thing at the center of my being. All other things change. And if I remember this, then it's far easier to let go of old stories, old roles, and ways of defining myself that no longer serve me. If I base my sense of self in I Am, then I am immune to judgment, to the pressure of roles and expectations, to the confusion that comes from trying to live a life based on the standards of others.

If I remember that I Am always growing, changing, learning, and making new decisions, then criticism, challenge, and crisis can help me to grow. These things can help me to honestly assess blind spots in my current approach. If I can remember that in the moment, I'm less likely to become defensive.

I am not my role, my story, my personality. These things are tools I use to regulate my interactions and navigate through this experience of consciousness. When my role or story falls short of my needs, I know that I have grown enough to be humbled by the shortcomings of this story and begin to write a new one. In surrendering and admitting my shortcomings I can begin to let go of old, outgrown patterns and make space for new ones.

I know that criticisms do not describe me; they are someone else's perspective on something that has happened. I am not that person anymore. Even if their assessment was accurate, I have learned and grown, and I can use my past oversights to help guide my actions in the future.

I am. I am right now. I am choosing, aware of the fact that I am building and creating with each decision. Every choice that I make has an impact upon the world, often tiny, sometimes massive.

Each of us is the steward of our own choices. If we are not aware of our choices, then we do not have freedom. And if we do not have freedom, then we have not begun to reclaim our power to make different choices.

Without a conscious connection to my I AM core, my freedom is lost to programming. My power is scattered, self-limited, and applied to things I do not truly want to create.

This is how we all begin the journey, seeing the world the way we have been taught, the way we have learned to see it. We react to the things in front of us in these habitual ways, and we come to know the world through a single lens. We play the role of the victim, dropped into a situation about which we had no choice, just doing the best we can to survive it.

When we do not know the I AM at the core of our being, we seek out substitutes. We may become attached to certain roles, like that of the partner, sporty one, pretty one, smart one, the helper, the one who gets things done. We might become attached to things that we enjoy. Creature comforts and momentary pleasures that colonize our attention. When we identify with outer things, we stand in resistance to the world, cling to things, run from things, and generally expend loads of effort in ways that don't give back to our quality of life.

With consciousness of the I AM at the core of our being, we have an unshakeable inner strength. We carry a rock of presence and Being that we can rely upon throughout all of the trials we face and all of the beautiful moments. We have the ultimate in resilience, or at the very least, the path to transform every crisis into wisdom and compassion. We have a choice as to how to spend our energy, how to engage with our Now. We can take action with consideration of the trails we leave upon the world and upon the hearts of our loved ones.

It should be clear, by now, that consciousness, in these terms, is not simply the state of being awake and alert rather than unconscious. There are different states of mind, different frequencies of consciousness. For example, you are in a different state of mind when actively engaged with a task versus when you are on the verge of falling asleep. You are conscious in both cases, but the quality of consciousness is more inward with the one, and more tightly focused in the outer world with the other.

To be conscious in the manner that I describe here is really to be conscious of *being*, with all that entails. Our emotions are a part of our being. As are our thoughts. Our actions and the consequences they create. The stories that we use to make sense of the world, and the very fact that our perception of the world is modified by these stories.

To be conscious in this manner is to know with certainty only that I Am, and to cultivate a habit of presence in *Being*. This brings peace, and grace, love, and a depth of clarity into our lived experience. Or, more accurately, this state of joy, peace, and freedom is our natural state. When we remember that we are *Being,* we return to this natural state.

Consciousness and the Ouroboros Point

Our global technological society is at the Ouroboros Point, the point where our pursuit of knowledge has circled back around to its beginnings. We have explored the world in terms of scientific materialism, and it has been an incredibly useful perceptual frame.

Our avenue of exploration into the world has been to view it as a machine operating on universal principles. We have observed and formed hypotheses, tested these hypotheses through objective measurement, and used empirical exploration to turn these hypotheses into theories about the workings of the universe. With these theories, we have been able to master chemistry, engineering, and biology. We have developed a physical technology unparalleled in history.

This mastery of the physical world is due in a curious way to the influence of Galileo. Galileo Galilei is known as the Western world's father of observational astronomy. He is also recognized for his investigations into physics, engineering, and mathematics. Galileo was one of the first Western thinkers to view the laws of nature as mathematical and discoverable from an observation of the world.

Galileo contributed massively to the development of Western science. And, in the process, he left us a legacy of scientific materialism. His approach – observation and measurement – is unmatched in matters of the physical world. And, for a long time in our history, it decisively separated science from philosophy and spirituality from questions of consciousness and subjectivity.

The working paradigm for our global culture is scientific materialism. We make space for God and philosophy in church or college, but major decisions are based upon science, upon the objective world and the things we can measure.

This was a massive step in the development of clarity in Western culture. It helped us to explore all aspects of a situation which could be measured, to look at the situation objectively and identify patterns. Hypothesis and observation are ideal for exploring the outer world, and it was a game changer to use fresh observation and human understanding (instead of theological doctrine) to unlock the mysteries of the world around us.

That said, our mastery of the world has left us with more power than wisdom. And, with all the power at our command, we are living more destructively than ever. We are overtaxing the land, acting without consideration for the beings that share the planet with us. Without consideration for our own future, and often with little thought beyond the next quarter's profits.

This approach has left us clueless as to how we can live a life that means something to us. Or, for that matter, how we as individuals can do something significant in the face of massive global forces.

We have sidestepped the fuzzy questions, like those of consciousness, mostly because they're very difficult to answer in measurable terms. But consciousness is central to morality and ethics, fundamental for the discovery of authentic values.

In fact, all of the machinery of society could be seen, from one perspective, as the body of the human race. A body formed entirely for the purpose of housing the spirit. For the purpose of housing consciousness. To fulfill our physical needs without looking deeper would be like building a home and preventing people from living there.

At this point, our culture faces a crisis of meaning. We have so much information, so much knowledge, so much power. Power to reshape the world. But in the face of all this abundance, all this information, we are disconnected from our sense of self, from our needs, passions, inspirations, and the things that would make all that power worth having.

We're distanced from the world, insulated in a way that makes us feel separate, isolated, insignificant. Like what happens to other people doesn't impact us and what we do doesn't make a difference in the world. From these places, it's easy to make self-destructive and inconsiderate decisions, and with such power, these decisions can have heavy, long-lasting consequences.

Our culture has progressed down the path of scientific materialism so far that we have hit the Ouroboros Point. The snake has begun to eat its own tail.

What is the Ouroboros Point?

So what is the Ouroboros point, anyway?

In order to understand this, consider the image of the Ouroboros, the snake eating its tail and forming a circle with its body. At the end of the snake, you're right back at the beginning again. Ouroboros is a symbol of infinity and cycles, a demonstration that often the end of the journey brings you right back to where you started from.

We began our scientific journey into the nature of the universe by taking consciousness out of the equation. By removing the subjective and seeing if we can explain what remains the way we would explain a machine. We have laid out the construction of the material world in terms of elements, atoms, and molecules. Cells, tissues, organs, even the phenomenally complex coding of genetic material.

Then we get to quantum physics. And suddenly, we discover that the behavior of physical matter is dependent, at least at extremely tiny levels, upon the observer. The observer brings one thing to the situation: consciousness. Subjective perception. When the situation is observed, it condenses from many possibilities into one actual situation. And the consciousness of the observer is central to this process.

In some way, consciousness is linked to how physical matter unfolds, how it moves from potential to actual. The easiest way to think about this is in terms of the future. There are infinite paths forward, but we can make choices, engage our consciousness with a particular outcome, and we align with that outcome. We make it more likely to occur within the field of our experience.

This is the Ouroboros point, the turning point in our cultural development where we are forced to return to the problem of consciousness. In order to go further in quantum physics, in order to come to a more human understanding of our experience, in order to make the next revolutionary leap in our understanding of the world, it's time to recognize consciousness as the new center of the universe.

Consciousness navigates us through possibilities. In the now, consciousness engages with possibilities to produce one concrete experience. We align with one outcome over another with our attention, our emotional charge, our actions, perceptions, and communications, all expressions of consciousness. When we set a goal and take action to make that goal happen, we are using consciousness to direct our actions towards the fulfillment of that goal. We use our conscious intention to navigate through possibilities.

When we recognize our entire experience, and perhaps all of reality itself, as an expression of consciousness, we have a new basis for the Real. Instead of a real world composed of atoms and molecules, we have a human experience, a conscious experience of the world and our journey within it. When we make consciousness the basis of our Real, we create a new, living relationship with our own personal experience and with all the conscious beings with whom we share this living ecosystem.

This is the Ouroboros Point, the point at which we realize that *consciousness is the fundamental force which brings order to the world we experience.*

A cautious observer might also note that this planet and the fundamental forces of the universe seem precisely calibrated to bring forth life. Life itself is an expression of order in the universe, an expression of the tendency of self-organizing patterns to emerge in sufficiently complex open systems. And the more sophisticated the form of life, the more completely it can reflect consciousness.

Rather than being an unexplainable accident of the material universe, it is quite possible that consciousness is the underlying force and direction behind the fabric of physical reality. That consciousness informs matter to produce life, perhaps to produce the universe itself.

Certainly for a human being, our conscious experience is everything to us. Consciousness deserves a central place in our understanding of the world and ourselves. When we tune in to the feeling of being, and when we learn to recognize being in both ourselves and others, we create a very different relationship with the world.

The Hard Problem of Consciousness

This is an exciting time in the field of neuroscience. Our technology is allowing ever more precise monitoring of the electrical activity of the human brain. We are currently mapping out neural correlates to conscious experience.

In other words, we can see that the brain functions like *this* when you're unconscious, like *this* when you're happy, like *this* when you're hungry. We're even getting to the point where we can decode neural activity to read into conscious activity. We are learning to read thoughts through the neural correlates of consciousness.

Explaining the function of the neurons, the different structures of the brain and the different activities of these structures, showing how they correlate with consciousness, all of this answers the *easy problem of consciousness*. This question is, "How does brain activity reflect consciousness?"

And that's an awesome start. But as we build up a model of consciousness based on neural activity, we inevitably get to an explanatory gap, a point where we say, "... and then consciousness happens." For example, would you describe a single neuron as conscious? How about a small cluster of them? When it shifts from a cluster of living tissue to a source of consciousness, what's actually happening there? Where does the consciousness come from?

According to some materialistic views, consciousness itself is no more than an illusion. A random accident that only seems to be consciousness, but is actually a series of programmed instinctive responses. Or portions of the brain monitoring and speaking with other portions.

In other words, "It's not really consciousness; it just looks like it." This is, quite frankly, an insane conclusion for a conscious being to come to. We can find physical correlates to every level and function of human consciousness, and it would in no way eclipse the magic of the conscious experience.

Consciousness is qualitatively different from the medium that produced it, a whole greater than the sum of the parts. From the perspective of physical matter, consciousness is an emergent property.

An emergent property manifests not from any single source, but from the interaction of the entire system.

Consciousness is not found in physical matter, so much as expressed through it. At the same time, all fluctuations of consciousness have their reflections in the physical medium in which they're expressed. We can see consciousness in the actions of our neurons not because they produce it, per se, but because their function reflects the influence of consciousness.

Consciousness and Relativity

Scientific materialism and the use of the quantifiable to make sense of our experience is incredibly valuable. But it was not intended to dissolve the subjective nature of the human experience in a puff of logic.

The objective world is no more than an abstraction. Our experience is composed of conscious beings with subjective experiences. And, in some very sneaky ways, our high-level physics brings subjectivity back into the game.

We've already touched upon quantum physics and the role of the observer. But relativity reiterates the importance of the conscious observer with the concept of the *frame of reference*.

Relativity is perhaps one of the most misunderstood concepts. In simple terms: Everything is Relative. There are no absolute qualities to the universe. All qualities are relative. We only have position relative to other things. We only have velocity relative to other things. In other words, there is no fixed center of the universe, no fixed point from which to establish absolute values.

Everything is moving all the time, so the "true" qualities of a thing observed are dependent upon its relation to the observer. There are as many true and valid (and potentially different) experiences as there are observers. The true and valid experience of a thing depends upon *how* it's being observed, upon where you stand in relation to it. And there is room for infinite different relations between an observer and any given thing observed.

Many generations ago, it was believed that the Earth was the center of the universe. This was a frame of reference which showed a flat earth. We could conceive of all of space as a three dimensional expansion, sky above, earth below, and on forever. Even when the earth was recognized as a globe, it was at first thought to be the central globe in the universe. This made the center of the earth a common, "true" frame of reference, a fixed point we all share and against which we determine all values.

When we began to see that the earth revolves around the sun, we lost the earth as the center of the universe. Instead, the sun forms the center of our solar system, just one of trillions of solar systems in our galaxy alone, which is just one of trillions of galaxies. We lost our throne at the center of the universe. We lost our fixed point. Everything is moving, everything is the center of its own gravity. And all these points of gravity cooperate in a common field to create the motions we observe in celestial objects.

With everything moving, the only way to make sense of the world is to choose a frame of reference and look at everything around you from that particular vantage point.

Say, for example, your frame of reference is your position on the earth. If you move forward at a walking speed, you are moving forward relative to this frame. In a car, however, you may be sitting still relative to the frame of the vehicle, while moving forward relative to the frame of the earth. None of these speeds is more true, than any other. The quality of velocity arises from the relation between two things.

We are each the center of our own frame of reference. We are each the center of our perspective of and relation to the universe. We are the point of observation, and all qualities we observe in the things around us are relative to us. In other words, we don't see *what something looks like*. We see *what it looks like to us*. We don't know *what it means*, in any sense that extends beyond ourselves. But we know *what it means to us, in that one moment.*

All meaning comes in relation.

This leads to a few different implications. First, when we look at a situation, it means something unique and specific from our perspective, through our unique vantage point. Each person makes meaning in their own way, so we don't know what the situation we shared with another meant to them. And there is no "true situation," at least from one perspective. There is just *my* relation to the situation, and *your* relation to the situation, a valid and different experience of the "same situation." Relativity, on a human level.

Another implication is that each conscious observer is the center of a completely valid psychological universe of sense, history, will, and meaning. And when we interact with one another, it is as if we bridge a gap between two worlds. Two little bubbles of order and meaning, tended by two expressions of one consciousness.

We can find some points of overlap in our universes, some common frame of reference for our interaction. But we are only ever dimly aware of the inner experience of those we interact with, of how they engage with their experience and what it means to them.

Relativity places each conscious being at the center of their own personal frame of reference. And quantum physics suggests an intimate interaction between consciousness and the movement of reality from potential into actual.

This is just the beginning. Consciousness is the source of magic and spirituality, a dimension of experience which brings life and depth and which allows us to engage with the world in surprising ways. When we begin to explore different states of consciousness, different frames of reference and ways of perceiving the world, we unlock genius, authenticity, and creativity. We begin to see that the world is infinitely bigger than we had imagined.

Intriguing New Ideas on Consciousness

Have you ever heard the current scientific theory regarding the initial formation of life on this planet? Chemical evolution, they call it.

Just so happens, just the right precursors for biological life were brought together in just the right liquid medium, with just the right clay substrate, and with just the right activation energy in the form of lightning or ultraviolet rays. If you put the right mix together in a lab and zap it, you can get it to begin forming RNA. Basic genetic material. Voila! Life, in an elementary form, has been formed from abiotic materials.

But here's the thing. There are massive steps in complexity that need to be addressed along the way. Between RNA and the first cell, you'd need cell walls, diverse use of proteins, and a number of structures to maintain the internal condition of the cell. In short, our best guess is that these things began somehow to self-organize from the chaos of their initial conditions. As magical as that may sound, that's our scientific approach to the origin of life altogether.

Life essentially manifests as an emergent property, an ordered arrangement that emerges spontaneously. It is formed from the abiotic world and brings order to the chaos of energy in its surroundings. Life orders energy relative to itself, its needs, and its medium of existence. It is formed from the abiotic world, and yet is qualitatively different from the operations of the abiotic world. A whole greater than the sum of its parts.

Any universe that produces life as a spontaneous emergent property, as a byproduct of universal laws, is a true marvel indeed. Of course, I'm biased. As a living thing, I will tend to value life. I marvel at the capacity of life to use entropy as a source of energy, and from this energy to crystalize into form, shaping the physical world with being and action. Life creates order.

The story of consciousness in living beings echoes the story of life from abiotic materials. The more complex the living being, the more consciousness it will tend to express, and the higher degree of order reflected both in the physical body of the life form and in its tendency to order the environment.

Where does consciousness come in? With animals? Are plants conscious in some way? Again, we are confronted with the explanatory gap: "... and somewhere in there, things become conscious."

A Copernican Inversion of Consciousness and Matter

From the perspective of scientific materialism, it is natural to ask how matter produces consciousness. But it seems to me that we can get much more out of turning the question around. How does consciousness produce or inform matter?

The simplest explanation, to my way of thinking, is that the self-organization of physical matter reflects the influence of order or information. A template of forms, structures, and maybe even ideas. It is also possible that this order is a product of something we experience as consciousness.

Furthermore, it seems likely that this consciousness is somehow fundamental to the universe in a way that is deeper than physical matter. It may even form a foundation for all of time and space as we experience it.

If this is the case, we could perceive consciousness as a force that extends nonlocally (and atemporally) throughout the entire medium of our experience. It does, however, appear to be concentrated and focused in points of consciousness, in regions of greater complexity (beings).

From this perspective, life offers sufficient sophistication and complexity for consciousness to be expressed in a form that we can understand. But it doesn't stop there. The tendency of matter to self-organize under sufficiently complex conditions can then be seen as an expression of consciousness in its fundamental relation to physical matter.

It is possible that, in some subtle way, consciousness informs matter to produce ordered arrangements. The entire action of consciousness in the outer world could then be seen as a process of bringing order (information) to physical matter. We might even take it further and suggest that consciousness inspires in physical matter the ability to better receive, reflect, and express this order.

At a fundamental level, it is possible that this information is not generated or produced by life, so much as it is received and transmitted. Consciousness could then be described as an information-laden signal that extends throughout all space and time.

From this perspective, consciousness extends into (and might even form) the fabric of matter, both subtly creating and coalescing around points of sufficient complexity (like life forms).

Although I am aware of something I call consciousness, consciousness in a deeper elementary form interpenetrates my physical body, informing each cell and the body as a whole.

It is this specific signal, and how I tune in to it, which tells my body how to grow, which courses through my brain, and which expresses itself through the machinery of my being.

Seen this way, consciousness is a flow and handling of information which brings order to chaos and introduces higher-level patterns to physical systems.

Furthermore, consciousness, as a fundamental force to the universe, may even be singular in source and infinite in manifestation.

If this is so, then it means that all reflections of consciousness in the physical are expressions of the same consciousness, different mirrors of the same image. The same spirit (consciousness) which enlivens me enlivens you and all things.

We could call it the force, the source, or the foundation. Consciousness is information, order, and spirit. It is, after a very strange fashion, the creator of all patterns, structures, and life in the universe.

Resonance and Consciousness

"If you want to find the secrets of the Universe, think in terms of energy, frequency, and vibration."

– Nikola Tesla

One of our most exciting discoveries regarding consciousness is just now coming to light. With the development of the functional MRI (fMRI), we can now monitor the electrical activity of the brain while the subject is in action. We can watch what happens in the brain when a patient performs a specific activity, thinks of something in particular, forms a specific word, or responds to chemical influence.

Analysis of patients under the influence of anesthesia shows that neuronal firing patterns desynchronize. So, instead of operating together, each neuron is doing its own thing. As the anesthesia wears off, the neurons begin to synchronize.

To put it another way, waking consciousness as we understand it is linked to a synchronization of neural activity (neurons firing together). Asynchronous neural activity (neurons firing separately), is associated with unconsciousness. Our experience of consciousness is linked with the ability of the neurons in our brain to operate as a unit.

Just to break this down a bit further, let's look at what synchronization is. Imagine that you have two drummers, each playing their own rhythm and clashing with one another. Now imagine that those drummers synchronized. Now two drummers form one beat. They have come into resonance with one another.

It's almost as if each of our neurons was a drummer. When we are under anesthesia, each of those drummers is wearing earplugs, just making their own beat. And, when the anesthesia begins to wear off, the drummers can hear each other again. They start to find one strong beat. And when enough neurons start working together, we move back into waking consciousness. Neural resonance accompanies conscious experience.

Resonance establishes functional unity. All of our cells are individual beings, living their own lives. However, our cells are in genetic resonance. They behave as if they are one body, just like many drummers can form one beat. When the neurons in our brain come together in resonance, it's like we build up a symphony of activity all aligned with the same beat. In our brains, all those neurons come together to form a single functional unity. And in the invisible world, we experience consciousness.

One of the most amazing things about this is that it doesn't stop with a single individual. When you are in rapport with another, conversation flows and communication is easy. When this happens, your brain waves will tend to mirror one another, right along with breathing patterns, attention, posture, and body language. Two people interacting with one another can find resonance just like two drummers can find one beat. And when we work with others, we do just that.

Consider a time when you were doing a collaborative project or sharing space with others, and you just didn't jive. Everyone is playing to their own beat, and the beats clash.

Now consider a time when the whole team or family is on one page, if you are blessed enough to have experienced such a thing. It's almost as if the group forms one body, as if we all sync up to the same beat and come into resonance.

When things come into resonance, they behave as a functional unity. As if they were one thing. Resonance forms a whole that is greater, and somehow qualitatively different, than the sum of its parts.

A single body forms from cells because those cells are in genetic and chemical resonance with one another. Our inner experience of consciousness is associated with the resonance of our neuronal activity. And when we come closer into resonance with other people in a group, this group behaves more like a single entity.

We come into and out of resonance with different people, different thoughts, different emotions, places, etc. throughout the day. Anything that we tune in to with our attention pulls us into resonance with it. And, when we come into resonance with something, we can see it more clearly, feel it more immediately. It's as if we have tuned our radio dial to that station.

All of this sounds very complicated, so let's break it down even further. Everything has a speed or frequency. Everything has a beat. When you match your beat to the beat of the person you're talking to, you'll communicate more effectively. The conversation will feel smoother and flow more easily. In fact, you will tune in to that person's mental and emotional state far more deeply and effectively than is possible with words alone.

When you match frequencies with someone, it's as if the two people form one energy field. And each person has access to the entire field. Thoughts and emotions will tend to be shared contagiously, as if they arise spontaneously from both sides. It could be said that when we are in rapport, we share a certain inner space where similar thoughts and feelings occur to both and influence both sides equally.

On an immediate level, our breath and attention bring us into resonance with others. In terms of path through life, we are brought into resonance by shared well-being and a common narrative framework. In other words, by using the same stories to make sense of the world, and having the same or shared vested interest in specific outcomes. On a cellular level, DNA is a precise antenna that attunes each cell to a specific frequency of information, a specific pattern of growth and function.

So, to recap: On every level we can observe, when things synchronize, they act as a single thing. When they come into resonance, they behave as a functional unit. When the neurons in our brain synchronize, we experience consciousness. Some reductionist views of consciousness describe this as an illusion of matter, just a *perception of consciousness*. Which is a pretty surreal conclusion in itself. Perception requires consciousness.

That said, it seems that consciousness is not found in matter, so much as it is expressed through it. The operation of consciousness is reflected in the function of our brain, expressed rather than created.

And this expression is in the form of order, information patterned into a specific shape and function, like a collection of senses, feelings, memories. A Being. A functional Unity. Temporary. Not absolute or fundamental. But still pretty compelling from our perspective.

An Old Idea Getting New Attention

One very old perspective on consciousness, panpsychism, is the view that all material things, no matter how small, possess some sense of individual consciousness.

In other words, consciousness did not evolve to help us survive, nor was it magically created once our brains became sufficiently complex. Instead, consciousness is a fundamental feature of the universe. The universe itself is conscious and all things partake of this consciousness in their own way.

Consciousness is an invisible quality, a sense of being that could never be confirmed from the outside. With panpsychism, we consider every aspect of our experience to be an expression of consciousness.

There is nothing we experience which is not touched by our consciousness. Consciousness interacts with the field of potential at a fundamental level to produce actual outcomes. Therefore all manifest outcomes, whether they are living beings, or inanimate objects, or complex systems, all of these things are expressions of consciousness, to some degree at least.

Although this may sound far-fetched, panpsychism is gaining renewed attention from scientists at the forefront of quantum physics. This is because quantum physics has forced us to recognize the limitations of our conventional understanding of physics.

We have a relationship between observer and observed which cannot be accounted for in our classical model of reality, and we have yet to find a satisfactory replacement. But we're coming close; consciousness is the key to our new model of reality. Quantum physics has peered into the depths from which matter is produced from the field of potential by the influence of *consciousness*.

A Singular Consciousness

One intriguing implication of panpsychism is the possibility that all experiences of consciousness (all beings) express the same fundamental consciousness.

If consciousness is a fundamental feature of the universe, like gravity, then it stands to reason that like gravity there will be focal points of consciousness. As a bit of mass is a focal point for the force of gravity, a conscious being is a focal point for this fundamental force of consciousness. More complex beings are like objects of greater mass, each being a larger and more powerful focal point for their respective fields.

Let's put this in even simpler terms. This fundamental consciousness of the universe could be expressed as I AM. As being itself, prior to the forms that being takes. So, the I AM at the center of my consciousness may very well be the same as the I AM at the center of your consciousness, this same fundamental I AM that is at the center of all beings.

If consciousness is fundamental, then this I AM sense is likely shared by all beings, each one a unique expression of a singular consciousness. And we can connect with that fundamental consciousness by tuning in to our own experience of I AM. We can connect with it in one another by treating one another with compassion and respect, by honoring the I AM in them as if it were our own. As it very well may be.

From this perspective, consciousness could be seen as a shared field of information and agency (knowledge and will) that is linked to all conscious beings and, to some degree, to the entire universe.

This means that your thoughts are objects in the shared field of consciousness. Your emotions are vibrations or noises in this shared field of consciousness.

At the core of every conscious being, and even all things that we would not describe as conscious, is a fundamental sense of I AM that wills the universe into being and shapes it into the forms we experience. And furthermore, each human being can feel and engage with this I AM core personally, from within, and be in contact with the source of all beings.

Jung and the Collective Unconscious

In order to delve a bit deeper into the human experience of consciousness, let's have a look at the work of Carl Jung.

Jung was one of the fathers of psychoanalysis, a student of Freud and pioneer in the field of psychology. He also had interest in Western esotericism, astrology, the I Ching, tarot, dreams, and vision quests. Jung's area of special interest was the *symbol*, and it was a difference of opinion he and Freud had regarding the interpretation of dream symbols that led to their falling out.

Freud believed that the *meaning of the dream symbol* was the only important aspect of it. Jung, however, thought that there must be some significance in the *specific choice of dream symbol*. If a hundred different symbols would work equally well for a given meaning, why did one show up rather than another? This sent him on an exploration of the human use of symbol throughout different cultures.

Jung discovered that each person has a very unique and personal relationship with their symbols. At the same time, there are some symbols which have universal appeal. All human beings are tuned in to certain fundamental symbols, although our personal relationship with each symbol is customized from this common base.

For example, the symbol of *mother* has a fundamental meaning to all humans. And, on top of that we each have personalized meanings based on our life experiences. The symbols of the *masculine* and *feminine* are similar in this regard. They are symbols, objects in consciousness, which have universal meaning to all humans. **Jung called these universal symbols archetypes**.

So, in Jung's conception of the world, we have waking consciousness, the outer world with which we are all somewhat familiar in our own way. We also have the personal subconscious, which is the individual repository of thoughts, feelings, our personal history and memories. And, in addition, we have the collective unconscious, which is a repository of these universal symbols (archetypes).

There are certain ideas, things which do not exist in the world of matter, but which are incredibly valuable. Just consider the idea of justice. Or peace. Mercy. Love. These are ideas, stories. And yet these stories have universal appeal. They can inspire, move hearts, and call people to action.

These archetypal ideas are motivations which can be shared, which bring people together and foster healthy interaction. They are objects within the collective unconscious, which means that they speak to all people.

Let us say, for example, that a person's life experiences felt extremely unjust to them. They may develop charge around the symbol of justice and a tendency to react against injustice. They create and strengthen their relationship to the archetype of justice. As they speak, their words reflect their relationship with justice, their passion and belief in this archetype.

To the extent that this individual is able to align with the quality of justice, their passion and belief will be felt by others that hear them. Their words will trigger in others the charge that the listeners have around the archetype of justice.

It is as if our experiences, our challenges, are journeys through the collective unconscious. On these journeys, we encounter powerful ideas, deep feelings, and strong words that can touch hearts and move minds.

In our journey of individuation, we learn what we value, what we believe in, what we would like to serve, and what we want to create. We discover all of these things within ourselves and, at the same time, within the collective unconscious, within this shared field of consciousness and story.

Consciousness and the Spirit World

Another interesting implication of this perspective is the identification of the spirit world with this collective field of consciousness.

Consider, for a moment, that the difference between life and death is often described as spirit. It is the spirit which enlivens the body. Life is the intersection of matter and spirit. Life is matter which possesses consciousness.

Consciousness is spirit. It is the I Am spirit at the center of my being, just as it is the center of yours, and of all beings. By connecting consciously with my I AM sense, and by observing and acting with consideration of that I AM presence in others I connect with, I am able to interact with other beings in a way that transcends our roles. I can engage being-to-being, rather than story-to-story.

This is phenomenal. In seeing consciousness as spirit, and as a spirit which is expressed in all other living beings, I have a new and more life-affirming frame for my interactions with the world. I have a way to recognize the unity beneath the difference and act accordingly. And, by acting in resonance with my world, I create a stronger functional unity throughout my field of experience.

And yet this is still just the beginning.

I could also describe our shared field of consciousness as the spirit world. As a repository of information which contains the potential forms of all thought, all knowledge, all feelings.

Suddenly my inner world becomes a window from which to view the underside of creation. Through my inner journeys, I can come into contact with all the wisdom and understanding available within this field, at least to the extent that I am able to synchronize with this knowledge.

As soon as we see the spirit world as a shared field of consciousness, we have experiential terms that allow us to perceive and interact with objects in the spirit world.

The role of shamans as intermediaries of the spirit world takes on a new light when we view the spirit world as a shared field of consciousness. Archetypes in the collective unconscious could be said to behave as entities within this space. It could even be said that when we engage with these archetypes, we are in communion with these entities. The angel of mercy, the demon of jealousy. It is poetic, but the conscious space certainly behaves alive.

Within individual consciousness, these archetypes act as subpersonalities, like files copied from the internet that are stored in your computer files. These subpersonalities espouse certain values or powerful ideas. We could call them deities or angels, if we preferred an older language for describing them. They each act as a voice within us, a specific perspective and its attendant motivations, a chunk downloaded from the collective.

These inner dynamics become stronger as we relate with them more deeply. By consciously relating with our inner being in this way, we are able to access guidance on anything we ask, though some things are always beyond our view.

In practical shamanism, it is said that the shaman uses imagination as a faculty of perception. Once we see this shared field of consciousness as something that can be meaningfully traversed by our own consciousness, these descriptions become more powerful. Spirit flight or shamanic journey is a meditation, a way of shifting our attention to the inner world, and then through the lens of that inner world, tuning in to a specific bit of information or wisdom.

Jung's discussion of the personal and collective unconscious, in addition to the individual consciousness, reflects the shamanic conception of the three worlds.

Each person begins in the middle world, the outer world. Over time, we begin to see that our experience of the outer world stems from inner stories and charge.

This leads us into the lower world, into the realm of our personal subconscious. We reclaim our power by journeying through the lower world, transforming old pain and stories.

As we begin applying this power, we become aware of the need for guiding principles. This moves us into an exploration of our values, which takes place in the upper world of the collective unconscious. We then bring this insight with us in our return to the middle world.

A final note when engaging with information on this level: when we have an inner journey, it comes to us in the language we best understand, in our preferred story or frame. This means that we must use symbolic language to understand it, just as if we were interpreting a dream.

Our investigations of the collective unconscious come to us cloaked in the faces, forms, and voices of our own imagination. The messages we get must be spoken in a language we can understand, the language of our own perspective and symbol framework. Whatever insights we encounter must later be unpacked in the context of our mundane experience.

No story is true. They're not about being true. Stories are about helping us to understand and navigate our experience. Similarly, no inner journey is true in a fundamental sense. Our conscious understanding is limited that way. Inner journeys, no matter how vivid, are true only in a symbolic sense. They come to us interpreted through our network of story and charge.

Our journeys through the collective subconscious can illuminate aspects of our unconscious charge, access deep creativity, and connect with deep wisdom. However, it can sometimes be challenging to translate journey insights into practical answers.

When we learn the language of symbol, we are given a means to make sense of our journey work in a grounded way. Over time, we tend to develop a very personal working relationship with our inner realm and the journeys we take in this space. We develop and refine an inner language all of our own.

PRACTICES IN CONSCIOUSNESS

Practice 1: Tat Tvam Asi

Tat tvam asi is a Sanskrit term, part of the Hindu tradition as portrayed by the Upanishads. It is one of four Mahavakyas, or *great sayings*, which express the underlying philosophy of the text.

Tat tvam asi, loosely translated, means "I am that."

In the Hindu tradition, Atman is the personal soul. We might describe it as a personal experience of consciousness. And Brahman could be described as the fundamental consciousness of the universe.

In the most expansive sense, tat tvam asi means that there is no real separation between Atman, the individual experience of consciousness, and Brahman, the fundamental consciousness that extends throughout all time and space.

To put this in really simple terms, tat tvam asi means that the same consciousness is at the core of my being, and the core of yours, and the core of all beings. It means, at a very deep level, we are one. We are all expressions of the same consciousness. It means much more than that as well, but this is a good start for the moment.

There is a word used as a prayer and benediction in modern yogic practice: namaste.

Loosely translated, Namaste could be defined as follows: *The light that is within me sees the light that is within you, and when we are in that light we are one.*

This practice is for the first scope of time, for the living moment. This means that it is an understanding that we can keep in our present moment. We can strive to remember, and remember, and remember, that whatever and whomever we're looking at, we're looking at ourselves.

On the level of cognitive psychology, everything that we look at, all of the perceptions that we have regarding the world around us, are ours. Whatever meaning we make about the things we experience, whatever we feel regarding them, even what we perceive with the senses themselves, these things are ours. Our responses and internal modifications of the world. When we see something that we judge, it is because we have associated it with something in our inner experience linked with charge and stories of judgment.

Everything that we see is us. Everything that we notice about what we see is highlighted to our consciousness, not because it is what everyone would see, but because it stands out to us in particular. When we see something in the outer world that we cannot accept, it is because we link that thing with something in the inner world that we do not accept. The emotional charge and story we carry within predispose us to respond to certain things in certain ways, and we project this out into our perception of the world.

Every moment we think we're responding to the objective world around us (how it really is), we're actually responding to our subjective lens of the world (how we think it is to us). Everything we see and respond to is us, from the perspective that we all inhabit our own psychological reality.

We subjectively personalize our experience and our perceptions far more than we might expect. So, in a very practical, immediate way, all of the perceptions that enter my awareness are me. All of the stories that I use to make sense of these perceptions, all of the emotions they evoke within me, all of that is me.

When I use tat tvam asi on this level, it helps me to remain accountable regarding my own perceptions, my own stories and emotions. The alternative approach is to take the victim role, to act as if these perceptions, emotions, and meanings were forced upon me by the world.

When I say, *I am that*, I can take responsibility for my perceptions, for my judgment and charge. I can look at the outer situation, and use it to tune in to things within myself that I have judged, things that had been hiding in my blind spots.

Tat tvam asi can be used on an interpersonal level when interpreted like namaste. So first, I strive to tune in to my own I AM sense, to identify with this aspect of myself which is Being, which has all potential, all possibilities, and which is equally connected to all ways of being. When we get still and quiet, when we tune in to the sense of awareness beneath our name, beneath our stories and memories, we can feel the core of our consciousness, unformed Being.

To use tat tvam asi in your relating, remember that the *I AM* sense that you feel within is different from your stories, from your history. That *I AM* sense inside each of us is the source of all healing, redemption, and transformation. It is bigger than any definition. *I AM* is all we can honestly say about it. But it is enough.

Our small stories of self are pale shadows in comparison to the I AM sense at the core of our being. Also, our little stories of self tend to get lost, caught up in dramas, power plays, and attachments. This leads to fear and conflict, to selfishness and the perpetration of harm.

When we first remember that we are the light of consciousness within, it gives us a way to identify with Being, rather than with our description of ourselves. We can change, and Being remains. We can never lose Being and we don't have to fight to defend it. We don't have to make sure Being is perceived in a particular way. Being is its own reason.

Being – fundamental consciousness – is the rock at the foundation of personal experience, the only thing we can truly know, the only thing we can truly depend upon, and the only thing we need. When we operate from this space, when we feel and identify with our I AM sense, then we begin to see the world around us very differently.

With the *namaste* expression of tat tvam asi, we see the light of consciousness at the core of the other person that we interact with.

They have stories, ideas, and feelings. They have vested interests that may run counter to our own, or a different way of perceiving and relating to the world. But underneath all of that, there is consciousness. Being. That same pure, fundamental consciousness – that same spirit – which I find at the core of my own being.

No matter who I am talking to, no matter who I see, there is the same fundamental consciousness at the core of that person. The person running the cash register. The homeless guy on the corner. The employer who's always given me a rough time. Everyone, whether my little story of self portrays them as important or not, pleasant or not, everyone has this same core of consciousness, this same singular I AM sense.

When I remember this, it's much more challenging to be judgmental and much easier to be compassionate. From this perspective, I can more easily act towards the common interests, rather than getting defensive or advancing myself at the expense of others. And this is still just the beginning.

What about your cat? Or your houseplants? Or that gorgeous tree that's been holding space for the world for the last forty years, right in that spot? From tat tvam asi perspective, all of these things are expressions of Being. They may be far less sophisticated than ourselves, at least from certain limited perspectives. But every single living thing is a focal point of consciousness, of Being. Of the same I AM that's at the root of my being.

Every part of the natural world is alive and (in some way) conscious. And, when we act with respect for the consciousness of the beings we engage with, the relationship becomes healthier.

When we can see the consciousness – the Being – expressed in another organism, we can identify with it. And when we identify with someone or something, that sense of identification grows feelings of care and connection.

Absolutely everything in life is relating. We relate with our bodies, we relate with our history, with each of our senses, with our memories and our life experiences. All of life is interconnected, interrelated. We exist within a living network of relationships.

When we can see and honor the Being in others, those relationships become conscious. Healthy. Respectful. Mutual. We come into resonance and form a functional unity. Something larger than ourselves, beautiful and graceful and alive. We experience a flowering of Being like a symphony formed out of all the individual instruments and musicians.

When we do not see the Being in another, that interaction is unconscious. We get out of sync. The relationship becomes unhealthy, a power struggle, a battle of wills. Each beat tries to run the show without regard to the other beats in the sharing. This is what happens when we divide the world into self and other, and then make self more important than other.

Tat tvam asi, as a moment-to-moment reminder, teaches us that there is no other. All is one. And the more that we act as if this is so, the more we move past selfish, unhealthy, and unconscious ways of relating. And, in a beautiful way, all of our relations begin to come into focus as we practice this.

It takes time, humility, and a willingness to keep showing up. But the more that we can get over ourselves, over our small stories of self, the more we can step into a life filled with joy and truly worth living, on every level.

Tat Tvam Asi as a Practice

The practice of tat tvam asi need not be a mantra, or any visible practice at all. I AM THAT. Whatever you see, remember, I AM THAT. Whenever you judge someone, remind yourself, I AM THAT. Whenever you enjoy a moment of nature, a gorgeous sunset, remember, I AM THAT. All THAT, any THAT, every THAT.

All things are one, all expressions of the One Thing. On the biggest scope, it is the same I AM that shines out of my eyes that shines out of yours. That same I AM is expressed through every single living being on the planet. One consciousness rings through this planet, this universe, and expresses itself through all beings in creation. I AM is singular, and it is deeper and more fundamental than the faces it wears. One artist, many canvases.

All beings on this planet are formed from the matter of this planet. Our mother, the earth, births our bodies from her flesh. We are the earth, all of us sharing the same water, breathing the same air, enjoying the light and warmth from the same sun. We are sharing an ecological web of intimate interrelationship with one another, every being a vital part of this web of life and energy. All life we see, we can remind ourselves, I AM THAT, and act accordingly.

When we remember I AM THAT, we accord others with the care, consideration, respect, and acceptance that we ourselves would like to receive. We begin to see that even the life of our bodies is part of a family, tribe, community, ecosystem, part of a larger world. We begin to see that all things that impact that world, impact us. Our scope of self begins to expand.

Instead of thinking only of our personal future and interests, we feel and consider the impacts of our actions on the larger system upon which we depend. Upon the individuals that matter to us. First, our identity expands to include our partner, our family, then our tribe, and finally our entire world, whatever that looks like to us.

As we practice remembering I AM THAT again and again, whenever we'd like to judge, or turn away, or dramatize our situation, whenever we feel pulled into conflict, anger, jealousy, or envy, we find our feelings about the world changing subtly.

I AM THAT encourages us to feel our natural connection with the beings we encounter, to operate from the heart and with presence. As we cultivate this attitude, this view of the world, it inspires us to relate and collaborate consciously. It teaches us to respect one another, ourselves, and the network of life around us. We begin to strive for balanced, healthy interaction with all aspects of our world.

Practice 2: Match Frequencies

Resonance leads to functional unity.

This is perhaps the most powerful concept contained in this entire book.

An individual is a functional unity. A family is a functional unity. A body. A being. A species. A planet. A cell. Each of these things acts, for some time, and to some degree, as a *one thing*. The elements that constitute that one thing will pass and change. Eventually that *one thing* will be gone as well. But for the time that it is around, it is a functional unity, a micro-consciousness reflecting the macro-consciousness of the Absolute.

Your body is *your body* because of resonance, because all of your cells are tuned in to the same frequency, a frequency expressed by DNA and other factors. Your neurons operate in this same fashion. When their frequencies are out of sync, they do not cooperate to form a functional unity, and we do not experience self-awareness. When the neurons sync up, they form a functional unity, a one thing, and we experience what we describe as consciousness.

Your subjective awareness of self is similar, a network of story and charge, all bound together with a frequency, not so much of sound, but of information. Context, identification. All of these things would be scattered, disconnected, if not for the sense of self, a personal history which rings through all of these stories and imbues them with a common quality.

Consciousness as we experience it is a matter of functional unity.

And, to take it further, all things are one. So every individual thing that we see is a functional unity evoked from the common substratum of consciousness. Every thing, or person, even thought, is made a functional unity by resonance, by the information frequency that directs all parts of it. Resonance happens when all the parts share a common frequency. When the beats match up. Resonance establishes functional unity.

All this sounds crazy technical. How could it possibly be relevant?

Simple answer: everyone has a beat, a frequency. When our frequency matches the other person in the conversation, the interaction flows and we have a good working interaction. We form, in some small, temporary way, a functional unity. Human beings are social creatures, and we're hardwired to come into resonance with other people and things in our experience.

When many people gather together, we come into resonance in powerful and unpredictable ways. When tensions are high, it can be very much akin to forming a wolf pack, and people do it unconsciously all the time.

Just think of a mob. All the people in the mob can get so swept up in the action that it acts like a wave of chaos rather than a collection of individuals. An unconscious functional unity, driven by the deepest pain and loudest voice. The individuals in the mob get caught up in the action, a new dynamic moving through them. The temporary functional unity of the mob has different values and priorities than the individuals which compose it and it can supersede those values for a short time.

A company is a functional unity, as is a nation. For each of these examples, resonance is formed in slightly different ways. And for most human collectives, the individuals are unconscious of the functional unities that they form and how deeply those influences impact their decisions. If we are unconscious of our choices and our creative energy, we cannot really be conscious of how we are using our power and what we are creating with it.

On a more personal level, when we are aware of our own frequency, of the feeling and story we bring to our interactions, we have more freedom in those interactions. Becoming aware of our own frequency helps us to choose how and where to engage and it gives us a choice as to what we bring into our interactions when we do engage.

Just think of a time when you were walking with a friend. Perhaps the friend sees something exciting ahead, and they speed up. If you're like most people, you'll tend to speed up as well. Humans, when interacting with one another, tend to come into resonance. They will match pace, match breath, mirror body language, most of this on a subtle and unconscious level.

If you are aware of this, you can *pace and lead.* You can match the other person's speed, and then slowly, a bit at a time, shift to the speed you prefer. The same thing happens on an emotional and psychological level when we engage with one another. It requires respect and rapport to pace and lead with integrity, but it is one of the best ways to help someone through a moment of intense crisis.

If both people are unaware of their frequency, the loudest one wins. The strongest emotion, the loudest voice, the most pain determines the tone of the entire dynamic. However, when you are aware of your frequency, you can enter a situation like this, match pace, and de-escalate. This approach offers a deep level of freedom and an ability to stand in service without being crushed by intense emotions. It's gold.

The most direct way to connect with our frequency is through feeling. The way that we feel, both emotionally and through the subtle sensations of the body, reflects a precise and specific frequency. We must first learn this frequency from within, determining which feelings are supportive of the needs we encounter in daily life.

Consider the feelings of calm, confidence, enthusiasm, creative absorption, motivation. When you encounter these feelings in your day, take note of them from within. In as much detail as you are able. And then practice. Using intention, disengage from your outer situation, and engage with the desired feeling, the desired *resource state*.

When you disengage from the outer situation, you practice a *state change*, returning to baseline consciousness. This can be as simple as closing your eyes and taking a breath.

When you connect with and express a certain feeling, you set your frequency in resonance with that feeling. So, for example, when I contact the feeling of confidence and really feel it, all the way down, that feeling will be reflected in all the myriad details of my manner. The feeling I carry qualifies the energy around me in certain distinct ways.

Consider the next important conversation that you have, the next interaction with a loved one. When you enter the interaction, remember that you have a frequency, and they have a frequency. Like two drummers, each with their own beat. When you come into contact, the first thing you want to do is find a beat you can agree on.

When you match frequencies with the other person, it's as if your energy field and their energy field come together to form one field. And, if you understand how to adjust your frequency intentionally, then you have just gained the ability to influence the entire field. Not only that, you will feel that field, just as much as the other does. This means that there is, after a fashion, a shared space where thoughts and feelings occur equally to both sides.

This is not a common perspective, but it is an extremely useful one. From this angle, there is a common language of resonance and feeling that all things speak. Humans, animals, plants, and even things that we would not traditionally define as conscious. In order to establish meaningful, conscious interaction with *anything*, tune in to that person or thing with your attention, and then allow yourself to match frequencies with it.

Matching Frequency: The Practice

This is an extremely advanced technique. It requires a solid, visceral self-knowledge, a deep ability to focus and concentrate, and a degree of consciousness around things that many people have not yet learned to be conscious of.

That said, it's so natural and fundamental to the human experience that the practice gains momentum quickly. We are basically designed to synchronize with one another socially so that we can interact meaningfully and to mutual benefit. We do it without thinking about it, often without meaning to.

The key here is that we are learning to first be conscious of our frequency and that of those we interact with. Next, we are learning to shift our own frequency at will and in the manner we intend.

Prior to this, our frequency will tend to react reflexively to the people and situations around us and to the thoughts and feelings within. We are unconsciously reactive to the world, and our frequency shifts or sticks in the ways that are familiar to us, usually within a relatively fixed range. With this practice, we begin to exercise conscious intention in these realms. *The ability to intend our frequency is the foundation of actualized free will.*

First and foremost, our frequency is established with intention. You intend to move your arm and it moves. In a similar fashion, we can intend to match frequencies with anything we focus our attention on.

The process is simple. First, we place the focus of our attention on someone or something. Then we breathe and relax, maintaining awareness and inner *feeling* of the focal point. As we breathe and relax, we create space within, and our frequency will shift to reflect more fully the focal point of our attention. Don't force it. Don't try. Just feel the focal point, and relax, allowing that feeling to spread into your body.

Anything shared provides grounds for synchronization. And synchronization provides a common space where thoughts and emotions are more likely to occur to all parties involved. We can synchronize moment-to-moment at the level of breath. We can synchronize in terms of thought and language with the use of common stories, common narratives. We synchronize in some ways when sharing space with others, or when engaged in a common task requiring collaboration.

All of these synchronizations are natural examples of how people match frequencies with one another in different ways, and they all facilitate the formation, however temporary, of a functional unity.

So again, **tune in, feel, and sync up**. Try it, feel it out, and you may be surprised how natural it is.

Everything is a relationship, and everything has a beat. How do you like to dance?

Practice 3: Seed of Light

When we are young, the structures that we form in our consciousness are reflexive, unconscious. As we develop a stronger relationship with our inner world, we gain the opportunity to create conscious structures within.

Consider the kinds of structures you have seen others grow. The wounded child's role. The legacy of pain. The person of importance. Just like a garden, we can grow these structures, these images, stories, and the feelings linked to them. In the garden of our mind, we cultivate many stories, watering them with our attention. After we have nurtured them long enough, it's almost as if they start to overgrow the garden. Our stories can actually colonize our consciousness, leaving very little space for presence.

But once we understand the impact of our time and attention, once we begin to understand how we bring life to stories within our minds, we have the opportunity to create healthy structures. Stories that bring us into focus, that connect us with our highest potential, deepest resilience, and brightest joy. We grow stories within us, consciously or unconsciously, throughout our lives, and it is just a matter of awareness and intention to use this to enrich our lives.

For this practice of consciousness in the third scope of time, imagine a seed of light, a point of brilliance right in the center of your chest.

This seed of light is the core of your being. It is your fundamental consciousness, the seat of the I AM which forms the foundation for every moment of your experience. This seed of light connects you to the source of all energy, inspiration, and life. It connects you to meaning and purpose, to loving, healthy relation with your world.

Every time you cultivate presence, you strengthen this seed of light, fanning it like a spark. Every time you look upon others with compassion, or find wisdom in pain, you make this bright spark of consciousness a little bit brighter.

Each person has this seed of light within them. Even when you are in conflict with the person, you can speak to the seed of light within them with respect. When we act with authenticity and warmth, when we speak with love to the seed of light within others, they respond to it. It takes work to get past our stories and our roles. It takes work to really *feel* it. But if you do, it can work wonders.

We can also speak to this seed of light within us. We can ask for guidance and listen to direction. Even if this is no more than us talking to ourselves, it is a way of connecting with our highest wisdom and deepest integrity. A way of intending to be guided by that part of ourselves which is in healthy connection to our world.

Take some time each day to remember the seed of light at the center of your being. Take time to nurture it with presence. With kindness, connection, meaningful action, service, and joy. With story and exploration, learning and growth. Remember that this spark becomes brighter as we become more conscious of our connection with everything around us.

At a very deep level, what we do as conscious beings is qualify energy. We bring a specific order, vibration, and frequency to the space that we inhabit. When we cultivate a seed of light, we learn to bring an energy of presence and connection into our space. We learn to qualify our energy in life-affirming ways. And, from that simple act of intention, cultivated over time, chosen again and again, we shine meaning, love, and freedom throughout our lives and into the lives of those around us.

The End and The Beginning

In some forms of martial arts, a black belt was used as a symbol of mastery. The history of this is interesting. It's said that when the tradition began, the belt started off white. And, over years of training and practice, the belt became so grimy that it was near black.

At this point, the student was said to have mastered the art. But what mastery meant, in these terms, is that the student was responsible for their own further training. The black belt signified that they have learned enough to receive further instruction from within, from the student's personal practice and journey.

The journey never ends. For an individual truly dedicated to a martial art, each day brings practice, improvement, and cultivation of skill. You can never be perfect. It's similar to learning to play a musical instrument. It's never finished. You can just sit back and work with what you have, but if you're dedicated to learning to play, that learning can go on forever.

The big journeys are lifelong, and the cultivation of consciousness is the biggest journey of them all. We will never be finished learning, growing, developing, refining. And, rather than seeing that as a frustration, I've come to view it as one of the greatest joys in life.

When we dedicate ourselves to growth, we are always discovering new potentials, new ideas, new ways of relating to the world, to ourselves, and to others. It's rich, and full, and intensely alive.

The cultivation of consciousness is also confusing. And mystifying, and intoxicating, a path strewn with pitfalls and dead ends. Just remember, any time we have things figured out, it's time to see something new. Humility and open-mindedness can save us a great deal of time and pain.

Many Native American tribes use a symbol called the medicine wheel, just a simple circle with a cross in it. This symbol describes the journey of life, the journey of the seasons, the journey of the day. A quartered circle to show the phases as life begins with spring, moves into summer, graces autumn, and comes to rest in winter. And, as has happened for as long as we can remember, winter is followed by spring and another turn around the cycle. Round and round.

This is the archetypal journey of life, evident as much in our personal lives as it is in nature. We go in circles, taking a journey and going afar, learning, discovering, growing, and then returning home with these inner treasures. And, after one journey ends, another begins.

Some of these journeys are physical, but not all. We begin a journey when we enter into a new relationship, or when we change jobs or move house. We go on a journey when we get hurt or lose someone we love. Or when we get stuck in thoughts, feelings, or habits. Or when we begin learning something new.

We explore this new focal point of our attention, play it out, take action prompted by it. We engage in this journey, develop it, see where it takes us, how it feels. There are infinite paths in life, and consciousness is the means of navigating these paths. That said, we go in circles, returning again and again to the same kinds of experiences, the same dynamics and feelings.

But nothing is ever the same as last time. We're not just going in circles. We're spiraling upward, gaining ever greater scope and experience, applying this to the next turn round the spiral. There is no real end in experience. None that we need practically concern ourselves with, anyway. Every end just leads to a new beginning.

The Journey Thus Far

The purpose of this book has been to provide a clear, coherent review of human consciousness, amenable to the western mind and based on experience rather than theory. And, more than that, to offer a liberating, empowering paradigm for our relationship with our own consciousness.

The one language all human beings share, the one foundational story that unites us all, is the human body. Our bodies are all different, but we all relate to the world in fundamentally human ways.

We all breathe. We all have emotions come up, and these emotions color our experience. We all use attention to focus our efforts, and story to make sense of our extended moment. We all have a need to make peace with ourselves, to learn self-acceptance. We all have a voice, in some way. We all have dreams, ideas, thoughts.

When we speak in these terms, we speak in a language common to all human beings, fundamental to human experience. We are all different, and yet, in being human, we can learn beautiful human skills to bring mastery and grace to each aspect of the human experience.

Breath and the journey state, the emotional compass, the art of discernment, the gift of each module is a superpower which we can bring to every area of human life. Taken together, they offer a way of relating to self and world that can completely transform our experience.

My greatest hope is that this book, this training, can offer you the sword of no sword. This is a Zen term, and it relates to a union of will and consciousness, unformed, and yet made powerful by its alignment with the Tao. I have done my best to devote these pages to clear, open-ended perspectives on the living experience of the human being.

A big focus of this training, and perhaps of life itself, is to bring consciousness more fully into our lived experience. To align with the fundamental consciousness at the core of our being, and see what happens. In service to this we have explored how to work with our experience to achieve our highest potential. We have looked into how we can each live the most fulfilling, connected lives possible, in our own way.

What I have tried **not** to do is saddle you with yet another theoretical account of your place in the universe. We have too many stories like this competing for our belief already, and they cloud the air.

I simply encourage you to pay attention, and to make meaning in ways that work for you, whatever that looks like. The stories in these pages will offer the most benefit when viewed as allegories, offering symbolic insight into the nature of our experience. Or as working models subject to change when a more effective perspective comes along.

We are artists of our own lives. We fulfill our art not by describing it, not by putting it in a box or painting by numbers. We fulfill our artistry by living, by exerting our intention, observing the responses, and moving into deeper, more conscious connection with every moment, every act. By breathing our lives.

Stories support us in this journey, ideally. However, our stories can also bind us if we're not careful. Each person makes meaning in their own way, so each person has subtly or profoundly different stories about the world.

We don't need to have others agree with our stories. They're personal. Our stories just need to work for us, to help us live our lives and meet our challenges. It is a fine balancing point to honor the stories of others while still offering value and guidance to them. And again, the language of the human body is ideal for this, experiential, personal, and universal.

Chakras and Consciousness

From time to time in history, people have shared new dreams, new messages, and new practices. Those gifted in dreaming and storytelling peer beneath the skin of the world and translate what they find there into terms which (hopefully) those around them can relate to.

Patanjali is one such individual, a sage of ancient India and author of the Yoga Sutras. One point of genius in Patanjali's sutras is the eight limbs of yoga, a step-by-step training that each person can follow in order to cultivate consciousness.

This sequential path of training works so well because it is structured in parallel with the natural path of human development. The eight limbs of yoga are customized to the human experience of consciousness. They move us from the most basic and tangible level of our experience to the largest scope of awareness. By following the limbs sequentially, a student can first address their most basic impulses, then their desires, then actions, becoming more aware of each level of their being along the way.

Patanjali was able to structure the path of yoga so brilliantly, in part, because he was working with a very sophisticated understanding of the human experience. Hindu culture was steeped in studies of the human energy field and the chakras, the centers of subtle energy in the body.

There are hundreds of chakras in the body, each one a point where veins of subtle energy cross one another. According to many systems, seven major chakras line the spine, each associated with certain emotions, functions, needs, and ways of relating to the world.

The most basic and personal motivations are associated with the lower chakras, while the most creative and expansive motivations are associated with the upper chakras.

The lowest chakra, poised at the base of the spine, is related to survival and the body.

The next, the navel, is related to will and emotions and the things that flow through the body.

Next, the chakra at the solar plexus is related to our ego, our conscious story of self.

Then comes the heart with feeling and connection, and with the healing that results from it.

And the throat, associated with voice and expression.

And the third eye, centered at the eye level and associated with vision and inspiration.

The crown chakra at the very top of the skull is related to faith and consciousness.

In a way, this perspective of human nature is similar to Abraham Maslow's hierarchy of needs. Maslow noticed that human beings have some needs that are more basic, which must be addressed before others. We are first motivated by hunger, thirst, the needs and conditions of the body.

Next comes safety. We must have our dire hunger and thirst addressed before safety becomes a priority. And safety must be addressed before we prioritize human connection. Once we have met our needs for human connection, our self esteem becomes a priority. And, once this need is addressed, we can then move on to self-development and actualization.

Students in certain Indian traditions were directed to work through each chakra in sequence, filling them with the light of consciousness. Essentially, this is a conscious participation in the natural human growth process. We take conscious note of and responsibility for our physical needs and sense of safety with the first chakra, meeting and coming to terms with the primary emotion of this motivation.

Next, we look at our emotions and the actions to which they drive us, the purview of the second chakra. These emotions show up in a major way in our connection with other human beings, so this chakra is associated with intimacy and human connection in Maslow's framework. The chakra system, seen from this perspective, is a sequential expression of human motivation, from the most basic to the most fully flowered.

Each of the first seven limbs of yoga is related to one of the chakras, working from the root up. So, the practice of the yama, the first limb of yoga, helps us to overcome fearful decisions by practicing restraint, by engaging in faith rather than fear. This helps us to do housekeeping on the root chakra.

The second limb, niyama, guides us in the right use of our energy. It is intended to address the sacral chakra, which is connected intimately with our vitality and how we use our will.

The third limb, asana, brings consciousness into how we move our bodies. It helps us to become aware of where we are putting our attention right now and how we meet that attention with the body.

This is associated most closely with the third chakra. And so on, bringing consciousness to a finer and finer point.

Patanjali's approach is excellent not only for its structure, but for the movement and physical engagement required. Yoga is something you learn by *doing*. And, in the process of *doing*, we learn personal lessons. We go beyond parroting the words of others. The practice itself becomes the teacher. We learn to get quiet and listen to the body. And we learn a complex and deeply intuitive language of the body in the symbolic language of the chakras and nadis, the veins of subtle energy mentioned above.

It is beyond the scope of this work to offer a comprehensive description of chakras and the subtle energy system. There is a wealth of excellent material available, online and in print, for those who wish to explore the subject in greater depth.

For now, it's enough to say that *Only Human* was structured on the very same principles as those used by Patanjali. With each module, we engage with a fundamental aspect of human experience, from the most basic and personal to the most expansive and abstract.

The practices in each section are an opportunity to begin using these understandings, thinking *with* them instead of *about* them. Gaining skill at working with your own consciousness, rather than just knowing about it.

The stories prime the pump, but the practice is where we walk the path, where all the magic happens. The personal journey is *personal*. It's unique, customized to the individual by the individual. Through challenge, experience, growth, and healing, we each find our own way to relate in an empowering way to each aspect of our being, and to our being as a whole.

The Tree of Earth

The journey we have taken thus far could be described as the first tree of our growth, the Tree of Earth. From this perspective, each of the elements relates to an aspect of human experience. Earth is linked to the most tangible elements of human experience, like our body and the rhythms, conditions, and qualities inherent in the body and the senses. This is the first turn round the spiral, the exploration of what we have and how we can work with it.

The remaining symbolic elements, water, air, and fire, relate to the realms of emotion, thought, and will respectively. Just as we have explored the constituents of the immediate human experience (Earth), we can go back through each and explore the ideas and stories used to frame our relation with each. This could be described as the Tree of Air.

We then proceed into the level of feeling, into a deep exploration of our emotional nature. And, in so doing, we grow within us the Tree of Water. And finally, we come to the level of will and creation, where we can take charge of our creative energy, learning how to consistently use it with integrity and in alignment with our values. This could be described as the inner bonsai of will, the Tree of Fire.

You may wonder why we would use the image of a tree to describe this growth. One thing stands out to me after a lifetime of study into the different symbols used by different cultures to describe the invisible world. All cultures are describing the same invisible world. They use different language and symbols, relate with the world from different vantage points. It almost seems as if there is a convergent evolution of the core spiritual symbols.

This means one of two things: either these symbols were derived from a common source, or they are in some way fundamental to the human experience. The tree is one such symbol, used in different forms by nearly every culture to describe the invisible aspect of the human experience.

Sometimes this tree is called the axis mundi, the axis of the world. Sometimes it is called the World Tree, or Yggdrasil. Sometimes it is called the Tree of Life. Sometimes this tree is described similar to a Russian nesting doll, as a series of sheaths or, to use a Sanskrit term, shokas.

Regardless of the specific imagery or the culture of origin, the connection between matter and consciousness is a link, a thread, or a tree which brings these aspects of being into union. A common image used to describe this tree in depth is the rainbow bridge, the link between matter and spirit.

The chakras described in the previous section are one symbolic map of this tree of human experience. The most basic, perhaps most animalistic or instinctive, aspects of the human experience occupy the lowest portion of the tree. And as we climb higher, we encounter more abstract, creative, and refined aspects of the human experience.

Life is, after all, the intersection of spirit and matter, the union of body and consciousness. We have some concerns that are driven more by the body, and other concerns which are rooted more fully in our experience of consciousness, in our abstract sense of self and that which gives rise to it.

In exploring the Tree of Earth, we have come to a deeper understanding of the middle world, also known as the outer world. We have begun to recognize that our perception of the outer world is more personal and subjective than we had imagined, and that we must refine our awareness of our senses and the interpretive stories we generate unconsciously. We have begun to notice that our senses reflect the function and condition of our body, our breath, and our conscious focal point.

All that we perceive in the world comes through the medium of the body and the senses. And *anything worth doing in the world comes through action aligned with values*. This makes the body the natural place to begin the journey of consciousness in earnest.

In growing the Tree of Earth, we bring the light of our consciousness to a host of subtle signals, such as breath, muscle tension, visceral emotional and physical reactions. Body reflects everything that's going on in our minds and hearts, as well as our physical conditions. Therefore, in becoming aware of the body, we tune in to a language spoken by all parts of our being.

Before we can truly gain from emotional work or mental work, we must have the capacity to be grounded and present. We must learn to pay attention to where we are and what we're doing. To the subtle choices we are making.

When we tune in to the body, we gain the ability to be mindful. Out of story and into the living moment, the *Now* which the body reflects and attunes to so faithfully.

The entire world has a beat, just as we have the triple drum of our breath, heart rate, and brain rhythm. When we tune in to the body, we gain the ability to hear the beat of the world and attune to aspects of it intentionally. We can, at will, come into resonance with those we encounter. And resonance leads to functional unity. We can, on a practical and energetic level, become one being for a time, sharing emotion, thought, and will along with our shared rhythm.

If this sounds confusing or outre, don't worry. This isn't something you really learn about from words. If you'd like to explore it yourself, just make it a habit to tune in to your own body and breath. And make it a point to tune in to the rhythm of others when you engage with them.

When we tune in to the rhythm of the other, we can dance with them, just like when you are working closely with a friend and everything flows. We can either allow the dance of the world to support and strengthen us, or resist it at every turn. Learning to dance begins with slowing down and listening to the beat of the world. With letting go and letting flow.

The Widening Spiral

There are as many paths to the cultivation of consciousness as there are different minds to frame the journey. We all walk a completely unique path, attuned to our personal challenges, gifts, and points of emphasis. The structure of the path to come, then, is not a universal one. The path I describe is one intended for people in the modern world, a world replete with ideas, stories, and an intellectual frame of the world.

Because of this, the next step in our journey is a mental one. The Tree of Earth focuses on the human body and the universal elements of human experience. The Tree of Air emphasizes the stories that we use to make sense of the world.

We are filled so full of stories about the world, indoctrinated with them with the best of intentions since before our first memory. And there's nothing wrong with that. It's the life of culture to pass along the stories of our ancestors to the generation to come. These stories form a common thread of experience that helps our culture to learn and grow through the centuries.

That said, we have stories passed from one generation to the next, often without critical review, and treated as Truths rather than as ways to make sense of the world.

This brings the downside of story to the fore. When we have invested our belief in a particular story, a particular perspective on the world, we will tend to selectively perceive only those things that line up with this story. This severely compromises our cognitive capacity. It binds us to the world we believe we will see.

As we grow the Tree of Air within our consciousness, we look back over our stories, we strive to notice them and maintain awareness of them in the moment. We learn to question all of these stories, even the most ancient and treasured in our experience. We question not the truth of these things, but their living value to our experience. We question why we believe these stories. We question our understanding of these stories in personal terms. And we learn some open-ended stories which help us to make deep sense of the world without hampering our ability to perceive and reason.

In a way, it would be more natural and experiential to engage with the Tree of Water after the Tree of Earth. It would make more sense to the healthy, natural human to explore subtle energy, learn how to feel it, learn how to make sense of this most tangible layer of the invisible world.

But the modern human is so full of borrowed ideas that they are often unable to determine the difference between expectation and subtle perception. Because of this, we must address the modifications of the mind before we can do justice to the realm of subtle energy.

So, to look at the *Only Human* path of cultivation from the sky-view, we see a fractal journey, similar lessons played out in each layer of our being. First we refine the way we relate with our bodies, then our minds, then our hearts, then our will, each layer leading to the next and deepening the work of the previous.

We take the same turns round the spiral in the growth of each tree, the same steps on the journey, but emphasizing different elements in sequence. The overall path becomes a fractal expansion, each tree becoming a reflection and amplification of the previous.

With the Tree of Earth, we explore the full range of human experience from the most physical and tangible perspective. We become more attuned to both our bodies and the thoughts and feelings that visit us in the inner world.

We then turn our view inward with the Tree of Air, exploring the ways we craft meaning, the ways we interpret and frame our experiences. In the process, we will also begin to tune in to our body's natural ability to perceive and respond to the energetic fields around us. Our emotions, stories, and perception of subtle energy are linked, all moving with and reflecting one another.

When we begin to explore subtle energy with the Tree of Water, we begin to understand that this energy flows through our body, reflecting every action, thought, and emotion. Not only that, our subtle energy fields reflect and influence physical growth, communication, and the likelihood of certain types of experiences.

With an experiential awareness of energy, we have a window into the state of our entire being, physical, emotional, and mental. In addition, we have a tail-that-wags-the-dog means to influence every aspect of our being. By reviewing these aspects of the human experience, by learning to work with the subtle levels of being, we have become an adept.

At this point, we must decide what to do with this power, this clarity and self-knowledge. We come to the final tree, the Tree of Fire. It's here that we work to bring every action, every decision into alignment with our true values. It is here that we craft a legend from our lives.

The Tree of Fire is so absolutely personal, so unique to each person, that no one can guide you through this phase of the journey. It is the most individuated, and, at the same time, the most dedicated to service and collective wellbeing.

At this point, we have transcended the bulk of our petty and ignorant stories, our limiting habits and unresolved emotions, though we will need lifelong vigilance for our own tendencies to distort, project, and generate story.

We have dedicated ourselves to living in a meaningful and fulfilling way, in principle. We now tune in to how we show up in the world. We strive to take conscious creative action in a way that most fully, most beautifully expresses our unique message, our unique offering to the world. We strive to contribute to the world, rather than survive it, conquer it, or attempt to convert it. The Tree of Fire is the tree of service, as well as creation, power, and freedom. This is where the journey truly begins.

Gurudeva

How amazing would it be to be able to ask yourself a question, listen within, and receive words, thoughts, feelings, or gestalts that provide clarity? What would you do with the capacity to listen within and get solid answers? Or listen within and receive refined, wise instruction for any area or focal point of human experience, any specific situation?

You are far more amazing than you may realize. Within you, wisdom, grace, and power are waiting at the gates, ready to be called upon. We are capable of far more than we have imagined. To access it, we first have to believe it's possible, to make space for the possibility of new and unexpected potentials within ourselves. Next, we have to learn how to bridge the conscious and subconscious functions of our beings.

In alchemy, the science of transformation, this is known as a Hermetic Bridge. In yogic traditions, it could be described as the gurudeva, the teacher within. In many tribal cultures, the young of the tribe are taught to listen within for their guide, for the spirit of great wisdom that watches over them and guides their path. In Christian traditions, we are taught to pray, and to listen to that still small voice within, the voice of the Lord in our conscience.

In all of these instances, the little "I," the conscious ego, intentionally makes contact with deeper reserves of our being. In each tradition, it is recognized that this deeper aspect of our being has access to wisdom, knowledge, and strength that the conscious mind does not.

When we begin to make space between our thoughts, we (re) gain the ability to listen within. From one perspective, the conscious mind is only an interface, a means to orient bits of subconscious knowledge to the needs of the current moment. So, when we start listening within, we begin to hear quite a bit.

When we begin looking inward and exercising discernment with the insights we find there, we come into contact with the teacher within, a source of great wisdom and a different, less invested, perspective. We gain a new way of knowing and the ability to process our lessons more deeply.

From a psychological perspective, the subconscious mind is always recording, processing, filing, and selecting relevant focal points, all below the threshold of conscious awareness. We are only able to pay conscious attention to a fraction of these impressions at any given moment.

However, the computer within our being continues to process these things in the background. When we slow our brain frequency and enter a light meditative, journey, or prayer state, we are able to engage more intentionally with this wealth of latent inner knowledge.

Our subconscious minds are genius at instant recording and high-level multifactorial processing, but we require an interface before this information is available to the conscious mind. We must learn to look inward, to ask a question and listen for the answer.

We must also, in order to avoid delusion, view all that we find in the inner world as we would a dream, a symbolic or allegorical expression offering veiled insight into our situation. These inner intuitive hits are starting points that can then be fleshed out with the more practical, contextual functioning of our conscious mind.

We can bring the deep wisdom of our intuition together with the intellectual handling of our conscious minds to form a whole greater than the sum of its parts. This is because the mind works far more effectively when we allow each aspect to function to its strengths.

The conscious mind is a tool for our being to engage with the living moment. For high-level creative work and inspiration, the conscious mind just catches it as it comes through, figures the words to fit the meaning, the actions to fit the music. It is the subconscious mind which feels the music and tunes the entire being to it.

Although I have explained all of this in a psychological way, please do not confuse this with reductionism. The fact that our subconscious mind is connected to inspiration, knowledge, and wisdom beyond the conscious mind is miraculous in itself.

Nothing in life is just spiritual or just practical. All aspects of the world come together to form a *one thing*. Everything is connected, forming a living dance that all of us participate in, each moment, each breath. The spiritual and material expressions of the world mirror and reflect one another. Consciousness is itself magical. And looking into the nature of human consciousness leads to more magic, not less.

When this function is developed to the highest degree, we align with our inner teacher, with the source of wisdom within. We make a habit of creating space between our thoughts, so that we can see more clearly. And we learn to ask questions and listen within for the answer.

We also learn the language of symbol, both personal and universal, so that we can translate the wisdom we receive from within into practical contextual terms. And, as always, we begin to learn how we can stand in service with this knowledge and clarity. In so doing, we begin walking the path of the sage, the guide and keeper of wisdom.

A final word about the path of the sage: humility. We don't know everything. We are always learning, changing. Letting go of old things to make way for new, inside and out.

No matter how clear our conception or beautiful our story, it will eventually outlive its usefulness to us. No matter how complete our perspective, we will still have blind spots. Humility helps us to keep growing, rather than succumbing to the temptation of pride.

Clarity is a matter of perspective, and we can always see a new perspective, just as we can always be blindsided by things that aren't accounted for in our working perspective. Each time we humble ourselves, we open up to see the world with fresh eyes. We grow, in the ways that matter most.

The Light of Consciousness

Have you ever noticed that a car will break down faster when you're not driving it? Areas of your home that you rarely pay attention to tend to get dusty and have piles of stuff accumulate. Anything that you're not paying attention to will tend to resort to its most relaxed state.

There are plenty of practical reasons for this. We don't do upkeep and maintenance of these areas. We tend to avoid them, sometimes consciously, sometimes unconsciously. In the outer world we do not take the actions required to keep this focal point in good order. In the inner world, it becomes darker to our mind's eye. And, conversely, when we begin paying attention to these things, working with them, they become brighter to the mind's eye, more suffused with the light of our consciousness.

The imagery of light transcends cultures. It is fundamental to human experience. That which is dark, we cannot see. We are blind to it, ignorant of it, unaware of it. That which we are conscious of is lit to our inner awareness. We are conscious of it. We can see it.

This is one of the most useful perspectives for seeing how perception influences our experience of reality. We cannot, in any moment, be conscious of absolutely everything that we are experiencing. It's too big. We'll always miss things. But we can train ourselves to be more conscious in specific areas. Yoga postures train us to be more conscious of our bodies, for example. To become aware of the body on ever subtler levels, filling even the finest threads of our physical bodies with the light of awareness.

When we learn about a new subject, information on that subject becomes lit to our consciousness, and we can access knowledge about it intentionally, consciously.

When we learn a new skill, we bring the light of consciousness into both our bodies and in the body of knowledge related to the skill. We bring light into the medium in which that skill plays out.

Just consider the journey of learning to play a musical instrument. We painstakingly learn the physical dexterity and knowledge required to make the music, and we tune in to the world of sound and feeling in which music operates. These things were unfamiliar to us at first, dark and unknown. With time and exploration, they become lit to our mind's eye and easy to traverse.

Energy flows where attention goes. Wherever we place our attention, the conscious focal point of our light of consciousness, we see it in greater detail. This aspect of what we're experiencing, the focal point of our attention, becomes larger and more powerful in our inner experience, more detailed. Fleshed out.

When we first begin to learn a new subject, for example, it is a dark expanse stretching out before us. And, as we begin engaging with the material, it comes to life in our inner experience, linking bits of information, providing new perspectives and insights. This subject gains detail in the manner of fractal articulation, layer after layer of depth and interconnection, as far as we can see. In other words, we just see more details and more interconnection the deeper we go. We can carry the light of consciousness deep within any subject and explore its inner workings.

Observation has an influence on what is observed. The light of consciousness is the essence of observation. It has a creative force in our inner world, and it directs our creative energies in the outer world.

Wherever we place the light of our consciousness, we begin to transform. Through the medium of awareness and will, we begin to work with what we see. And it begins to take a new shape, reflecting the new energy that we bring to it.

Light is consciousness. It is the potential for intention, awareness, and understanding. When we feel old feelings and forgive them, we bring light into the heart. When we learn something new about a particular subject, we bring light into our knowledge about that subject. When we look at our decisions and what we build in life, we bring light into our relationship with our own power. When we pay attention to the body, its conditions and its functions, we bring light into the body.

We bring the light of consciousness to anything upon which we place our attention, to anything we're learning, exploring, discovering, or creating.

In addition to what we have discussed so far, there is an aspect of balance that pertains to the interaction of light and darkness. When we begin to cultivate awareness, we concentrate our light. We become more present, more able to see, feel, and respond intelligently to what is happening in any given moment. We wake up, incrementally and gradually, to depths of meaning and perception that are not consciously shared by all around us. And this light is a power, one which allows us to see and touch the inner world of another.

No gift comes without a challenge. The power of light and consciousness feeds an equally powerful shadow. We will become ever more gifted in surfing our minds and hearts, utilizing best fit stories for a given purpose, and crafting an impeccable legend to support our service.

But the inner journey is never over. No matter how far we have gone, there will be more lessons, more things hidden in our blind spots and yet to be revealed to the light of our awareness. And, since we tend to play in the collective sphere at this time, it becomes essential to cultivate vigilance and make a practice of personal shadow work.

Shadow work is the intentional exploration of the outer world in light of the inner misalignments that it reflects. We look at what's going on around us, knowing that we will see things that reflect our inner world. We take note of the kinds of interactions we have with others, the kinds of challenges we face, and we look to them for clues to lessons yet unlearned.

Gone are the days of the victim, when we could blame the world for being unfair, or specific people for being unreasonable or cruel. We participate in everything we experience. We have navigated to this exact moment, consciously or unconsciously.

The shadow is the part of our being which is creating things that we do not consciously wish to create. It is that part of our beings that acts without conscious awareness. And the more intelligent, powerful, or actualized we become, the more powerful this shadow becomes, right along with us.

This is another reason that humility is so essential. We will have times when our perception falls short, and we need to learn a new lesson. There will be times that we create challenges for ourselves

319

without realizing it, and with humility, we can actually see ourselves doing it. Thus relieving us of the necessity of replaying the lesson. Maybe.

All balanced energy flows in a circular pattern. And the journey of our lives involves many of these cycles, all overlapping and set within one another. When we have a lesson unlearned, we will play it out again and again as we travel around the cycle. Until we have a fresh perspective on this issue. Until we have learned how to navigate our journey so that we no longer create or align with this outcome.

We're doing it to ourselves. Which sucks to realize, in a way. But the upside is that doing something different is completely within our power. Shadow work is the key to making these unconscious activities and motivations conscious. And it is the work of a lifetime.

Alongside humility, we must cultivate a practice of vigilance, trying to take note of what we do, what we feel, in each moment. And it is important that this vigilance be blended with kind, gentle, and ruthless self-honesty. We can only truly move forward when we take complete accountability for our lives. Again and again, while we're tempted to slip back into the egoic victim mentality or the hero script.

One thing which can make this incredibly difficult is the fact that we get triggered. When we get defensive or hurt, we immediately change how we think and feel. We tend to get entrenched, defending ourselves and our perspective, closing our minds.

In times of challenge, we enter into a period of small-mindedness where we can only see down. We tend to lose sight of our lessons during these moments. Challenges bring intense feelings, and only the lessons we have learned deeply will be able to cut through the din.

If you have been so lucky as to have had a dark night of the soul, a time when everything fell apart, and if you have come out the other side, then you will understand this feeling of smallmindedness. In the depths of depression or despair, we can see only what we have lost.

All of the beautiful ideas seem to lose their power, and we're left only with the pain and the grittiness of our experience. We get invested in our justification, our conflict, our situation, invested in our particular egoic expression. We get the most invested when this way of relating to the world has the least to offer us, when it's on its last threads.

The ego fears change because it is a story. And when you change a story, you tell a different story. One story becomes dark to our perception, while another takes its place in our inner world. And, from the perspective of the little story of self that we cultivate unconsciously, that is tantamount to death.

To realize we're not who we thought we were, that we don't know what we want, that we don't want what we thought we wanted, these things are extremely challenging to our story of self. So we tend to blame the discomfort of these times on everyone and everything else, before finally getting down to the business of clearing our side of things.

This is natural. Human. However, it is a temptation which causes great and unnecessary conflict in our own lives and in the lives of others. Would you rather be right or be happy?

The cultivation of consciousness, to the furthest extent, leads to the deepest happiness. And it takes the road of stripping us of all the things we thought we needed to be happy to find the latent joy that was within us all along. Consciousness forces us to face our lives and make peace with what we find there. To *become* a light in the darkness.

The Medicine Path

It was many years of walking my own path before I came to a clear expression of my purpose. And, as with many things in life, that purpose was present to me from the beginning, framed in my earliest explorations of the world. The path that I walk, that many of my ancestors walked before me, can be called the Medicine Path.

I am not a doctor, not a member of the medical professionals of this culture. Medicine, in this context, is not about drugs and prescriptions. But it is about healing. About encouraging balance and the free flow of energy.

Healing is to make whole. Health occurs, in both body and mind, when we can flow freely, without tension, without darkened or unconscious areas in our being. To share medicine, in a tribal sense, is to complement the energies of a person or situation to help bring them into balance.

From this perspective, all things have their medicine. All things have a specific vibration or frequency, which can, in turn, be linked to certain aspects of the human experience.

Tribal cultures would look at how the animals around them behaved and how they met the challenges of the natural world. When they took lessons from these animals, they were partaking of their medicine. Plants have their medicines as well, as do features of the land, thoughts and feelings, stones, elemental forces, and the phases of the seasons.

We are all conductors in a sea of energy. As a conductor, we tune our vibration to different feelings, lessons, and experiences. We maintain a little bubble of order in a sea of chaos. We create this order with our actions, emotions, stories, habits. We choose. And when we learn to actualize this choice, we can bring the vibration we choose into our bubble of order. We can tap in to a specific medicine, after we have learned the feel of this medicine in our bodies and our beings.

In order to gain a close relationship with the medicine we carry within us, we tend the garden of our minds and learn to hold warmth in our hearts. We bring light to our stories. We become willing to explore them more deeply and come to know them consciously, in terms of personal, lived experience. We learn to choose whether we would like to feed these stories or tend to others. We cultivate a sense of loving connection with every aspect of the world that we encounter, inner and outer. At every moment, throughout every act, we strive to walk the walk and live in alignment with our values.

When we match frequencies with someone or something, we – temporarily and partially – become one with them on a practical and energetic level. We share in their field of thoughts and emotions, and they share in ours. And, if we understand how to navigate our inner space, we can do so, to a certain extent, for all involved. We can bring our medicine to the situation or interaction.

On the Medicine Path, it is vital to understand the Law of Sovereignty and the right use of power. Each being is responsible for their own journey. There is no one right way to live or to understand the world, so it is not right for us to impose our beliefs or specific dreams upon another, no matter how important or Real we believe they are. It is kind to inspire and empower. And, although people may ask for it, it is not kind to enable them or impose our will, our view, or our choices upon them.

Sovereignty, in part, means that we are all rulers of our inner space. We are responsible to ourselves for our thoughts, feelings, voice, and the use of our will. We decide for ourselves, not for others.

It is right for us to have clear boundaries, to make decisions that will lead us in the direction we'd like to go. And, no matter how awesome it would be if everybody followed our dream, it is not right for us to project or impose that dream upon others.

This becomes even more nuanced when we see that absolutely every story is an influence. We share stories with one another all the time, and each story we receive has the capacity to limit us or support us in our expansion. The limiting stories are only as true as we make them. When we hold a story true, we will behave as if it is. We will perceive the world through the lens of this story, seeing only what lines up with it.

Limiting stories are not beneficial to an individual dedicated to the cultivation of consciousness. They are good only for governing the behavior of children. And any story that says, "It's only this and not any other thing," is a limiting story.

To honor sovereignty is to honor the right of each person to craft meaning in their own way, to make sense of the world through their own stories. To blaze their own trail.

That said, no one is an island. Human beings communicate and share dreams with one another. We participate in creating meaning and inhabiting the abstract worlds that we have constructed together. We work together to create a dream of the world which we then confuse with the world itself. It is this last tendency which makes the Medicine Path so essential to the modern human.

Often, in order to promote healing, we must work with an individual's dream of the world, helping them to discover a new and more empowering, more life-affirming story. Without imposing this new dream upon them.

In standing in service, especially in teaching, we are often called to balance on a knife edge. The words we share have power in a way that the one who hears them is not likely to fully understand, at least at first. Our stories shape their world. If we see this, we have a responsibility to act with respect and to tell stories which expand and empower, rather than limit and govern.

Within our inner experience, and with each story we tell, we shine the light of consciousness. This is the Medicine Path. We feed the flame of consciousness within ourselves and in others, with each action, each decision, each story. We commit ourselves to living in the highest expression of our Freedom, Power, and Purpose, and to fostering this growth in others.

We dedicate ourselves to the personal experience of the divine in terms of Truth, Beauty, and Love, and to the expression of this experience, this message, with our lives. With every fiber of our beings, and throughout every moment of our experience.

Blessings.

AUTHOR BIO

I srael has spent his life in the pursuit of Truth, of the nature of the world, of humanity, and the Divine. This journey has led him to explore spiritual, religious, and magical traditions from peoples all across the world and throughout history.

He views each of these perspectives as an attempt to convey the same Truth, the same message. Different flashlights in the same dark room. His work is to share this wisdom in ways that inspire the human spirit and sing it to life.

"The time has come for us to remember our living connection to the earth, to one another, and to the I AM presence at the core of our Being. This is my mission, and one which I hope will find resonance in the living heart of the human race."

Israel Bouseman
only.human.wisdom.training@gmail.com

URGENT PLEA!

Thank You For Reading My Book!

I really appreciate all of your feedback and
I love hearing what you have to say.

I need your input to make the next version of this
book and my future books better.

Please take two minutes now to leave a helpful review on
Amazon letting me know what you thought of the book:

onlyhumanwisdomtraining.com/review

Thanks so much!

- ISRAEL BOUSEMAN